BOILERPLATE

Boilerplate, the fine print of standard contracts, is more prevalent than ever in commercial trade and in electronic commerce. But what is in it, beyond legal technicalities? Why is it so hard to read and why is it often so one-sided? Who writes it, who reads it, and what effect does it have?

The studies in this volume question whether boilerplate is true contract. Does it resemble a statute? Is it a species of property? Should we think of it as a feature of the product we buy? Does competition improve boilerplate? Looking at the empirical reality in which various boilerplates operate, leading private law experts reveal subtle and previously unrecognized ways in which boilerplate clauses encourage information flow but also reduce it; how new boilerplate terms are produced, and how innovation in boilerplate is stifled; and how negotiation happens in the shadow of boilerplate and how it is subdued. They offer a new explanation as to why boilerplate is often so one-sided and identify models for regulating the content of boilerplate. With emphasis on empiricism and economic thinking, this volume provides a more nuanced understanding of the "DNA" of market contracts, the boilerplate terms.

Omri Ben-Shahar is the Kirkland and Ellis Professor of Law and Economics at the University of Michigan and the director of the Olin Center for Law and Economics at Michigan.

Dr. Ben-Shahar teaches courses in contracts, electronic commerce, intellectual property, and economic analysis of law. He holds a B.A. in economics and an LL.B. from Hebrew University and an LL.M., S.J.D., and Ph.D. in economics from Harvard. He is the Chair of the Contracts Section of the American Association of Law Schools and a board member of the American Law and Economics Association.

Dr. Ben-Shahar writes in the fields of contract law and products liability. His work has been published in many journals, including the *Yale Law Journal, University of Chicago Law Review, University of Pennsylvania Law Review, Journal of Legal Studies*, and *American Law and Economics Review*.

BOILERPLATE

The Foundation of Market Contracts

Edited by

OMRI BEN-SHAHAR

Kirkland and Ellis Professor of Law and Economics
University of Michigan Law School

CAMBRIDGE
UNIVERSITY PRESS

CAMBRIDGE UNIVERSITY PRESS
Cambridge, New York, Melbourne, Madrid, Cape Town, Singapore, São Paulo

Cambridge University Press
32 Avenue of the Americas, New York, NY 10013-2473, USA

www.cambridge.org
Information on this title: www.cambridge.org/9780521859189

First published 2007

Printed in the United States of America

A catalog record for this publication is available from the British Library.

Library of Congress Cataloging in Publication Data

Boilerplate : the foundation of market contracts / edited by Omri
Ben-Shahar.
p. cm.
Includes bibliographical references and index.
ISBN-13: 978-0-521-85918-9 (hardback)
ISBN-10: 0-521-85918-2 (hardback)
ISBN-13: 978-0-521-67638-0 (pbk.)
ISBN-10: 0-521-67638-X (pbk.)
1. Standardized terms of contract. I. Ben-Shahar, Omri. II. Title.
K845.A34B65 2007
346.02′2 – dc22 2006101738

ISBN 978-0-521-85918-9 hardback
ISBN 978-0-521-67638-0 paperback

In Memory of Gili, 1965–2000

CONTENTS

PREFACE

Or: A Boilerplate Introduction

It is tempting to open this volume with yet another "boilerplate" salute to the challenge that standard-form contracts pose for contract law doctrine. You may have seen many tributes to this fundamental problem. If I were to offer my own variation on this familiar introduction, I would have perhaps tried to come up with an original spin to induce you to read forward another paragraph or two. I would probably have talked about a major divide within contract law between the "law of negotiations" and "product regulation." The former is the body of doctrines that determine the legal consequences of bargaining behavior; the latter is the assortment of substantive limitations on terms of bargains – some general to all contracts, others industry- or area-specific. I would then have argued that the study of standard form belongs to the latter, not the former, and that this distinction can help overcome many difficulties in contract law doctrine.

Such would surely be an appropriate overture for a discussion on boilerplate. Boilerplate, recall, is the building blocks of standard-form, nonnegotiated contracts. The enforceability of boilerplate is very much the legal locus where the philosophical debate over the regulation of markets hits the road. Boilerplate employment arbitration terms, for example, are the core of one of the most intriguing and fundamental debates in current contract law over the scope of the unconscionability doctrine.[1]

And yet, with boilerplate being the theme of this volume, there is a looming paradoxical feature with such an introduction: It would be, in and of itself, a boilerplate introduction! It would satisfy all the attributes that introductions-to-symposia are known to have. It would begin with a general reminder of the importance (and timeliness!) of the topic. It would demonstrate that the stakes are more than just conceptual-scholarly clarity, but also that the business world anxiously awaits academia's last word on the topic – here, the academic gospel concerning the efficacy of market contracts. The standard introduction would then maintain that the issues are not yet resolved, cite leading scholars who have acknowledged how difficult the issues are, and posit that this lack of resolution is manifested in inadequate development of the doctrine. And, finally, this hypothetical introduction would lay out a set of questions that ought to be addressed and the various ways in which the contributions to the symposium advance the answers to these questions.

You likely have read, by now, many such introductions-to-symposia and can recognize their boilerplate structure, their adherence to the how-to-write-an-introduction protocol. But if this hypothetical introduction – the one I eventually decided not to write – is indeed standard and predictable, it does not only introduce the topic of boilerplate; it also embodies that very phenomenon. Thus, ironically, it must satisfy many of the characteristics of boilerplate that the articles in this volume describe. Writing an introduction about boilerplate, it turns out, is also producing boilerplate!

Perhaps the most obvious analogy between boilerplate contracts and boilerplate introductions is the following. Like boilerplate contracts, boilerplate introductions-to-symposia are not read by anybody. (Why, then, are they written, you may naïvely wonder. I will say something about this later.) The "un-readness" property is of course a troubling phenomenon, both for contracts and for symposia introductions. Luckily, some of the contributions to this symposium address this un-readness feature of boilerplate. Robert A. Hillman, for example, investigates whether advance disclosure mechanisms can help consumers know what's in the contract or whether they would merely backfire against the interests of consumers;[2] Michelle E. Boardman suggests that in some industries the un-readness (and unreadability) of boilerplate is a perfectly reasonable – in fact, desirable – feature of a system in which contract terms are written not to expropriate value but to stabilize meanings.[3]

Here is a second analogy between boilerplate terms and symposium introductions: They appear objective, but they are often one-sided. You can probably recall some introductions to past symposia that you read (despite their un-readness . . .), in which the introducer put on a mask of neutrality, acknowledged all the relevant and conflicting perspectives, provided broad-as-possible context and normative appeal, and yet planted in all of that objectivity his or her own controversial agenda, building on a set of selective assumptions and skewed observations. I am sure I can recall some such introductions, and I'm pretty sure I even wrote one.[4] Similar to introductions, this buried one-sidedness is also a very familiar feature of boilerplate contracts. Disguised by "legalese," they are often unbalanced, favoring their drafter. Although the one-sidedness of consumer contracts is hardly a discovery, several contributions to the volume offer a new understanding of this phenomenon. Lucian A. Bebchuk and Richard

A. Posner, in one chapter,[5] and Jason Scott Johnston, in another chapter,[6] argue that self-serving boilerplate terms may not be as bad as they seem. They argue that one-sided terms are a general feature of contracts written by firms who care about their reputations and who do not intend to strictly enforce such terms. These two chapters argue that firms write one-sided terms in order to have the option to enforce them selectively to fend off consumer opportunism but otherwise let their honest clients off. Johnston nicely calls it "tailored forgiveness"; Bebchuk and Posner attribute this feature to the observability but nonverifiability of opportunism – that is, to the difficulty of proving it in court. Both these articles portray a reality in which one-sidedness poses less of a concern than previously thought.

Against this view, Ronald J. Mann examines one-sided boilerplate in credit card contracts and concludes that they continue to burden debtors.[7] He suggests that contract law doctrine may be inadequate in dealing with this problem and explores the case for prohibitions against some such terms or even a regulatory promulgation of more balanced mandatory clauses. Along this line, Clayton P. Gillette explores an intermediate form of intervention. Instead of regulating terms, the government can preapprove standard terms. The approval will shield the drafter from ex-post judicial scrutiny.

Paradoxically, the only way to know if the un-readness of boilerplate indeed leads to one-sidedness is to read the terms (in the same way that you are currently reading a normally unread Preface). Several studies in this symposium do just that. They measure the bias of terms in specific sectors, such as software licensing and heavy manufacturing. Surprisingly, they find that in areas where everyone would have expected there to be a bias, it does not exist;[8] and, in areas where a bias should not exist, it is substantial.[9]

There is another, more subtle feature of introductions-to-symposia, which they again share with boilerplate terms. In a typical introduction, the collection of articles in the symposium being introduced is not a result of a tournament or competition between able scholars. The list is solicited and tailored, and the writer of the introduction is usually the person who put together this list and shaped it to correspond with what he or she perceives to be the ideal agenda. In the same way that the introduction describes a substance that is not negotiated but rather unilaterally tailored, the boilerplate contract stipulates a substance of a transaction that is not negotiated or bilaterally dickered but, rather, dictated – unilaterally drafted. Of course, this raises difficult questions about the relationship between boilerplate and the power to dictate. Douglas G. Baird demonstrates in this symposium some of the fallacies that have become all too common in addressing this relationship.[10] He argues that the evils of concentrated economic power have nothing to do with boilerplate. Revisiting some of the classic cases from the folklore of contract law, he shows that it is not the fine print that makes some clauses troublesome. But in a rich and original chapter, David Gilo and Ariel Porat show a variety of previously unrecognized ways in which boilerplate terms do operate in an anticompetitive fashion, such as to price-discriminate, facilitate collusion among sellers, and deter entry by new sellers.[11] The unilateral drafting of boilerplate is also studied by James J. White and me in a merchant-to-merchant context. We examine the contracts between automotive companies and their suppliers, one of the most important form contracts (in terms of economic stakes) ever drafted.[12] We uncover several ways in which the drafters of these contracts prevent negotiations and tailoring from ever occurring to bolster their economic rents.

If there is a significant boilerplate element to the craft of writing an introduction – if introductions are indeed standard and predictable – this raises the question: Why bother writing them? Similarly, if a form contract is boilerplate to be used and replicated by many similarly situated parties, why would any single individual have the incentive to draft it? A boilerplate contract is a public good – an item that is copied freely by others – and we should therefore expect a problem of underproduction. This question is studied directly by Kevin E. Davis, who identifies the production paradox and looks at the role of nonprofit organizations in generating boilerplate contracts.[13] It is also studied by Stephen J. Choi and G. Mitu Gulati, who look at the incentives of boilerplate drafters and define their crucial role in giving interpretive meaning to boilerplate.[14] Choi and Gulati's study is even more ambitious: It suggests that a better way to understand the emergence of boilerplate – and to interpret it when ambiguous – is to conceive of it as *statute* and apply statutory interpretation techniques to dispute resolutions.

I have noticed another thing about published symposia: Readers rarely sit down to read an entire symposium from the introduction to the last article. Rather, most readers may bump into one or a small subset of individual symposium articles that are of particular interest to them. This suggests that, other than for the participants in the conference, there is really no audience for introductions. Summarizing to the hypothetical symposium reader what the articles of the symposium are about is a service that future readers do not really need and of which very few would make use. In other words, symposia introductions are a wasteful – *inefficient*? – scholarly effort. This conclusion is every bit as unorthodox as the idea that boilerplate contracts also may be inefficient. And yet the claim that boilerplate could be inefficient is a more difficult proposition to defend. There is a long tradition in law and economics arguing for the efficiency of standard-form contracts. Several of the contributions in this volume, however, suggest otherwise and provide either evidence or new theoretical underpinnings for the inefficiency conjecture.[15] Choi and Gulati, studying the evolution of boilerplate in sophisticated transactions, show why it is often unlikely that boilerplate converges to the most efficient terms.[16]

If I somehow got you to read this far, you may recognize that this introduction includes two types of information. The first type is specific to the forthcoming symposium and conveys its particular context (for instance, my references to the specific articles and to the prior standard-form contracts literature). The second type of stuff you read is more general and can be used, with almost no changes, to introduce other symposia on a variety of topics. This distinction roughly corresponds to what Henry E. Smith, in his important contribution to this symposium, calls intensive and extensive communications.[17] Contracts, when drafted ad hoc, are highly intensive information-rich rights. Property, in contrast, is less context dependent, less information specific, and therefore more extensive. Smith suggests that boilerplate represents a shift of contractual rights toward the status of property. He argues that the *modularity* feature of boilerplate is what allows it to have its extensive appeal.

Finally, in many contracts that are otherwise skewed in favor of their drafters, we nevertheless find boilerplate terms that appear to accord some balance. For example, one of the "hidden roles" of boilerplate that Gilo and Porat discover in their article is the provision of true and accessible benefits – but only to those who labor to read the unreadable contract.[18] Likewise, two contributions to this volume are aimed at providing more balance – and more fairness? – to the otherwise dominant law-and-economics presence but, like boilerplate, can be accessible mainly to readers who will labor to read through most of the other chapters. I have asked two of the more influential scholars that have studied standard-form contracts using other approaches to comment on the ideas that are advanced in the volume. Accordingly, Margaret Jane Radin, whose recent work identifies new challenges posed by standardization of contract in the digital age,[19] and Todd D. Rakoff, whose seminal work on contracts of adhesion continues to provide a baseline for the study of form contracts,[20] responded to this challenge.[21] Note that these commentaries are anything but the boilerplate commentaries that sometimes are affixed to symposium articles. Rather, this symposium provides a platform for Radin and for Rakoff to examine the emerging inventory of new ideas about boilerplate – an inventory that is hopefully richer after this symposium – and to reevaluate their own thinking on the topic.

As occasional market transactors, you surely know that many important details of transactions you are about to enter are buried in boilerplate, but you often prefer to read sellers' pamphlets to figure out the big picture – what the bargain is about. What, then, is the big picture coming out of this volume?

What can we write on our pamphlet? I think we can safely say this symposium is breaking new ground in the study of boilerplate and standard forms beyond the general claims about market power, competition for terms, and network externalities. On a theoretical level, boilerplate is shown to be a legal phenomenon different from contract. Is it a statute? Is it property? Is it a product? On an empirical level, boilerplate is studied in specific contexts, including insurance, credit cards, auto manufacturing, debt financing, and electronic commerce. The contributions to the symposium reveal subtle and previously unrecognized ways in which boilerplate clauses encourage information flow – but also dampen it; increase competition – but also reduce it; how new boilerplate terms are produced – and how innovation in boilerplate is stifled; how negotiation happens in the shadow of boilerplate – and how it is subdued; and offer new explanations as to why boilerplate is so often one-sided. With emphasis on empiricism and economic thinking, this symposium provides a more nuanced understanding of the DNA of market contracts – the boilerplate terms.

This volume presents a collaborative effort by leading scholars of private law to provide a richer understanding of the relation between contracts and markets. Many of the chapters in this book were previously published in full article length in a *Michigan Law Review* symposium issue, Vol. 104, No. 5 (March 2006), which was dedicated to the conference on "Boilerplate" that took place in Ann Arbor, Michigan, in October 2005. The current volume provides a revised and abridged version of these articles, focusing on the theme of this book, along with additional, new contributions.

LIST OF CONTRIBUTORS

Douglas G. Baird is the Harry A. Bigelow Distinguished Service Professor of Law and formerly the Dean at the University of Chicago Law School. He is the author of numerous books and articles on bankruptcy, contracts, and law and economics, including *Game Theory and the Law* (Harvard University Press, 1994) (with Robert Gertner and Randall Picker), *The Elements of Bankruptcy* (Foundation Press, 4th ed., 2006), and *Cases, Problems, and Materials on Bankruptcy* (Foundation Press, 3rd ed., 2000) (with Barry Adler and Thomas Jackson). Baird earned a B.A. from Yale University and a J.D. from Stanford University.

Lucian A. Bebchuk is the William J. Friedman and Alicia Townsend Friedman Professor of Law, Economics, and Finance and Director of the Program on Corporate Governance at Harvard Law School. He is also a Research Associate of the National Bureau of Economic Research, and an Inaugural Fellow of the European Corporate Governance Institute. Bebchuk holds an LL.M., S.J.D., and Ph.D. in Economics from Harvard University. His main areas of research are corporate governance, law and finance, and law and economics. Bebchuk's recent writings include *Pay without Performance: The Unfulfilled Promise of Executive Compensation* (Harvard University Press, 2004, with Jesse Fried), "The Case for Increasing Shareholder Power" (*Harvard Law Review*, 2005), and "The Costs of Entrenched Boards" (*Journal of Financial Economics*, 2005, co-authored with Alma Cohen).

Omri Ben-Shahar is the Kirkland and Ellis Professor of Law and Economics and the director of the Olin Center for Law and Economics at the University of Michigan. He holds a B.A. in economics and an LL.B. from Hebrew University and an S.J.D. and Ph.D. in economics from Harvard University. Ben-Shahar teaches courses in contracts, electronic commerce, intellectual property, and economic analysis of law. He writes in the fields of contract law and products liability. He previously edited the conference "Freedom *From* Contract" (*Wisconsin Law Review*, 2004).

Michelle E. Boardman is an Assistant Professor of Law at George Mason University. She holds a J.D. from the University of Chicago Law School. Boardman clerked for Judge Frank Easterbrook at the Seventh Circuit Court of Appeals and served as Deputy Assistant Attorney General in the Office of Legal Counsel at the U.S. Department of Justice. She writes in the area of insurance law and contracts.

Stephen J. Choi is the Murray and Kathleen Bring Professor of Law at New York University. He previously taught at the University of Chicago Law School and at University of California, Berkeley, where he was the Roger J. Traynor Professor of Law. He holds an A.B., J.D., and Ph.D. in economics from Harvard University. Choi is the author of *Securities Regulation: Cases and Analysis* (Foundation Press, 2005) (with Adam Pritchard) and more than forty articles, primarily on corporations and capital markets.

Kevin E. Davis is Professor of Law at New York University. Davis received his B.A. in Economics from McGill University, an LL.B. from the University of Toronto, and an LL.M. from Columbia University. He previously taught at the University of Toronto. Davis writes in the areas of contracts, commercial law, and law and development.

Clayton P. Gillette is the Max E. Greenberg Professor of Contract Law and Vice Dean at the New York University School of Law. He was previously a Professor of Law at the University of Virginia and Boston University. Gillette earned his J.D. from the University of Michigan and a B.A. from Amherst College, and he clerked for Judge J. Edward Lumbard of the U.S. Court of Appeals for the Second Circuit. Gillette writes on commercial law and local government law. He is the author of casebooks on local government law (with Lynn Baker) and payment systems and credit instruments (with Alan Schwartz and Robert Scott) and a textbook on municipal debt finance law (with Robert S. Amdursky).

David Gilo is an Associate Professor of Law at Tel Aviv University, where he teaches antitrust and corporate law. He earned a B.A. and LL.B. from Tel Aviv University and an S.J.D. from Harvard University. He writes in the areas of antitrust, regulated industries, and industrial organization.

G. Mitu Gulati is a Professor of Law at Duke University Law School. He previously taught at University of California, Los Angeles, and Georgetown University. Gulati writes in the areas of securities regulation, international debt transactions, corporate law, employment discrimination, and judicial behavior. His most current research is on odious debt. Gulati earned an A.B. from the University of Chicago, M.A. from Yale University, and J.D. from Harvard University Law School.

Robert A. Hillman is the Edwin H. Woodruff Professor of Law at Cornell University Law School. He has written extensively on contracts and commercial law and is the author of several books, including *Principles of Contract Law* (West, 2004), *The Richness of Contract Law: An Analysis and Critique of Contemporary Theories of Contract Law* (Kluwer, 1997), and *Contract and Related Obligation: Theory, Doctrine,* *and Practice* (with R. Summers) (West, 4th ed., 2000). A graduate of Cornell University Law School, Professor Hillman clerked for Judges Edward C. McLean and Robert J. Ward, of the Southern District of New York. He is currently the reporter for the American Law Institute's Principles of the Law of Software Contracts.

Jason Scott Johnston is the Robert G. Fuller, Jr., Professor of Law and Director, Program on Law, the Environment, and Economics at the University of Pennsylvania Law School. He previously taught at the University of Vermont and Vanderbilt University. Johnston writes in the areas of contracts, environmental law, law and economics, and natural resources law and policy. He recently organized a conference on the law, economics, and science of liability for global warming. He earned an A.B. from Dartmouth College and a J.D. and Ph.D. in economics from the University of Michigan.

Ronald J. Mann is the Ben H. and Kitty King Powell Professor of Business and Commercial Law and Co-Director of the Center for Law, Business, and Economics at the University of Texas at Austin School of Law. A graduate of the University of Texas School of Law, Mann clerked for Judge Joseph T. Sneed on the Ninth Circuit of the U.S. Court of Appeals and Justice Lewis F. Powell, Jr., of the U.S. Supreme Court. He previously taught at Washington University in St. Louis and the University of Michigan Law School. Mann is the author of several books, including *Charging Ahead: The Growth and Regulation of Payment Card Markets Around the World* (Cambridge University Press, 2006), *Payment Systems and Other Financial Transactions: Cases, Materials, and Problems* (2nd ed., 2003), and *Electronic Commerce* (with Jane Winn) (2nd ed., 2005). He recently served as the reporter for the amendments to Articles 3 and 4 of the Uniform Commercial Code.

Florencia Marotta-Wurgler is an Assistant Professor of Law at New York University School of Law. Previously the Wagner Fellow for Law and Business at New York University, she earned a B.A. from the University of Pennsylvania and a J.D. from New York University. Marotta-Wurgler writes in the areas of contracts and commercial law.

Ariel Porat is the Alain Poher Professor of Law and former Dean at Tel Aviv University Faculty of Law. He earned his LL.B. and J.S.D. from Tel Aviv University. Porat taught as a Visiting Professor at the University of California at Berkeley, the University of Chicago, Columbia University, and the University of Virginia. He writes in the areas of torts and contracts and is the author of *Contributory Fault in the Law of Contracts* (1997), *Tort Liability under Uncertainty* (with Alex Stein) (Oxford University Press, 2001).

Richard A. Posner is a judge on the U.S. Court of Appeals for the Seventh Circuit (since 1981). He previously was the Lee and Brena Freeman Professor of Law at the University of Chicago Law School, where he is now a senior lecturer. Judge Posner has written a number of books, including *Economic Analysis of Law* (6th ed., 2003),

The Problematics of Moral and Legal Theory (1999), *Antitrust Law* (2nd ed., 2001), *Law, Pragmatism, and Democracy* (2003), *Catastrophe: Risk and Response* (2004), and, most recently, *The Little Book of Plagiarism* (2007).

Margaret Jane Radin is the William Benjamin Scott and Luna M. Scott Professor of Law at Stanford University. She received an A.B. from Stanford University and a J.D. from the University of Southern California. Radin writes in the areas of property theory, intellectual property, contracts, and the jurisprudence of cyberspace. She is the author of *Contested Commodities* (Harvard University Press, 1996) and *Reinterpreting Property* (University of Chicago Press, 1993).

Todd D. Rakoff is Byrne Professor of Administrative Law at Harvard University Law School. He earned a B.A. from Harvard University and Oxford University and a J.D. from Harvard University Law School. He writes in the areas of contracts and administrative law. Rakoff is the author of *A Time for Every Purpose: Law and the Balance of Life* (Harvard University Press, 2002) and numerous casebooks, including *Cases and Materials for the Course in Contracts* (3rd ed., 2004).

Henry E. Smith is Professor of Law at Yale University Law School, where he teaches in the areas of property, intellectual property, natural resources, and taxation. Previously, he clerked for the Hon. Ralph K. Winter, U.S. Court of Appeals, for the Second Circuit and taught at the Northwestern University School of Law. In 2003, he was awarded a Berlin Prize Fellowship by the American Academy in Berlin. Professor Smith has written primarily on the law and economics of property and intellectual property, including *Self-Help and the Nature of Property*, *Exclusion and Property Rules in the Law of Nuisance*, and *The Language of Property: Form, Context, and Audience.* He holds an A.B. from Harvard University, a Ph.D. in Linguistics from Stanford University, and a J.D. from Yale University.

James J. White is the Robert A. Sullivan Professor of Law at the University of Michigan Law School. White has written on many aspects of commercial law and has published the widely recognized treatise, *Uniform Commercial Code* (with Robert Summers). He is also the author of several casebooks on commercial, bankruptcy, and banking law. White has served as the reporter for the Revision of Article 5 of the Uniform Commercial Code and has served on several American Law Institute and National Conference of Commissioners on Uniform State Law committees dealing with revision to the Uniform Commercial Code. White earned his B.A. from Amherst College and his J.D. from the University of Michigan Law School.

PART ONE

WHY IS BOILERPLATE ONE-SIDED?

Perhaps the most robust feature of fine-print terms in contracts is their bias in favor of the drafter. It is a puzzling feature because one-sided boilerplate accompanies not only "bad" consumer contracts but also almost every contract, including contracts for the sale of high-end goods and contracts between sophisticated parties. Why, then, are contracts often "worse" than the products with which they come? Does one-sided boilerplate have a role that goes beyond simple rent expropriation? The first five chapters in this volume provide novel insights on this fundamental question. They document the extent of the phenomenon of one-sidedness and explore its role in market contracts.

ONE

One-Sided Contracts in Competitive Consumer Markets

Lucian A. Bebchuk and Richard A. Posner

Editor's Note: *This chapter shows that "one-sided" terms in standard contracts, which deny consumers a contractual benefit that seems efficient on average, may arise in competitive markets without informational problems (other than those of courts). A one-sided term might be an efficient response to situations in which courts cannot perfectly observe all the contingencies needed for an accurate implementation of a "balanced" contractual term when firms are more concerned about their reputation, and thus less inclined to behave opportunistically, than consumers are.*

The usual assumption in economic analysis of law is that in a competitive market without informational asymmetries, the terms of contracts between sellers and buyers will be optimal – that is, that any deviation from these terms would impose expected costs on one party that exceed benefits to the other. But could there be cases in which "one-sided" contracts – contracts containing terms that impose a greater expected cost on one side than benefit on the other – would be found in competitive markets even in the absence of fraud, prohibitive information costs, or other market imperfections? That is the possibility we explore in this chapter.

We focus on the following asymmetry between seller and buyer in cases in which the latter is a consumer rather than another business or comparable entity: The seller in such a case may be deterred from behaving opportunistically by considerations of reputation; the consumer is not constrained by such considerations because he has no reputation to lose, assuming that his opportunistic behavior in a particular transaction will not become known to the market as a whole. This difference is important whenever it is difficult to specify contractual terms to cover every important contingency that courts could accurately and easily enforce. In such circumstances, opportunistic buyers might try to use "balanced" terms to press for benefits and advantages beyond those that the terms were actually intended to provide.

Slanting the terms of the contract in favor of the seller is, we show, a way of redressing the balance. The existence of a one-sided contract does not imply that the *transaction* will be one-sided but only that the seller will have discretion with respect to how to treat the consumer. A seller concerned about its reputation can be expected to treat consumers better than is required by the letter of the contract. But the seller's right to stand on the contract as written will protect it against opportunistic buyers. A one-sided contract may thus be preferred ex ante by informed parties as a cheaper mechanism for inducing efficient outcomes, should contingencies arise during the performance of the contract, than a more "balanced" contract, which, because of imperfect enforcement, could create costs as a consequence of consumers' enforcing protective provisions in the contract.

When firms are influenced by reputational considerations, contracts that appear on paper to be one-sided against the consumer may in reality be implemented in a balanced way. The distinction between contracts on paper and their actual implementation is one that has received much attention from the literature on relational contracts between businesses.[1] As our analysis highlights, however, the distinction is also relevant to contracts that businesses enter into with consumers who are not repeat players. As long as the business is a repeat player with the consumer side of the market, its expectation of doing business with other consumers in the future may dissuade it from enforcing a one-sided contract to the hilt against a particular consumer even though the business does not expect to have further dealings with that consumer.

I. Explaining One-Sided Contracts

We consider a competitive market in which sellers offer boilerplate contracts that include terms that appear to impose on buyers expected costs that exceed expected benefits to the seller. Examples are predispute mandatory-arbitration clauses, holder-in-due-course clauses, forum selection clauses in cruise-ship ticket contracts, and shrink-wrap licenses.

Contracts that contain such terms and, as is typical of such contracts, are offered to consumers on a take-it-or-leave-it basis are described by critics as "contracts of adhesion." An older, and pretty well discredited, scholarly literature thought the absence of bargaining showed that the seller must have monopoly power, enabling him to foist on consumers whatever terms he liked. But transaction costs plus agency costs, relative to the modest stakes in most consumer transactions, are sufficient explanations for why sellers prefer a form contract to individual negotiations.[2] Nor is it obvious why a monopolist would offer suboptimal terms rather than just charge a monopoly price for balanced terms, a price that would be higher because the consumer was receiving greater value.[3]

But this leaves unexplained the one-sidedness of many form contracts. Scholars often try to explain them as a result of informational problems. Consumers could be inadequately informed about the provisions included in the contracts or their consequences.[4] Consumers' understanding could also be distorted by the kind of cognitive problems that are receiving increasing attention from economists.[5] Or sellers could be induced to offer one-sided contracts by the presence of adverse selection, as we explain in Part IV.[6] Scholars who advance these explanations oppose judicial enforcement of contracts of adhesion in the name of unconscionability or similar doctrines.[7] Some courts have agreed,[8] but most have not.[9]

Must the presence of one-sided contracts in competitive markets be a result of informational problems? Are courts that enforce such contracts failing to intervene when they should? Or might there be an explanation that does not depend on assuming asymmetric information in favor of sellers or other possible sources of market failure? We show that such an explanation does exist and that, as a result, the normative inferences that can be drawn from such contracts are far from being clear and straightforward.

Many one-sided contracts are found in consumer markets that have the following characteristics: The seller side of the market consists of repeat players who have a sunk cost in a reputation for dealing "fairly" with consumers, in the sense of not taking advantage of one-sided terms as long as the consumer deals fairly with them. The buyer side of the market consists of parties that – because they do not have repeat dealings with particular sellers (the market is competitive, so consumers can switch easily among sellers) and because privacy rules or other barriers to pooling of information among sellers prevent sellers from comparing notes about the behavior of individual buyers – do not have a sunk cost in reputation and, hence, have no incentive to deal fairly with sellers in the sense of honoring the terms of the contract.

In such a situation, the optimal set of contract terms does not depend only on the relative costs and benefits associated with particular terms. It also depends on the relative propensity of the parties to behave opportunistically, that is, to take advantage of contractual terms and, in so doing, impose a cost on the other side that will exceed the benefit to the opportunistic party.

In the asymmetric-reputation case, the seller has little or no incentive to behave opportunistically because if he does, he will suffer a loss of reputation, which is a cost. The buyer, however, is not deterred by concern for reputation.

Nor is he dependably deterred by threat of legal action because, given feasibility limits on drafting contract terms that are free from uncertainty, courts cannot always determine when a party is using a contract term opportunistically.

In this situation, seemingly one-sided terms may not be one-sided after all. The expected cost of the term to the buyer must be discounted by the likelihood that reputational considerations will induce the seller to treat the buyer fairly even when such treatment is not contractually required. This cost will sometimes be reduced further by sellers' disinclination to sue consumers even when they have an ethically as well as legally solid case. Sellers may still worry that a suit will injure their reputation for fair dealing (because the term *is* one-sided), or that the cost of the suit will be disproportionate to the expected benefit. If, therefore, we assume that a court would be able to determine only whether the litigated contract term is *on average* efficient – that is, on average, it burdens the bound party less than it benefits the obligee – a rule of unconscionability that condemned one-sided terms would systematically favor opportunistic buyers without protecting fair buyers because the latter are protected by the sellers' investment in reputation.

Consider by way of example the following provision in the standard contract that Harvard University Press enters into with authors: "[i]f the Author fails to return the corrected proofs sheets by the date set by the Publisher, the Publisher may publish the Work without the Author's approval of proof."[10] Clearly, given the importance of accuracy to the author, the publisher's enforcing this provision to the hilt would impose on the author an expected cost greater than the benefit to the publisher, especially given that the agreement does not limit the publisher's discretion in its choice of "the date set by the Publisher."

What could explain the inclusion of this provision in an agreement recently signed by this publisher and one of us and his coauthor? It could not be the publisher's market power. The publisher was seeking in this case, as in many others, to compete with other publishers on other aspects of the agreement. Nor could it have been the publisher's expectation that this provision would not be noticed by the authors. Authors are in general likely to read carefully the short publication agreement. Furthermore, the authors in this case did notice the provision and asked to amend it, but the publisher indicated that its policy was not to make amendments to this provision.

Notwithstanding the publisher's insistence on retaining the provision, the publisher's agent assured the authors that they do not have to worry about this provision and other seemingly one-sided provisions included in the agreement. Although this assurance had no legal significance, the authors signed the agreement without worrying that the publisher would abuse the power given to it by the provision. Indeed, when the authors were a bit late in returning the proofs, the publisher, as expected, waited for the corrections rather than enforcing the provision.

Our explanation is that the provision is intended to protect the publisher from circumstances in which the author's delay in returning proofs is egregious. But if the provision were explicitly limited to those circumstances, enforcement would be a difficult undertaking for a court because determining "egregiousness" might well depend on information available to the parties but not easily and accurately observable by the court. The one-sided provision obviates this concern, whereas the publisher's reputational interest protects the authors from the publisher's taking advantage of the literal meaning of the provision.

In the circumstances on which we focus, a one-sided provision allows the business discretion whether to provide the individual with protection in any given circumstances. In contrast, because a balanced provision cannot be written in an unambiguous way, whether protection will be provided in any given circumstances will be influenced by the court's discretion. In some circumstances, a strategy of discretionary protection is superior to a strategy of judicial discretion.

II. A Simple Model

Assume a competitive market in which one side (the seller side, consisting of many sellers) faces stronger reputational constraints than does the other side (the buying side, assumed to consist of many individual consumers). The sellers are repeat-playing firms, and consumers have information about their behavior. As a result, sellers are concerned about their reputation. Buyers, however, are not concerned about investing in reputation because they buy infrequently from a given seller and sellers do not exchange information about consumers.

In some markets, of course, buyers are not indifferent to their reputation. They may be firms that are repeat players with powerful incentives to protect their reputation, whereas the sellers may be individuals that transact infrequently. An example is the agreements that university presses have with new authors. Our analysis applies to such markets as well. It can explain, for example, why the agreements that those presses have with their authors include provisions that seem one-sided against the author even though authors are likely to read the terms of these agreements and there is competition among the publishers. For simplicity of exposition, however, we will assume in the model that the sellers' side of the market is the one composed of firms with reputations to protect.

Similarly, not all consumers are well informed about the behavior of sellers. Indeed, the cost of becoming informed may exceed the benefit, resulting in rational ignorance of hidden traps in contracts that competition may not dispel.[11] The novelty of the present analysis is that the same contract forms that are widely assumed to be based on consumer ignorance can be shown to be consistent with competition under conditions of full information.

When a contract term is on average efficient, then each buyer's expected benefit, B, exceeds the seller's expected cost, C: $C < B$. But "on average" implies that the term won't be efficient in all the circumstances to which it literally applies. Assume it will be efficient in state θ, which has a probability p of occurring, but not in any other state. Assume that the benefit to the buyer will be $B_2 > C$ in state θ but only $B_1 < C$ in the non-θ state, so that the average benefit to the buyer is:

$$p(B_2) + (1 - p)(B_1).$$

Assume further that courts will be unable to observe whether the state of the world in which the contract dispute arises is θ, but the parties will, although all that is necessary for our analysis to hold is that the parties have better information about the presence or absence of θ than courts have.

Sellers in our model offer to buyers identical take-it-or-leave-it contracts and are not prepared to renegotiate when the time for performance arrives. One can think of the sellers as large firms that do not trust their agents to negotiate contract changes or (a point to which we will return) that mistrust consumers who try to negotiate over terms.

If a seller fails to comply with a contract term, the consumer will be able to obtain from a court an award of expectation damages equal to B. Because the court will not be able to distinguish perfectly between consumers who derive a large benefit from the term and consumers who derive only a small benefit, there will be a tendency to award damages equal to the average benefit of the contract term that the seller has violated. For the sake of simplicity, we assume that the same damages are awarded in all cases in this class.

Because $B > C$, if sellers' behavior is not constrained by their concern for their reputation, the protective term will be included, for without it the seller would have no incentive to confer B and so the value of the contract would not be maximized. Inclusion of the term produces an efficiency gain of $B_2 - C$ in state θ and an efficiency loss of $C - B_1$ in the non-θ state, but the net gain is positive because:

$$p(B_2 - C) + (1 - p)(C - B_1) = B - C > 0.$$

Sellers in a competitive market will offer the term because although they will be charging a price for the contract that is higher by C (because that is the cost to the seller of the term), the expected benefit to consumers will be greater and so consumers will shun sellers who fail to offer it.

This is the standard result when courts cannot observe the exact circumstances of a given case and there is no contract renegotiation; a term will be included if the average benefit exceeds the average cost. But it is no longer the case when reputational considerations are in play. For then, provided sellers' practices are known to consumers, sellers will offer only a contract that omits the term benefiting the buyer, but they will have a policy of honoring the (nonexistent) term whenever the parties are in state θ.

For example, the term might be that the buyer can return the good and get his money back, and θ might be the state in which the buyer returns it promptly without having used or damaged it. Sellers will charge a price that is higher by pC because they expect to incur a cost C with probability p, in cases in θ. But buyers will have an expected benefit of pB_2 and thus a net expected gain of $(pB_2 - C)$. When some sellers offer such contracts while following the policy just described, no seller who fails to provide such a combination will be able to attract any consumers without losing money.

It might seem that because buyers value the policy, sellers would make it a term of the contract even if they were constrained to follow the policy by their investment in reputation. But this is incorrect because, as a contract term, the policy would require adherence by the seller even when it was inefficient to provide the benefit, that is, even when the parties were in the non-θ state. Thus, if the contract provided that the buyer could return the good if dissatisfied with it, the seller would be obligated to accept the return even if the buyer, rather than actually being dissatisfied with it, had used it as much as he wanted to or had damaged it so that it was no longer valuable to him. Of course, the seller might include some qualifying language such as "reasonably dissatisfied," but the uncertainty created by such language would give the buyer some probability of being able to get away with returning the good in circumstances not intended to be covered by the clause.

III. Positive and Normative Implications

Our analysis has both positive and normative implications. On the positive side, it can explain the large number of cases in which sellers dependably treat consumers much better than their contracts require them to do. Sellers often accept returns in circumstances in which they are not obligated to do so. Similarly, hotels usually do not charge a guest for checking out of his room shortly after the check-out time; publishers commonly do not send a manuscript to the printer without waiting for the author's corrections when the author is late and usually overlook other small breaches as well; airlines sometimes give people double mileage credit if a flight is delayed; and restaurants allow substitutions although the menu states "no substitutions." Such concessions are not properly regarded as advertising or price discrimination because consumers expect them and often would be indignant if they were withheld.

But because they are not legal entitlements, the seller is not at the mercy of a buyer who would abuse them but not be amenable to legal sanctions. Suppose, for example, that instead of fixing a rigid checkout time, the contract between a hotel and its guests provided that the guest must leave at the checkout time (or pay for another day) unless he has good cause to delay his departure for a reasonable amount of time. Such a provision could be (ab)used by a guest who decides cavalierly to stay in the room, watching TV, until the evening news. With the rigid checkout rule, the hotel will be able to charge this overstaying customer for another day while waiving such charges routinely for customers who miss the checkout time in good faith and for good reason.

In the circumstances that we study in this chapter, courts would do well to take a hard line in enforcing the terms of one-sided consumer contracts in the absence of evidence of fraud. Suppose the contract that a seller has with its customers does not promise them some protection X (say, forgiving charging for an entire day in the event of a short delay in checking out as a result of circumstances beyond a customer's control), but there is evidence that the seller does commonly accord them X. Should a court view the common practice as an implicit promise to do so? Our answer is no because this would sacrifice the benefits of an unenforceable policy that allows the firm discretion to withhold a normally expected benefit.

There will be borderline cases because courts frequently use evidence of past practice or custom to interpret a contract. However, this is done mainly in cases in which a contractual term is ambiguous.[12] If the term is crystal clear, as the drafters of one-sided contracts will endeavor to make it, courts will generally enforce the term as written.

IV. Alternative Information-Based Explanations

We enlarge briefly here on the alternative explanations mentioned earlier for one-sided contracts. These explanations are based on informational asymmetries between sellers and buyers. One explanation assumes that consumers are at an informational disadvantage. They are uninformed about the costs that the contract may impose upon them or suffer from cognitive limitations and biases when assessing these costs.

The other explanation assumes that there are two types of consumer between which the seller cannot distinguish; in other words, consumers have the informational advantage. One type, who would value a protective provision more than the other, also happens to be the one that is costlier to serve. In these circumstances, even if the protective provision is efficient for all consumers, in equilibrium, no consumer might ask for it out of fear that doing so would make the seller suspect that the buyer was of the type that is costlier to serve.

Our explanation for one-sided contracts has two different implications, one positive and one normative, from those of the alternative, information-based explanations.[13] The distinctive positive implication is that when our explanation is applicable, firms will not take advantage of the one-sided contracts: Only in exceptional cases will they stand by the letter of the contract. In contrast, when one of the two information-based explanations applies, firms will always (or, at least, almost always) stick to the letter of the contract.

The normative implication is that when our explanation is applicable, the law should not intervene and provide protection not supplied by the contract, whereas if the seller has and is exploiting an informational advantage, there is an argument for implying protective provisions in the contract to make it less one-sided. Similarly, in the presence of inefficient pooling produced by adverse selection, imposing protective provisions could sometimes (though not always) improve matters. The challenge for future research is to try to distinguish between the domains of our explanation and the information-based explanations.

We emphasize, finally, that our analysis is limited to the case of repetitive selling of consumer products under conditions of good consumer information about sellers. With infrequent sales or poor information about sellers, sellers will not be constrained by reputational concerns. Our analysis is likewise inapplicable when the buying side consists not of individual consumers but rather of firms that have their own reputational stake in fair dealing, so that sellers have less concern about being taken advantage of by buyers who are not reputation-constrained. It is the asymmetry of reputation concerns in the case of the repeat seller selling to a consumer that drives our analysis. The potential existence of such asymmetries is a factor to which scholars and judges should, we contend, pay close attention.

TWO

Cooperative Negotiations in the Shadow of Boilerplate

Jason Scott Johnston

Editor's Note: *In this chapter, Jason Scott Johnston argues that one-side boilerplate serves as a baseline for performance-stage bargaining during which firms accord customers benefits beyond those required in the contract and forgive some of the customers' obligations that are unreasonable. Firms nevertheless include the boilerplate in order to have the legal right to differentiate between legitimate and opportunistic ex-post requests by customers. Johnston argues that the practice of granting ex post concessions reinforces the relationship more than if the same concession were drafted into the initial terms of the contract.*

Among attorneys, judges, and legal academics, there is virtual consensus that the widespread use by business firms of standard-form contracts in their dealings with consumers has completely eliminated bargaining in consumer contracts. I believe that this perception is false, that rather than precluding bargaining and negotiation, standard-form contracts in fact facilitate bargaining and are a crucial instrument in the establishment and maintenance of cooperative relationships between firms and their customers. On this view, firms use clear and unconditional standard-form contract terms not because they will insist on those terms but because they have given their managerial employees the discretion to grant exceptions from the standard-form terms on a case-by-case basis. In practice, acting through its agents, a firm often will provide benefits to consumers who complain beyond those that its standard form obligates it to provide, and it will forgive consumer breach of standard-form terms. Firms do this because they have an interest in building and maintaining cooperative, value-enhancing relationships with their customers. Were firms legally required to extend such benefits or forgiveness – as would result either from judicial invalidation of the tough standard-form performance terms or legislatively mandated generous standard-form performance terms – then both firms and their customers would be worse off.

My analysis generates some advice for courts employing common law contract doctrines. Courts should presume that standard-form contract terms are a valid and enforceable part of the bargain among business firms, their customers, and their employees. At the same time, however, courts must recognize that opportunistic firms will use standard forms to renege on promises to offer the tailored and flexible forgiveness and accommodation offered by good firms. To prevent such behavior, courts should enforce additional promises or concessions made by agents of the firm that go beyond standard-form obligations, provided that there is clear evidence that such promises were actually made. Courts should also ensure that standard-form arbitration clauses do indeed offer uniform and predictable remedies, rather than no remedies at all.

I. From Contracts of Adhesion to Market Assent

In its core doctrines, the common law of contracts was already well developed when standardized consumer contracts appeared on the scene. One of those core doctrines is that a legally enforceable contract requires a manifestation of mutual assent to the exchange – a bargaining process culminating in an offer and an acceptance. The paradigmatic standardized consumer transaction does not, however, involve an individualized negotiation but, rather, mass retailing with standardized terms and prices.

Many courts and commentators view with alarm the absence of negotiations over such standard-form terms. Particularly disturbing to these critics is the uniformity often displayed across different forms. This uniformity is regarded as further evidence of the absence of meaningful consumer choice.[1] On this traditional view, which may be called the exploitation theory, standard-form terms in consumer contracts represent the exploitation of consumers by manufacturers and retailers who possess superior information and/or market power.

In the 1980s, law and economics scholars advanced a new, alternative view that standard forms must respond to competitive pressures. Schwartz and Wilde famously argued that a small proportion of smart consumers who actually read boilerplate induce firms to adopt efficient terms.[2] Priest showed that the warranty terms do in fact allocate liability efficiently.[3] Without bargaining, it seemed that standard forms give rise to the same terms that negotiations would have produced. This was the theory of market assent. And even the Supreme Court bought into it.[4]

Recently, a new and rising body of scholarship applying findings from experimental psychology of widespread and serious human cognitive limitations gave new life to the old exploitation theory of standard-form terms.[5] It is again founded on the view that standard-form contracts are not designed to encourage bargaining but to preclude it. The view that I advance in this chapter accepts the fact that most (or all) individuals do not read the terms. I argue, however, that although there is no bargaining over standard-form terms, there is plenty of bargaining in the shadow of those terms. I begin with some empirical evidence supporting this view and then provide a theoretical model explaining the emergence of this practice.

II. Bargaining around Standard-Form Terms: Some Evidence

Virtually every firm that sells goods or services or extends some form of credit to consumers has certain standard-form contractual terms governing such things as when and how payment is due, when and if a good can be returned, whether charges are made for services beyond those originally contracted for, and other related matters. Although set out in contractual forms that are standard in all the firm's dealings, the evidence shows that the actual implementation of these various policies must be done on a case-by-case basis, whether by firm employees who work at particular stores or by staffers in centralized call centers. Typically, the firm's standard-form terms set out clear and unconditional consumer obligations. But the common practice is to accord discretion to a supervisor (and sometimes lower level employee) to forgive part of the obligations and to depart from these standard-form terms, if it is deemed in the firm's best interest to do so. Let me begin by offering some selected evidence on the pervasiveness of this pattern of contracting, which I call a *two-part, or discretionary, standard-form contract.*

A. *Hospital Bills*

A major problem for hospitals and ambulatory-care facilities is nonpayment of medical bills by outpatients. A *USA Today* article noted that "[h]ospitals can raise charges to any amount the market will bear, but it's an odd market because most hospital customers negotiate discounts off charges."[6] This statement is borne out by exchanges on The Dollar Stretcher, a mediated online-discussion board, on which a patient who inquired about negotiating over hospital bills received a variety of responses such as, "[t]he thing to do is immediately upon receiving the bill is [*sic*] call the accounting office at the hospital and doctors [*sic*] offices ([if] they send their own bills) [and] explain that you do not have the funds to pay in full but would like to make monthly payments."[7]

Following the recommendations of industry consultants, many, probably most, hospitals have dedicated "assistance officers" or "financial counselors," whose jobs are to work out payment plans with patients. On The Dollar Stretcher, a hospital employee noted that these hospital financial counselors "often will negotiate the charges.... [P]hysicians will do the same thing, especially if they know you don't have insurance." Another hospital employee stated, "I would explain your financial situation, and offer a lowball sum, mayby [*sic*] 25%. I would not expect to pay less than 50%. They will often discount to 2/3." The Web site for the American Academy of Family Physicians also recommends negotiating payment plans with hospitals and doctors.

In the case of hospital bills, there is systematic survey evidence that confirms the anecdotal evidence of widespread negotiation around standard-form payment terms. A Harris Interactive survey shows that although negotiating over hospital bills is not quite ubiquitous, it is common.[8] Seventeen percent of all adults reported having talked to their pharmacist to see if they could pay a lower price than billed, with lower numbers reporting doing the same with doctors (13%), dentists (12%), and hospitals (10%). Of these, about half reported success in paying a lower price. The poll also showed that if hospital costs continue to rise, many more people would seriously consider negotiating over their medical bills.

B. *Consumer Credit Cards*

Credit-card contracts are full of terms that epitomize the pairing of bright-line borrower obligations with discretionary creditor forgiveness. A typical credit-card contract grants a grace period during which time balances may be repaid without the borrower incurring the stated finance charge, and grace periods are typically stated as, for example, "not less than 20 days," thus giving the issuer the option to extend the grace period beyond twenty days. As described by Ronald Mann,[9] issuers reserve much discretion, including the power to shift spending limits, and to change rates, fees, and other terms of the account, at any time and for any reason. Notoriously, they reserve the right under the Universal Default Clause to base the modification on default information acquired from other creditors. Clearly, in a number of key terms, the consumer credit-card contract is written with minimal bright-line borrower guarantees but lots of room for "tailored forgiveness" by the issuer.

While I have not yet found any systematic empirical data on how often credit-card issuers renegotiate debt, the existing informal and anecdotal evidence suggests that this practice is common. A raft of best-seller books on consumer finances recommend negotiating around credit-card contract terms including the interest rate, annual fee, late payment fee, payment moratoria, and repayment schedules.[10] The frequency with which repayment obligations are renegotiated is perhaps most strongly evidenced by the fact that repayment negotiation – consumer credit-card "workouts" – has been prominent among several credit-card industry practices that have recently been under very high-level regulatory scrutiny. In July 2002, the four federal regulatory agencies with jurisdiction over credit-card issuers put out a draft "Account Management and Loss Allowance Guidance" ("Draft Guidance"). This document criticized credit-card companies for a variety of practices that extended credit to borrowers beyond the borrowers' ability to pay, increasing creditor risk exposure to very high levels. The Draft Guidance criticized the way that issuers were handling their "workout" programs – programs set up to allow borrowers to pay off the outstanding balances on (closed) credit cards – for not reducing interest rates, fees, and finance charges sufficiently to allow borrowers to extinguish their debts within "reasonable time frames."

Credit-card issuers responded almost immediately to the Draft Guidance. They correctly noted that it was essentially calling for a dramatic change in credit-issuer operations, from one focused on "portfolio review and management of the millions of consumer loans . . . to an increasing supervisory review of individual loans."[11] Issuers complained that, even as they seemed to require such costly individualized management of millions of consumer loans, financial institution examiners would interpret the Draft Guidance's recommendations as bright-line rules barring overlimit authorizations under any circumstances and requiring repayment of borrower workouts within forty-eight days.

Interestingly, issuers claimed that their existing policy of offering overlimit authorizations in certain circumstances was an important customer-relations tool in getting and keeping the business of good, low-credit-risk customers who occasionally had emergency credit needs that caused them to exceed their limits. Without such discretionary overlimit authorizations, issuers would need to grant higher initial credit lines or else risk losing their best, lowest risk customers. Similarly, the issuers argued in favor of a "reasonable and prudent timeframe [for a repayment period]" that would retain issuer discretion to "address each consumer's individual needs and circumstances."

C. *Retail Sales Return Policies*

Legally, the default rule in retail sales provides no right to return items for a refund. However, most large retailers have adopted a policy that grants consumers a right of return. Until recently, retailers also generally granted their on-the-ground employees discretion in liberalizing their official return policies so as to please consumers – so much that opportunistic consumers were taking advantage and obtaining free product rentals. This is a dramatic illustration of the reality of getting around the standard-form term and the firm's need to use its agents to screen for consumer type.

Even though a consumer may have no idea what a retailer's formal return policy might be, consumers clearly like liberal return practices such as allowing long return periods, giving cash rather than just store credit, and allowing for the return even of sale items. A recent poll found that 91 percent of customers considered return policies and processes as very important to their decision about where to make a purchase[12] (although only about 25 percent of customers make returns at all). Liberal returns keep consumers happy, generating repeat business and positive word-of-mouth.

To reduce customer abuse of liberal return policies, retailers have recently undertaken measures to both identify and refuse return requests by opportunistic consumers and to limit employee discretion in granting returns. Retailers such as Kmart and Target have started to strictly enforce their standard-form policy of granting returns within the specified return period and only if the customer has the product receipt. Retailers have begun to implement point-of-sale information systems that allow them to quickly identify repeat returners. Services such as the Return Exchange maintain databases that track customers whose buying patterns make them look like return abusers, enabling retailers to refine their real-time response to return requests.

III. Explaining Observed Behavior: Designing Standard-Form Terms that Are Meant to Be Forgiven

In all of the empirical examples, a business uses a standard-form contract that establishes a clear, bright-line obligation, but the business gives its supervisory employees the discretion to do more for the customer than the standard-form obligations require. A very strong economic logic motivates this very common contracting practice: The desire of firms to maximize not only short-term profits but also long-term value.

The strategy of allowing employees the discretion to grant case-specific benefits beyond those that are required by the standard-form contract can be seen as a sophisticated way for the firm to grow its revenues by gaining the loyalty of existing customers and establishing a good reputation that will attract new customers. There are, in fact, two slightly different aspects to this strategy. In the first, the good or service provided was not up to the customer's expectation, and the customer complains, seeking some kind of compensation from the provider. I shall refer to this as the strategy of awarding discretionary benefits. In the second case, the customer has not lived up to her obligations under the standard-form contract, but the provider forgives her technical breach. I shall refer to this as the strategy of discretionary forgiveness.

A. *Discretionary Forgiveness as Ex-Post Customer Screening*

The key to understanding why a firm can benefit by allowing its employees to forgive some customers' contract breaches lies in the recognition that not all existing customers are worth keeping. Some consumers are honest, some are not. Some consumers have a highly secure economic base and ability to pay, whereas others have jobs and income flows that are much more uncertain. The strategy of adopting bright-line standard-form terms and then granting discretionary forgiveness allows businesses to identify or screen for good, high-value customers under circumstances when they could not do so with the contract term itself.

To see why this is so, consider the important example of repayment terms. Creditors more generally renegotiate these when their agents have determined that there is a good reason for the borrower's failure to make timely payment. A "good" reason is something beyond the borrower's control, such as an illness or loss of a job (or, for a business, a sudden downturn in market conditions). A borrower who has fallen behind only because of such an unusual and extraordinary event is a valuable customer, someone who is basically a very good credit risk and on whom the creditor will, on average, make money.

A creditor can successfully screen for such "good" types by setting clear standard-form terms that are sometimes waived (or not enforced) when it could not do so by using a simple standard-form contract without renegotiation. Suppose, for instance, that the creditor eliminated its managers' discretion to forgive and altered the standard-form terms to require a shorter repayment period and/or a higher interest rate. By demanding such harsh terms up front, in the standard-form contract, the creditor would lose the business of "good," lower-income borrowers who will keep their promises to make timely repayments while doing nothing to lose the business of "bad," opportunistic borrowers who borrow with no intention of repaying on schedule. By the same reasoning, we can see the trade-off that the creditor confronts in arriving at the optimum, profit-maximizing combination of standard-form terms and discretionary forgiveness. On the one hand, the lower the standard-form interest rate and the longer the standard-form repayment period, the greater the number of good, honest borrowers who sign on and the lower the probability of costly, forgiving renegotiation with such borrowers. On the other hand, a lower interest rate and longer repayment period mean lower revenues from such borrowers. Conversely, were the creditor to raise the interest rate and shorten the repayment period, it would increase revenues from good borrowers but also decrease the proportion of good borrowers and increase the probability of costly renegotiation with good borrowers. The optimal terms result from solving this trade-off.

What necessitates the two-part contract – clear standard-form terms plus managerial discretion to renegotiate – is a fundamental economic problem of adverse selection (or hidden information).[13] Adverse selection refers to the problem of designing a contract when the contract may attract different types of contracting parties – some honest, some opportunistic, for example – who bring correspondingly different costs and benefits to the relationship. Tailored forgiveness deals with the problem of hidden customer types. In dealing with the hidden-type problem, tailored forgiveness is a substitute for ex-ante screening. That is, a firm that has tough standard-form terms and then delegates discretion to renegotiate when its managers believe that the customer has not behaved opportunistically does not have to worry so much about identifying opportunistic types before entering the contract. If it turns out that the customer behavior was indeed opportunistic, its manager will insist upon adherence to the unforgiving standard-form terms. In fact, it can be shown that a lender will set a lower interest rate and more generous repayment terms than it would if denied the legal ability to use its discretion to forgive breach of the standard-form terms.

Interestingly, although economists have recognized the adverse selection problem confronting creditors and other providers of consumer goods and services, they have failed to discuss two-part contracts as a market solution to this problem. Rather than ex-post forgiving renegotiation, economists have focused on ex-ante mechanisms that creditors use to screen out bad credit risks, such as requiring collateral or lending only to consumers with whom they have had ongoing personal contact (referred to generally in the lending context as "credit rationing"). Compared with ex-post renegotiation, such ex-ante screening has the disadvantage of making it hard for "new" consumers – those without an established reputation – to obtain credit. Rather than screening ex ante on the basis of wealth or relationship, two-part contracts in effect say, "We do not know you, but we will give you a chance." In this light, it is clear that two-part contracts serve a very important social as well as economic function: They make it economically rational for creditors and other providers to do business with consumers who, because of their age, ethnicity, or nationality, have not yet had an opportunity to establish either accumulated wealth or valuable personal relationships.

B. *Individualized versus Algorithmic Renegotiation*

In the empirical examples discussed earlier, the seller or creditor does not incur the high cost of having its employees individually renegotiate forgiveness but, rather, relies on general rules of thumb or algorithms that all employees use in determining whether or not to forgive breach.

On my analysis, there is no reason for regulators to insist on such individualized bargaining at the forgiveness stage of a two-part standard-form contract. After all, a seller or creditor is using the second stage to determine whether or not the buyer or borrower is or is not worth keeping as a customer. From the evidence discussed earlier, providers that have a relatively small number of accounts to manage – such as hospitals – seem to find it economical to engage in a more individualized forgiveness renegotiation than do providers – such as credit-card issuers – who have millions of accounts and rely on generalized algorithms that, for instance, extend additional credit x number of times automatically. In reasonably competitive markets, the lower the cost of forgiveness, both the provider and its consumer clients are better off.

Were regulators to make it too costly for providers to engage in ex-post forgiveness, they might well make the two-part contract uneconomical for providers. As just argued, if restricted to a one-part contract in which only price and other standard-form terms may be used to screen customer types, it is on my analysis very likely that providers would increase price and toughen payment terms. Thus, as the credit-card issuers argued, adoption of regulations that make forgiveness of late or inadequate payments too costly would indeed likely cause some institutions to stop making new credit loans to subprime borrowers, thus restricting credit availability to many low- and moderate-income families.

C. *Discretionary Benefits and the Potential Instability of Consumer Screening through Two-Part Standard-Form Contracts*

Another version of the two-part contract involves the awarding of discretionary ex-post customer benefits. For many firms, the most important type of customer to keep happy is the customer who is relatively knowledgeable, persuasive, and strategic – a sharp bargainer. Such customers are likely to be a lucrative source of repeat business if they remain satisfied with the firm's services. By the same token, if they terminate their relationships with the firm because they are dissatisfied with the quality of the firm's services, they are likely to be an especially influential source of negative word-of-mouth advertising. The strategy of allowing its employees to respond to complaints with various forms of compensatory benefits is a cost-minimizing way for the firm to increase the probability that it will keep the business of such consumers. By waiting for the consumer to make the first move – by complaining – the company effectively lets the high-value, high-information consumers identify themselves. That is, the consumers who will complain most often and loudest are presumably those who are most inconvenienced by the failure of the product or service to meet their expectations. Other consumers may not even be aware of the possibility of obtaining relief by complaining to the company. The firm would like to give the benefits to this first group but not to the second.

This works to the benefit of the demanding consumers when they are in a minority and there are lots of naïve, uncomplaining consumers. The price of the lower quality good or service may be low enough so that the sophisticated consumers are better off with the lower-quality good (plus complaint-based compensation when things go wrong) than they would be with a higher-quality, higher-price good. When these conditions hold, the complaint-based benefits strategy not only allows the firm to retain and add sophisticated, influential customers but also effectively gives those customers a price subsidy that is paid for by well-informed or simply more acquiescent consumers.

By this same token, however, the complaint-based benefits strategy creates an opportunity for new firms to enter and offer the good or service on a simple one-part contract that offers no discretionary benefits but charges a lower price to attract the low-value consumers who do not demand discretionary benefits. The entry into the market of low-price, "no-frills" providers will destroy the cross-subsidy offered by the two-part contract, and with such entry, that market may segment into low-price, no-frills providers and high-price, quality providers. In such a segmented equilibrium, there will no longer be any reason to use bargaining around the standard-form, no-frills terms to screen out high-value consumers. The two-part standard-form contracting practice should exhibit long-term survival only in industries that are relatively noncompetitive.

This does not, however, imply that it is only in such relatively noncompetitive industries that we will observe such a contracting strategy. Even if undermined from below, as it were, by the entry of no-frills providers, the discretionary-benefits strategy may have been a valuable, albeit temporary, instrument for firms. The strategy allows firms to identify and attract high-value, sophisticated consumers. Hence, even if firms using such a strategy eventually lose their low-value consumers to low-price, no-frills entrants, the discretionary benefits strategy may well have accelerated growth in firm size and sales for a number of years, thus increasing the firm's stock-market value.

IV. The Value of Discretion: Distributional Issues in the Regulation of Standard-Form Contracts and Their Renegotiation

An immediate implication of the preceding analysis is that the effect of laws or regulations mandating generous standard-form terms would be to replace a system in which firms extend a wide and trusting invitation and then enforce standard-form terms only against those whom its on-the-ground managers have found to have violated that trust with one in which firms use only attorney-drafted standard-form terms to control their exposure to contractual risk. Such a move from individualized ex-post screening to crude ex-ante screening may well harm the very groups – such as generally poorer, economically disadvantaged racial minorities – that it was designed to help. It is also true that mandating generous terms might prevent the cross-subsidization of high-value, sophisticated consumers by low-value, less sophisticated consumers that is entailed by the discretionary strategy. But by mandating generous standard-form terms, the firm's cost, and hence the competitive price, would increase.

Such a price increase will almost surely be higher than the increase in value that any consumer type gets from the mandatory terms. The reason why this is so is crucial to understand, for it sharply distinguishes this analysis of mandatory standard-form terms from earlier law-and-economics work on the topic. When the law mandates generous standard-form terms, it is possible that it is giving low-value, low-sophistication consumers terms that they value at more than their cost, but which they did not get under the discretionary strategy because they lack the sophistication or simple willingness to complain and bargain ex post. However, if this is true, then it would seem that firms would have been better off simply offering and advertising the generous standard-form package in the first place. When, however, the firm promises all customers these generous terms, it has lost the ability to screen for customer opportunism. Such opportunism is costly. Hence, when the firm sells a standard-form package with all the various benefits and forgiving adjustments that it would otherwise have made on a discretionary basis under the tough standard-form contract, non-opportunistic customers must pay for the costs of opportunism that the firm can no longer control. Although low-value, low-sophistication customers might indeed value discretionary benefits at more than they cost the firm when they are not opportunistically claimed, such customers may well not value the benefits as highly as their cost to the firm when it can no longer control opportunistic claims.

Thus, when opportunism is a serious concern, low-value customers will be priced out of the market if policies that were discretionary with the firm become part of the firm's standard-form obligations. Alternatively, when opportunism is not so serious as to price out the low-value customers, mandating generous standard-form terms may eliminate the cross-subsidization in favor of high-value, sophisticated customers. In this case, all customers may end up getting the benefits that before accrued only to the higher value customers.

Such a happy outcome is, however, not likely. For one thing, because opportunism becomes a more severe problem under mandatory generous standard-form terms, the firm will have an incentive to instruct employees to behave in a noncooperative fashion when customers bring complaints by insisting on very narrow and legalistic interpretations of the firm's superficially generous obligations. Thus, whereas under the discretionary strategy, high-value customers were met with an ex-post willingness to bargain, in the world of mandatory standard-form terms, they will often encounter precisely the opposite. As a result, high-value types are more likely to switch their business to a more expensive higher-quality provider, which the low-value customers cannot afford. In such a case, mandating generous standard-form terms may induce a kind of adverse selection; as higher-value customers drop out, the ostensibly generous standard-form terms offered to remaining customers are, in practice, degraded further and further.

V. Standard-Form Terms and the Doctrinal Control of Firm Opportunism

A. *The Complexity of Opportunism*

It may quite aptly be objected that opportunism cuts both ways; just as consumers and employees might opportunistically invoke generous standard-form contractual rights, so too might opportunistic firms harshly and unfairly enforce harsh standard-form clauses. Although this is indeed possible, such behavior would alienate and drive away customers. And if word-of-mouth is indeed as important as many contemporary marketing experts increasingly believe, by unfairly driving away their current customers, such firms would do much to ensure that they do not get future customers. Thus, firm opportunism is possible only where the firm is selling a good or service that consumers buy infrequently and in small quantity and where the firm makes its sales in widely diffuse locations that are not part of the same consumer word-of-mouth network.

Furthermore, real firm opportunism would seem to consist not in being a literalist about form contract rights and obligations but rather in creating a false appearance of pursuing a policy of forgiveness or complaint-based benefits by mimicking the behavior of a firm that really does implement these strategies.

The truly opportunistic firm would take steps to appear to pursue a nice, forgiving strategy, while eventually reneging on those promises for various technical or legalistic reasons that are burdensome or impossible for most consumers, even quite sophisticated ones, to sort through.

B. *Doctrinal Implications*

The possibility of good and bad types on both sides of the firm-consumer divide raises an obvious question about the potential for laws and regulations to improve the performance of two-part standard-form contracts. My general answer to this question is that courts should support the standard-form, discretionary benefits/forgiveness market equilibrium. To get more precise prescriptions for judicial action (or inaction), the key thing to see about the market equilibrium is that in it, whereas all firms have very strong incentives to actually discipline customer opportunism, only those firms that are long-run players in the game and really seek to build lasting customer relationships have an incentive to actually confer discretionary benefits beyond what they have promised in their form contracts.

For firms that are opportunistic short-run players, the second stage is too costly. Such opportunistic firms will instead rely on onerous standard-form terms to extract consumer rents, refusing to renegotiate them at all, or fraudulently promising but then failing to forgive. Indeed, and most seriously for the viability of two-part contracts equilibrium, if, by invoking complex legalese, firms could renege on promises to forgive or to extend benefits without customers being able to determine whether there is a valid legal reason for reneging, then all firms would have an incentive to pursue such a highly opportunistic strategy. The market equilibrium posited earlier would then unravel.

It is, unfortunately, far from clear that courts can do much to prevent such firm opportunism. One's first thought might well be that courts could reduce firm opportunism by holding firms to their agents' ex-post promises offering discretionary forgiveness or complaint-based benefits. The critical doctrines here are those governing the enforceability of relatively informal promises made apart from or in the process of renegotiating the standard-form contract. Candidate doctrines would include those determining the enforceability of an express warranty made outside a standard-form contract that by its terms excludes any such warranties and the enforceability of an oral modification of a standard-form contract that by its terms precludes any such oral modification.

It is possible that, through such doctrines, courts could increase the cost to opportunistic firms of inducing consumers to make more payments by promising but failing to deliver discretionary benefits or forgiveness. But it is the opportunistic consumers who will file lawsuits claiming that such promises were made when they in fact were not. Contract-law rules that presume that the terms of a present contract are affected by prior course of dealing or past performance tend to facilitate plaintiff opportunism and raise the risk that a defendant firm will be erroneously held liable for a forgiving promise that it never made. This may increase the cost to the firm of pursuing two-part contracts, so much so that firms might no longer allow discretionary forgiveness/benefits, thus destroying what is, in general, a socially desirable market outcome.

This argument suggests that if courts are to get into the business of enforcing promises of discretionary forgiveness/benefits, then they should do so only if there is very strong evidence that the promise was in fact made. Although some courts have followed this recommendation, others have been, if anything, too cautious in enforcing such promises. My analysis suggests that with sufficient evidentiary safeguards, oral misrepresentations by a firm's agent that deviate from standard-form contract terms are a form of opportunistic exploitation that should be deemed fraudulent and, hence, should constitute grounds for rescinding a contract. State high courts, however, appear to be split on the issue of whether general standard-form merger clauses[14] and/or language that disclaims reliance on oral representations bar actions for fraud claiming that oral representations by the firm's agents in fact induced such reliance.[15] On my analysis, standard-form disclaimers and merger clauses should not bar persuasive proof that oral representations were indeed made. Such an approach is precisely what courts have taken in dealing with a closely related issue, the enforceability of oral agreements modifying written standard-form contracts that by their terms prohibit oral modification. Here the courts have held that whereas detrimental reliance or partial performance may make enforceable an oral promise modifying obligations in a standard-form contract that precludes such modification unless in writing, such reliance or performance must be "unequivocally referable" to the oral modifying promise and must not be "compatible" with the original agreement.[16]

Courts have dealt with consumer-sales contracts falling under the Uniform Commercial Code in a somewhat more liberal way. On the one hand, under section 2–316(1) of the Uniform Commercial Code, standard-form terms attempting the "negation or limitation" of express oral warranties are "inoperative" to the extent that they conflict with the express warranty. On the other hand, to address the concern that consumers might falsely claim that a seller's agent made an express warranty, comment 2 to section 2–316(1) explains that "[t]he seller is protected under this Article against false allegations of oral warranties by its provisions on parol and extrinsic evidence and against unauthorized representations by the customary 'lack of authority' clauses."

Neither of these points is convincing. A standard-form clause stating that an agent lacks actual authority can and sometimes should be overcome by showing a pattern or practice of agent representations and promises that establishes apparent agent authority. The Code's parol evidence rule is, moreover, very liberal in allowing for the admission of evidence of "course of dealing or usage of trade" to "explain" or "supplement" standard-form terms. Especially given the language of section 2–313 that a buyer need not show any "particular reliance" for oral express affirmations of fact "made by the seller about the goods during a bargain" to become part of the parties' contract, the courts have generally admitted parol evidence of such affirmations and have ruled that they override the warranty exclusion clause of a standard form.

Turning to consumer-credit transactions, the Uniform Commercial Code's liberal attitude toward course-of-performance evidence has led some courts to be too ready to find that a pattern of forgiving conduct has overridden standard-form terms. This is dramatically illustrated by the split of authority on the issue of whether a consumer creditor who has accepted late payments as a matter of course may still insist upon the validity of a standard-form clause stating that such a pattern of behavior does not waive its rights to insist on timely payment (an antiwaiver clause). One general approach holds that if the creditor has, in fact, induced the consumer borrower to rely on the ability to make late payments, then the creditor is estopped from reasserting its standard-form rights unless it first notifies the borrower. An alternative view holds that on basic Code principles of assent, a secured creditor's course of conduct may effectively change the meaning of the contract so that regardless of reliance, by accepting late payment, a creditor has waived its own standard-form antiwaiver provision. In such case, the creditor can reinstate its right to insist upon timely payment only if it gives the borrower reasonable notice that it is reverting back to the original, standard-form policy (and then only if the borrower has not materially changed its position in reliance on the waiver).

On my theory, both of these approaches to creditor waiver of a standard-form no-waiver clause fail to recognize the informational, screening function of creditor forgiveness. Creditors allow late payments as a kind of experiment even though they are not obligated to do so by their standard-form agreement. What creditors are trying to discover is borrower type: Is this a "good" borrower, one with a temporary problem only and whose business we want to keep as a customer, or is this a "bad" borrower, one who really cannot make the agreed-upon payments and who is not worth keeping as a customer? When the creditor discovers a bad type, it will revert to the standard-form right to timely payment, which when not forthcoming will then allow it to declare the borrower in default and exercise its various standard-form default rights. On the margin, the risk that courts will find that tolerating late payments has entailed a loss of standard-form contractual rights makes forgiveness a riskier strategy for creditors. If the risk is significant enough so that creditors find forgiveness too costly, then they will respond by making the basic credit terms – interest rate, repayment period, and the like – tougher, thereby excluding from the market precisely those good faith but ex-ante risky consumer borrowers that the courts are undoubtedly anxious to help, not hurt.

Finally, turning to standard-form choice-of-law and arbitration clauses, my analysis suggests that the recent trend of hostility toward them is misguided. In some states, courts are increasingly striking down arbitration and choice of regime clauses as unconscionable. Such hostility toward mandatory arbitration clauses is, in my view, ill-founded and inimical to the kinds of cooperative consumer-firm and employee-employer relationships that two-part standard-form contracts can generate. True, there are opportunistic employers and sellers who attempt to write arbitration clauses that effectively take away the other side's right to press her dispute. These worst-case clauses should be and are invalidated as unconscionable. They should not be used as grounds for a general rule against contractual choice-of-regime terms. Instead, legal enforcement of arbitration clauses is crucial to the ability of firms and consumers and employers and employees to pursue the kind of tailored forgiveness and complaint-based benefits strategies that govern the performance of their ongoing and continuing relationships.

The reason why legal enforcement of arbitration clauses is so important is that for the system of tough standard-form terms coupled with tailored forgiveness and complaint-based benefits to work, it must be that the firm is free to deny the forgiveness or the benefit. If, upon denial, the firm would face a risk of being sued in the civil liability system, the two-part system will break down. For one, if the firm's practice of sometimes paying benefits and sometimes not is litigated in court, the firm may be found to have established a new, standard practice of paying such benefits or may be estopped from denying the grounds for liability. Moreover, the large variation in civil-damage awards makes expected ex-post liability outcomes, rather than the perceived business value of cooperative resolution, a key determinant of what firms are willing to do. Firms have too great an incentive to resolve "cooperatively" complaints of questionable validity involving large customer or employee loss and too weak an incentive to resolve much more clearly valid, but small, customer and employee claims.

Arbitration resolves these dangers. The proceedings are not public and so the firm does not have to worry that cooperative resolution of employee and customer complaints, or forgiveness of customer or employee contractual shortfalls, will establish a binding precedent that converts these discretionary acts into mandatory obligations applying to all employees and customers with legally similar situations. And, in terms of outcomes, arbitration allows plaintiffs to prevail at a much higher rate, and, because of the litigation cost saving, find attorneys to represent them more often. They end up getting about the same median award in both civil trial and arbitration but a higher mean award and much larger damages in big, catastrophic cases in civil trial than arbitration.[17]

The two-part contract model suggests that under arbitration, the firm's incentive to accommodate and maintain an employee's or customer relationship is influenced largely by the value of ongoing relationship, not by the threat of costly civil liability. When the value of the continuing relationship has little to do with the employee or customer's loss in a particular instance, both the firm and the employee/customer are better off when it is the potential future value of the relationship, rather than the damages in a particular case, that determines their joint behavior in promoting its continuation.

THREE

Boilerplate and Economic Power in Auto-Manufacturing Contracts

Omri Ben-Shahar and James J. White

Editor's Note: *This chapter examines the boilerplate contracts used by automakers to procure parts from suppliers. It identifies drafting and negotiation techniques that are used to secure advantageous terms. It also explores some prominent specific arrangements as evidence that firms with bargaining power are exploiting their position to dictate self-serving but inefficient terms. Finally, it shows how standard contractual clauses solve the problem of ex-post hold-up by suppliers.*

Manufacturing contracts in the automotive industry have served a canonical role in the economic theory of contract and bargaining. The famous story of General Motors' relationship with its supplier Fisher Body in the 1920s is a landmark illustration of the problem of contractual hold-up, underlying a prominent theory of vertical integration and the nature of the firm.[1] The theoretical fascination with automotive procurement contracts is well deserved. There may be no other merchant-to-merchant contractual template that governs such fantastic economic stakes – hundreds of billions of dollars per year – and implemented through a process that involves almost no negotiation of the legal terms. Boilerplate rules these transactions.

There is a long line of law-and-economics scholarship studying the attributes of standard-form terms in contracts between sophisticated parties in high-stakes transactions. One of the benchmark predictions in this literature is that contractual terms have to be efficient if they are to be consistently used by the parties. Any rent-seeking power that a party has should be translated into a price advantage; it should not be used to dictate selfish but inefficient performance terms. Furthermore, because legal terms such as warranties and remedies affect the costs borne by the parties, we expect that sophisticated parties will be "pricing" the terms and will be ready to redraft terms that cost more than they save. A study of automobile contracts provides an opportunity to test these predictions. These are transactions in which economic power is unevenly distributed; much dickering takes place over prices and product design; but everything else is packed into boilerplate. Every party reads the boilerplate and understands its legal effect and its economic consequences. Do strong parties dictate efficient boilerplate and extract rents through prices and other purely distributive clauses? Do they tailor their terms to maximize their net gains from the transactions?

Moreover, automotive-supply contracts are the paradigmatic long-term relationships that require a great deal of relationship-specific investments in the form of machinery, location of plants, and precontractual technology research. As the economic literature predicts, the interdependence of suppliers (who must invest in specializing for their buyers' needs) and buyers (who need specialized parts from their suppliers) gives opportunities for hold-up.[2] These dangers make the contracts the primary tool for deterring hold-up and encouraging investment. What are the contractual techniques used to address the risk of hold-up?

In answering these questions, we have taken a simple, almost naïve approach. We read and compared industry boilerplate contracts and talked to lawyers who drafted these forms and to some nonlawyer industry participants. We provide a case study, but it yields some general insights. For example, the boilerplate contract terms between the Original Equipment Manufacturers (OEMs) and the tier-1 suppliers show how economic power is translated into transactional advantage. From the contract terms, we can identify ways the OEMs extract value from their suppliers. Contrary to the fabled GM–Fisher Body story, we find no real problem of hold-up by suppliers. The claim that suppliers with a long-term contract can hold up the OEMs is based on a misunderstanding of the terms of the deal, the rules of contract law, and the structure of the market. Moreover, comparing the terms that appear in the purchase orders (POs) of the various OEMs reveals ways in which they differ and, surprisingly, it suggests that some of these terms may foster inefficiency. Finally, studying the way the form contracts are drafted gives a detailed understanding of how and when tailoring of terms takes place and how internal organizational features are harnessed to affect the outcome of negotiations over contract terms.

I. The Contracts

The automotive-supply industry is sometimes described as a pyramid built in "tiers." At the top are the OEMs. This study focuses mostly on the "Big Three" OEMs – General Motors, Ford, and DaimlerChrysler – but it also looks at six foreign OEMs that assemble cars in the United States. Directly below the OEMs are the tier-1 suppliers – anyone who sells directly to an OEM. These companies usually sell sophisticated assemblies or parts, and most of them specialize in designing and manufacturing automotive-specific products. They purchase their supplies from tier-2 suppliers who in turn purchase from tier-3 suppliers, and so on. Because there are only a few OEMs at the top but roughly six hundred to eight hundred tier-1 suppliers, the main issues that need to be governed by the contracts between OEMs and tier-1 suppliers are different than in lower tiers.

Supply contracts in the automotive industry are made through competitive bidding. An OEM issues requests for quotations for a particular part or assembly. The supplier whose bid is picked would ordinarily make a significant capital investment in R&D and production assets and supply this part for the duration of the car model in which the part is assembled, a period that normally lasts four to eight years. The winning bidder, however, does not always get the security of a long-term, fixed-price contract. Although some OEMs accord the supplier a long-term sourcing commitment, the actual POs are issued on a short-term basis. Shorter contracts give the parties opportunities to renegotiate aspects of the deal such as price and quantity estimates; OEMs commonly demand (and receive) price reductions every year. Technically, most of these adjustments are not modifications of the contract but, rather, renewals of short-term POs, all entered into under a master long-term agreement.

Each OEM has a single form, titled either "Global Terms" or "General Terms," that is used almost without exception for procuring all of the manufacturing parts. General Motors, for example, enters into roughly one million procurement contracts every year, at a total amount in excess of $80 billion – all governed by a single contract form containing thirty-one paragraphs, translated into six languages.

We expected little variation in the OEMs' forms. What we found was a different reality. There is significant variance across the OEM contracts. We examined the boilerplates of nine North American OEMs and recorded the many ways in which they differ. These differences were also confirmed in discussions with representatives of tier-1 suppliers and of the suppliers' trade association, who emphasized that the differences in the legal terms represent in some cases significant variations in the economic consequences of the deals. According to all of our interviewees, the most important issues in the OEM boilerplate contracts are the following: termination rights, warranties and remedies, service parts, intellectual property rights in technological innovations, and tooling (the ownership of the production assets). We consider each of these issues.

Termination. In all purchase contracts, OEMs secure the right unilaterally to terminate the agreement. This right to terminate, which is not available to suppliers, is almost unrestricted. Either for no cause at all or for reasons stated ambiguously as "competitiveness of price and quality," the OEMs can, with short notice, terminate the contract. In fact, the cancellation rights are so one-sided that they might render the contracts unenforceable on the ground that they lack consideration or fail to state a quantity term under the statute of frauds.[3] There is variation among OEMs' forms regarding the payments to which suppliers are entitled upon termination. Whereas all OEMs provide some recovery to suppliers for their squandered investments, some, such as GM and DaimlerChrysler, are stingy – they pay only for finished parts, work in progress, and raw materials. Others are more generous: They will pay for a combination of other termination costs, such as suppliers' obligations to their own subcontractors and investments in capital. None of the OEMs cover suppliers' unamortized investment in R&D and engineering – a great source of agony for suppliers who expect to cover their fixed costs only after several years of supply.

It is difficult to identify the exact inefficiency that broad termination rights create, particularly because it is not clear how often these rights are exercised. Still, contracts containing harsh termination terms represent a de-facto transformation of the long-term commitment into a series of short-term agreements. In this reality, suppliers anticipate pressures from OEMs to reduce prices even after they have been awarded a contract. This creates a risk of hold-up by OEMs – "reduce your price or be terminated" – that makes relationship-specific investments less valuable.

Warranties and Remedies. Warranty provisions determine suppliers' liability for design defects, intellectual property infringements, and the cost of precautionary recalls. There is significant variation across the contract in the sharing-of-liability clauses, which reflect true differences in the cost allocations and which correlate with different systems for monitoring of defects. It appears that OEMs with the most self-serving warranty allocation terms are also those that take longest to detect and resolve a defect. That is, they are the ones for whom the total costs of defects are, on average, greater. One of our interviewees quoted the warranty cost per vehicle to be roughly $1,000 for an American OEM that uses the harshest warranty allocation terms[4] but only about $250 for a Japanese OEM that applies a more balanced approach.[5] Furthermore, he pointed out that the American OEM takes, on average, 180 days from the time of the first indications of a parts defect until it is resolved; the Japanese OEM takes only forty days. Of course, Japanese cars may simply be better built than American cars. But other figures suggest that if there is a quality gap, it is not as significant as the gap in warranty costs. One way to measure intrinsic quality is the average number of problems per one hundred vehicles. Toyota and Honda, for example, in 2003 reported 101 problems per 100 vehicles; GM, Chrysler, and Ford reported between 120 and 127 problems per 100 vehicles.[6] This quality gap is much smaller than the warranty-cost gap, in which an American OEM suffers a cost roughly four times as high as that of the Japanese OEM.

These figures are consistent with the prediction that parties who believe that they can shift the cost of liability onto others would do less to reduce this cost. Put differently, in situations in which joint precautions by both supplier and buyer are necessary to prevent liability from mounting or in which suppliers can efficiently cure a defect, it is not surprising that the allocation of greater liability to the supplier reduces the OEM's need for a quick solution to any quality issue. What is surprising is that not all contracts are designed to induce more participation of the suppliers in the warranty process and thus fail to achieve efficiency. Compared, for example, to the boilerplate purchase contract drafted by the German Association of the Automotive Industry (VDA), which applies to all tiers, the American OEM's warranty is much harsher. The VDA contract gives the supplier a greater role in assessing any damage claim, participating in repairs and replacements, and limits the scope and duration of warranties.

Service Parts. Service parts are sold in the retail market at a large premium. If the OEM alone may sell these parts, the supplier is deprived of a share of potential profits. And if the supplier is obligated to supply the OEM's requirements for these parts for years after the model production ends (when it is expected that volume efficiency, materials, and skilled personnel will no longer be available), the burden on the supplier can be large.

Almost all OEMs require the supplier to agree to supply service parts for a period of ten to fifteen years after current-model production ends. Some OEMs, however, share the surplus that this production will yield. Honda and Toyota, for example, stipulate that the service-part prices will be negotiated by the parties when the time comes; that translates to a profit-sharing deal. Others (for instance, GM) require prices to remain at their low, production-phase price for an initial period, say three years, after which a higher negotiated price would be agreed on. Most harsh are terms that require suppliers to commit to fifteen years of postproduction supply and to refrain from raising prices above the production-phase prices. These provisions leave the supplier with the high cost of maintaining a production line but without the ability to recoup the expense through high sale volume.

The service-parts provisions also have efficiency implications. Maintaining the production line and the skilled labor to produce the parts will be expensive. Pricing the parts based on the cost structure prevailing when volume is much higher is a poor way to reflect the true wholesale economic price and may lead to suboptimal purchase decisions. OEMs are reluctant to hold minor inventories of parts and instead make frequent small-volume purchases. This requires the suppliers to "turn on the machines" repeatedly to produce small, highly inefficient quantities of parts.

Intellectual Property. The production of assembly parts often requires the development and application of new technologies that have high value as intellectual property beyond that particular application. Much of this technology passes over to the OEMs in the course of designing the parts and assembling them into the vehicles. The contracts grant the OEMs legal rights in these valuable information assets, not only to use them in production but also to control other uses. The most extreme position, found for example in Ford's contract, accords the OEM unlimited rights to all intellectual property of the supplier that is disclosed in the course of trade, except for patents registered before the supply. Suppliers also waive their trade-secret protection and assign to the OEMs all copyrightable works created under the contract without any royalty rights. The more restrained position, as in GM's contract, limits the OEMs' right to sublicense intellectual property and protects the confidential information of the supplier.

Some suppliers refuse to grant such rights in their intellectual property. Companies whose main business is information technology (IT), such as the makers of software, are stubborn about this, and OEMs have learned to expect that they will not be able to dictate their terms to such suppliers. Indeed, some OEMs have specially drafted IT contracts that accommodate the expectations of their IT suppliers for more balanced terms.

Suppliers that have the ability to develop new technologies but who cannot enjoy the full value of the technology they develop once appropriated by the OEM will have a weaker incentive to make investments. We can only speculate that OEMs that insist on harsh IP terms end up with cars that incorporate fewer technological advances. Some of the suppliers' representatives suggested that this is the case.

Tooling. Representatives of tier-1 suppliers voiced many complaints against the tooling provisions. A repeated complaint was that OEMs who often pay for and own the tooling refused to allow the use of production assets to serve multiple clients. The strict ownership terms and the restriction against commingling and co-serving can lead to wasteful duplicity of investments and, of course, to inefficiency. Moreover, this strict control of the machines makes the OEMs' potential threat to terminate a contract (and haul away the production line) more credible. The fear that relationship-specific investments by the suppliers would be squandered increases.

What can be learned from these examples of fundamental variations in the contract terms? Differences in corporate culture may explain the persistence of this variation and the lack of convergence. Furthermore, contract terms do not always reflect actual practices. The actual behavior under the contract may not vary as much as the variation in contract language. Generally, variation of terms across vendors does not itself indicate inefficiency. There may be varying efficient ways to do business. But looking at individual terms in their context, we believe that some of the boilerplate terms are inefficient. Warranty terms of some OEMs do not appear to solve a surplus maximization problem but rather to place the greatest ex-post burden on the seller. Likewise, intellectual property (IP) terms and service-parts arrangements of some OEMs do not reflect an optimal sharing of a resource that is jointly created but instead provide one-sided gains. Given the enormous stakes, we expected that economic power would be used to dictate low prices, not selfish boilerplate. But that is not what we found.

The boilerplate terms are not necessarily the *cause* of the inefficiency. The legal terms in the forms is the tail that is wagged by the business dog, not vice versa. It is plausible that many of these provisions are tailored to leverage the OEMs' economic and bargaining power in the negotiation stage into advantages at the performance stage, in which the parties are locked in a classic bilateral monopoly. American OEMs' record-breaking losses have driven them to capture any opportunity to shift costs to suppliers. But if indeed they do so in a way that reduces the overall surplus of the contracts, the shifting of costs ends up hurting the OEMs more than helping them.

What we may be witnessing is a classic agency problem: Agents find ways to save costs in the domain that they control but often neglect to consider the effect of these cost-saving measures on activities that they do not control. If the pressure on suppliers is strong enough, they will accept harsh terms and low prices. And if there are inefficient consequences, they may eventually be counted on the scorecard of a different internal division. The lawyers and purchasing officials who write and negotiate the supply contracts invest much effort in tightening up the legal terms and in leveraging the OEMs' bargaining power in securing adherence to these terms. It is possible that this exercise of their power will degrade suppliers' cooperation and performance in ways that become clear only later.

II. Drafting of Boilerplate

One of the striking features of automotive-supply contracts between OEMs and their tier-1 suppliers is their simplicity. Each OEM has a single form used for procuring all of the manufacturing parts. General Motors, we mentioned, enters into roughly one million procurement contracts every year with suppliers all over the world. With few exceptions, these deals are governed by GM's "Global Terms" – terms that are never challenged, neither at the negotiation stage (say, by battle of the forms) nor in litigation.

Another notable feature of these boilerplate forms is their durability. DaimlerChrysler, for example, is still using the form that was drafted in 1985; GM's form goes back to 1986. Ford's old form had been in place since the 1950s, until it was recently revised in quite dramatic fashion in 2004. Although minor revisions addressing new problems are occasionally patched onto these forms, the main terms and conditions remain unchanged over a long period of time.

These boilerplate contracts are simple. The terms are written in plain English. Although most of the tier-1 suppliers are large corporations with sophisticated legal counsel who read every word of the OEM contracts, and although each provision in these contracts can have significant effects on the division of the surplus, the clauses are drafted in a much simpler and shorter form than ordinary consumer contracts, which are usually lengthy, cumbersome, and legalistic. Perhaps this difference owes to the greater government regulation of consumer warranties; perhaps it has to do with the identity of the drafter – a buyer or seller. A seller-drafter needs to avoid the sweeping warranties of the UCC, whereas buyers like the OEMs need only to strengthen the pro-buyer UCC warranties. Note, also, that the difference between warranty terms in the auto-production context and other, consumer-related contracts cannot be explained by factors such as trade usage and course of dealing. The supplier's warranty to the OEM is governed solely by the express warranty term.

Because boilerplate terms have to deal with many different types of situations and address many possible contingencies, drafting the standard form from scratch would seem a daunting task. It is often perceived, therefore, that the drafting of boilerplate language in mass contracts involves not much more than a cut-and-paste task, whereby the drafter identifies similar forms used by other organizations that do similar business and – on the premise that "if they work for others, they'll also work for me" – borrows their language.[7] Interestingly, the American OEM supply contracts were not drafted in this fashion. Each OEM contract was drafted by in-house attorneys in a concentrated effort over a short period of time with very little revision since.

No Authority to Dicker. A principal way in which OEMs prevent deviations from their own terms is by restricting the authority of agents within the organization to approve different or additional terms. Suppliers in the chain periodically try to negotiate or change the terms of the boilerplate imposed by the OEMs or other buyers. Both OEM and supplier representatives agree that changes in the boilerplate resulting from negotiations with an individual seller are as rare as hens' teeth. Ford, for example, has erected a clever and conscious barrier to such negotiation: Only the global vice president for purchasing has the authority to change the terms on the form contract.

Equality of Treatment. Another factor that limits the incidence of variation from the boilerplate terms is the strong formal commitment of OEMs to treat all their suppliers equally. Of course, transactions with suppliers vary significantly with respect to the goods purchased, prices, volume, and the like. But all suppliers – from the mega corporations who produce car frames to the sellers of nuts and bolts – must take the same legal terms: payment provisions, termination rights, warranties and remedies, and so forth. OEMs believe that the fact that these terms are presented as nonnegotiable and that variations are not approved provides their suppliers with assurance that there is horizontal equity, that everyone is treated the same.

Open-Ended Provisions

OEMs use such open-ended provisions to address some of the issues that would otherwise be most troubling for suppliers. With respect to some of these issues, the OEM elected to implement open-ended terms, thereby postponing the dickering of the actual resolution of individual cases to the postperformance stage.

The Dissemination of Boilerplate Terms across Tiers. OEM contracts with their tier-1 suppliers affect the contracts entered into in lower tiers. Tier-1 suppliers, being strapped to the onerous OEM terms, turn around and offer the same terms to their own tier-2 suppliers. A striking metaphor that a tier-1 representative used is "contractual DNA." Looking at contracts down the supply chain, one can identify the OEM for which a given supply is eventually intended by the terms of the lower-tier contracts. With each tier buyer copying some of the terms it had to accept as a supplier, the OEM's terms are "genetically" replicated down the chain.

Exception I: Information Technology Transactions. All of the OEMs reported that their relationships with IT providers were different from their relationships with conventional suppliers. Some OEMs have drafted different forms for IT suppliers. Ordinarily, IT suppliers insist on terms that grant them greater ownership in the intellectual property. They also successfully limit their liability and cap it at a level far below the liability that conventional suppliers may face, usually not to exceed the price paid for the component. Finally, they are reluctant to provide the same types of extensive warranties that OEMs usually demand.

It is hard to explain this exception. It may have to do with the concentration and leverage of the IT suppliers, led by Microsoft and other superpowers. But that would not explain the fact that even less powerful IT suppliers enjoy the more favorable terms. It may have to do with the importance of intellectual property clauses to IT firms because this is their only asset. Standing to lose more from the OEMs' IP provisions, their resistance to these expropriatory clauses is therefore more credible. But that would not explain the fact that IT firms succeed not only in securing better intellectual property terms but also far more lenient warranty and remedies provisions. Or, it may simply have to do with the fact that, unlike the ordinary tier-1 assemblers, IT firms do not buy parts and therefore do not have many tier-2s to which they can turn around and dump similar antiseller terms.

Exception II: "Backdoor" Negotiations. Staff attorneys within the OEMs are, of course, the organ that keeps the tightest control on the boilerplate terms and guards against deviations. Other organs – specifically, engineers and purchasing agents – may have slightly divergent goals and motivations. The purchasing representatives are interested in the cost of the item and their performance is measured by their success in getting the lowest price. Engineers are interested in quality and uniqueness of features and operation and are less interested in cost. A time-honored but relatively crude way for a supplier to get better legal terms is to convince the OEM engineers that the supplier's part is the only acceptable part and to get the engineer to write the specifications to exclude others. Or one might get the OEM engineers to agree to "engineering change orders" that modify the specification of the part, enable the supplier to quote a new price (without going through a competitive bidding process), and increase the profit on the sale of the part. These ploys that result in higher prices offset some of the cost of unfavorable boilerplate.

III. Economic Power

At the outset of this study, we hypothesized that OEMs' bargaining power would be strongest at the bidding and contract formation stage and weakest once relationship-specific investments were made and performance began. We imagined that once the OEMs became dependent on a supplier, they would face instances of hold-up, in which the supplier demanded a better price and other terms. The standard hold-up account seems to fit this situation perfectly – in fact, the hold-up theory was developed in the context of the GM–Fisher Body saga, which was an OEM–tier-1 relationship. This hypothesis, we explain later, turned out to be misguided.

We also hypothesized that economic power would echo down the supply tiers, with tier-1 suppliers being dominated by OEMs but exercising their own dominance over tier-2 suppliers. This, too, turned out to be only partially true. Some powerful companies, such as Exxon and General Electric, are in the tier-2 levels and are able to wield power because of their size and product mix. Other tier-2 suppliers have power because of their wide base of clients, extending beyond the automotive industry, and can afford to pass on automotive contracts. Yet other low-tier suppliers have power that is supported by the uniqueness of their technology. Finally, the financial integrity of a firm turned out to affect its economic power in ways that are more subtle than we expected.

How far can OEMs go in drafting one-sided terms? Surely, if suppliers have choices, they can bargain away these clauses. But, for automotive suppliers who sell a large chunk of their output to OEMs, in a market in which suppliers suffer severe overcapacity, there does not appear to be much choice. Even collective efforts by the suppliers through their trade association to draft a form more favorable to sellers have not, as far as we can tell, influenced even a single term of the OEMs' contract forms.

When we move down from OEM contracts to lower tiers in the supply chain, bargaining power is no longer one-sided. Tier-1 suppliers cannot exert the same influence on tier-2s as OEMs exerted against them. For one, tier-1 suppliers do not offer the same magnitude and rarity of deals as OEMs do. If an OEM turns down a bid by a manufacturer of passenger seats, a big chunk of the business cannot be salvaged. By contrast, if the same manufacturer of seats breaks the negotiations with the supplier of leather, that supplier would have many other business opportunities.

Switching Costs and Hold-Up. An important factor that influences the contracts among the OEMs and suppliers was the OEMs' significant switching costs. All of the OEM representatives acknowledged that the suppliers may have some power in the course of carrying out a long-term contract. Many current contracts are for intricate subassemblies that will be installed wholesale into a finished automobile. For example, an OEM might buy the entire heating and cooling system from a supplier, and the supplier might be the principal designer of the system. Because any such system must integrate with the car's electrical and other systems and must conform to the physical location that is set aside for it in the completed automobile, the "part" may be unique. It is this uniqueness that accords the supplier the power.

If an OEM who abandons a supplier would suffer prohibitive costs in finding and qualifying a replacement, the original supplier will have some economic power over the OEM for the contracted goods or services for some period – perhaps even to the end of the model run of the vehicle in which the part or assembly is installed. This power, we should expect, would be at its height shortly after production commences when the supplier looks forward to five years of work and the competing bidders have turned to other things. In fact, this conjecture – that a tier-1 supplier can exert hold-up power against an OEM after production begins – is widely recognized as *the* benchmark example in economic theory for the general problem of contractual hold-up. The standard account of the hold-up problem was developed and generically illustrated in the context of the very same OEM–tier-1 contracts that we explored. It suggests that in the 1920s, Fisher Body (a tier-1 supplier of automotive bodies) had a ten-year requirements contract with General Motors. When GM's requirements increased due to the greater demand for closed-body cars, Fisher Body enjoyed an "intolerable" position to hold up General Motors and to refuse to make adjustments that were overall efficient and was therefore acquired and vertically integrated into GM.[8] It is not clear how much evidence substantiates the GM–Fisher Body hold-up story,[9] and yet it seems plausible that in light of the high switching costs, OEMs would indeed be vulnerable to rent-extraction. As one leading economist explains:

> Why did GM and Fisher Body not simply write a better contract? Arguably, GM recognized that, however good a contract it wrote with Fisher Body, [...] contingencies might occur that no contract could allow for. GM wanted to be sure that next time around it would be in a stronger bargaining position; in particular, it would be able to insist on extra supplies, without having to pay a great deal for them.[10]

Our own findings suggest that, at least in the automotive business, this bargaining position–hold-up account is misguided. Even without looking into the contractual language, this account ignores the fact that each individual transaction is only part of a larger portfolio of business, both concurrently and into the future. Even for unique goods, the power of the supplier to hold up its buyer is effectively limited. If the seller uses its power to engage in explicit hold-up (for instance, "Give me an increase in price or I won't ship"), it knows it will lose in the long run. Such threats by a seller would surely count against it in the award of new contracts. If hold-up by the supplier causes a disruption at one OEM, it is likely to become known and to be considered by other OEMs when bids are being evaluated. Thus, the short-term benefit from extracting some concession by hold-up would be more than offset by the long-term reputation sanction.

The myth that suppliers can engage in hold-up overlooks a very basic fact. Suppliers trying to hold up OEMs must threaten to halt production of a part that is necessary to keep the assembly line working. Such a threat, if carried out, would lead to enormous losses, constituting an entire meltdown in the industry. If the OEM can show that such hold-up amounted to breach of existing obligations, the tier-1 supplier would be subjected to potentially bankrupting damages, some of which can be set off by the OEM against the supplier's account as a matter of self-help. Moreover, the OEM would likely be able to get injunctive relief,[11] thus barring such a threat from being carried out in the first place. In other words, given that suppliers make contractual commitments prior to acquiring the hold-up power, successful hold-up must assume lethargic contractual obligation and legal enforcement, which is probably far from reality.

Moreover, in his rebuttal of the Fisher Body myth, Ronald Coase speculated that problems of supplier hold-up can be addressed by OEMs contractually.[12] We have seen some evidence for such contractual arrangements. First, OEMs have almost unconstrained authority to terminate contracts. That is, if anyone has the contractual power to threaten to walk away, it is the OEM, not the supplier. True, they may not want to terminate a contract for supply of unique parts, but they can threaten to terminate other contracts with this same supplier, to phase out its business.

Second, OEMs maintain significant property rights in "tooling," namely, in the machines and production assets at the suppliers' plants, and they can haul these assets away once the contract is terminated, often with only stingy compensation for suppliers' sunk investment.[13] This ownership-of-tooling mechanism can be regarded as a subtle version of vertical integration, conforming to the Klein-Hart hypothesis of the boundaries of the firm. However, if it is an ownership solution to the hold-up problem, it is not one that rises to complete integration but rather a mechanism that accords OEMs partial ownership rights that gradually diminish over the life of the contract as the hold-up scare diminishes. The supplier is, in effect, posting a bond against hold-up; its investment will be amortized in the course of production but only if it sticks around for the long haul.

Third, OEMs reserve for themselves, in other boilerplate terms, the right to control the very profitable market for service parts for years, sometimes decades, into the future, and to potentially share this profit with suppliers. Suppliers that hold up the OEM in the short run will lose in a big way in the division of the aftermarket surplus.

Coase is correct in asserting that contractual provisions can protect OEMs from hold-up. But a more important aspect, we believe, and one that is also recognized by Coase, is that the "concern for their reputation would also have deterred the Fisher brothers from engaging in [hold up]."[14] The explanations we heard from all the participants confirmed that it is indeed the OEMs' long memories and the sanctions they can levy upon bad suppliers in future deals – that is, reputation sanctions – that render hold-up a bad strategy for tier-1 suppliers.

Thus, if long-term contracts confer power on the weaker seller but the seller cannot engage in hold-up, how is that power used? First, the power ameliorates the standard contract termination or cancellation terms. If the buyer cannot find a replacement, it cannot exercise its legal right to cancel. Second, particularly with a weak supplier, the contract may mitigate an OEM's setoff or hold-back of funds earned when the OEM claims that the supplier broke the contract. If the supplier is in a weak financial state, the OEM risks losing the supplier's production if it reduces the supplier's cash flow by setoff. We suspect that the seller's power is also expressed in more subtle effects on the buyer's use of its boilerplate. For example, we can imagine buyers hesitating to be as aggressive as they might be in using the boilerplate indemnity provision against an important seller. As we suggest earlier, a seller needs to be felicitous in its use of this power (for instance, "Can you give me some help with my increased material costs?") to escape identification as a chiseler who should be avoided when new contracts are awarded. Furthermore, because many tier-1 suppliers produce a portfolio of parts, they can leverage the power they have in the supply of one crucial component to secure additional deals for other parts.

Bankruptcy. The picture of a weak tier-1 supplier, squeezed by powerful OEMs that demand ever-growing discounts, can change dramatically when the supplier experiences insolvency. When this happens, suppliers' threats to stop performing critical contracts become credible. They are credible because they come not from a company that is concerned with long-term business but from stern bankruptcy workout specialists who have no attachment to next year's business or even to next month's if current crises can be surmounted. In the automotive industry of today, in which suppliers' bankruptcy has become a real danger[15] and their threat to file in Chapter 11 more credible, many suppliers who are known to be suffering losses have a more powerful negotiation position vis-à-vis their buyers.

Ironically, at times when the supplier's costs increase unexpectedly, it is that very weakness of the supplier's economic power and its inability to secure modifications to the contracts with the OEMs that can send it to bankruptcy and eventually bolster the credibility of its threat. Threats from the weak and desperate are more powerful than threats from the strong and rational. Indeed, the increasing hardship of the American automotive industry provides ample examples of this unfortunate dynamic.[16] These examples confirm that tier-1 suppliers have no power to hold up the OEMs when the OEMs know that their suppliers regard the costs of long-term retribution as greater than the near-term gains from improved terms. But when retribution loses its effect, hold-up can be significant. Still, suppliers generally believe that even if it is bankruptcy that drives the price renegotiation, the victorious supplier will suffer significant detriments in future dealings.

Conclusion

So there you have it – sophisticated companies use rigid boilerplate forms to govern tens of billions of dollars of sales every year. The drafters of these forms are not the least embarrassed in admitting that they draft every term in a one-sided, self-serving manner. It turns out that such unrestrained economic power in contracting is exercised not merely against the weak and ill-advised but also against sophisticated partners to relational contracts. And yet, claims of "unconscionability" do not surface in this industry. Obviously, there is no element of duress or unfair surprise in the formation of these contracts.

Our study has obvious limitations. Because our primary interest was the boilerplate contracts, the evidence we collected came from "legal" sources – the contracts, the lawyers who draft them, the lawyers representing the parties to the purchase agreements, and the very small body of case law. In the shadow of this legal cloud, there may be a different business reality in which transactions occur in a more balanced way, and OEMs exercise their power and their contractual entitlements in a selective and less selfish manner. Yet we found no evidence for such a gap.

What are the lessons that can be drawn from this study? We do not claim any general conclusions about contractual behavior, nor do we aim any critique at the law or advocate any legal reform. The automotive production business is sufficiently idiosyncratic that much of what we have learned may be applicable only to this industry. For one, it is clear that much of the bargaining power account stems from the specific structure of the industry, in which specialized tier-1 companies are "captives" – they have immense investments in production capacity and can sell only to a handful of clients. The study does identify the important role that internal organization structures play in the formation of form contracts. That is, forms are a way for principals to exert control over terms offered by their agents. But what we found here was the flip side of this account. The internal hierarchy is not the *reason* for the forms but rather an instrument in implementing the forms as-is, without allowing any erosion of the terms. Constantly under pressure by counterparties to vary some terms, buyers have erected artificial internal structures to prevent purchasing agents from yielding to such pressures. This internal rigidity also explains the absence of "menus" – the refusal of the drafting party to set prices under which its counterparties can "buy" better terms.

Although some of our findings can be explained with clear economic logic, for others we did not find a compelling explanation. We do not offer a satisfactory explanation for the variance of terms across the different OEM contracts or for the conjecture that some of these terms are inefficient. If we are right in suggesting that there is inefficiency in the legal provisions, it is possible – given the enormous stakes in this industry – that a lot of money is left on the table. Clearly, the OEMs are using any means to reduce costs and are pressuring their suppliers to the maximum extent. But, by using such harsh terms, the OEMs may be creating (or, at least, not eliminating) the deadweight loss. Another finding that left us puzzled is the IT forms; these are a remarkable exception to the otherwise one-sided boilerplate in the industry. We can offer only guesses as to why IT firms succeed in securing better terms. We leave this question for future inquiry.

Finally, this study reinforces some doubts about theories of asymmetric information in contracting. We mentioned that a prominent line of thought in economic theory identifies contractual failures as the reason why firms organize the way they do and why some activities are outsourced and others are done in-house. Because auto-production contracts have served an important role in demonstrating these insights (the GM–Fisher Body story), we took a closer look at the actual contracts. We discovered a reality in which more things are "contractible" than previously suggested; where asymmetric information and imperfect verification are rarely obstacles for contracting; and where reputation sanctions quickly fill any void that the contracts may have left. And yet, the familiar economic story of vertical integration is not necessarily undermined. Although it is not manifested through outright takeover of supplier firms, we discovered that integration in production occurs in more subtle ways, such as contingent control over production assets and technological innovations.

FOUR

"Unfair" Dispute Resolution Clauses: Much Ado about Nothing?

Florencia Marotta-Wurgler

Editor's Note: *This chapter takes an empirical look at boilerplate terms that stand in the midst of much current controversy – the dispute resolution clauses. Using a dataset compiled from software license contracts, it finds no indication that these terms place hardships on consumers. Vendors choose governing law and forum, not to bar consumer protections or to deter lawsuits, but most often for simple convenience, directing the dispute to be resolved in their home state. Moreover, these terms are used less often than prior commentators feared.*

Standard-form contracts governing consumer transactions often include clauses that specify how disputes will be resolved. Such dispute resolution clauses (DRCs) spell out which law should govern and in which forum a dispute should be heard. The choices made are important because they help determine whether a party will find it worthwhile to seek legal redress on being injured. And the possibility that such clauses specify laws and fora that are not mutually convenient for the buyer and the seller has multiplied with the growth in online commerce, as such commerce involves transactions between buyers and sellers that are often distant.

The use of DRCs in mass-market transactions, both online and traditional, has sparked controversy among academics and legislators. One position that some have taken is that liberal enforcement of DRCs is desirable. DRCs help sellers minimize costs associated with legal complexities of transacting in many states at once. Sellers protect themselves from the risk of being sued in whichever jurisdiction buyers reside, safeguard from having to comply with the laws of inconsistent jurisdictions (a pervasive problem in online transactions), and economize on legal representation by having to be familiar with the law of only one state. This arrangement also benefits consumers because they would receive the cost savings in the form of lower prices. That is, although the DRCs often limit consumers' options of legal redress *ex post* (by, say, restricting class actions), consumers receive the value of the foregone option *ex ante* in the form of lower prices.[1] Moreover, granting the parties flexibility in contractual choice of law and fora would encourage competition among states to provide more efficient contract laws.[2]

An opposing position is that sellers' use of DRCs puts the general public and small business users at a disadvantage. Forum selection clauses do not represent a joint effort between buyers and sellers to maximize surplus by reducing commercial uncertainty but rather the sellers' own prescription of the most advantageous forum. Sellers exploit their superior bargaining power by requiring disputes to be heard in a forum convenient to them, where they have business ties or political influence to benefit from local favoritism.[3] They choose seller-friendly laws and procedural rules or mandatory arbitration that impairs buyers' ability to seek court relief and might preclude class actions.[4] This inability to seek legal redress is particularly problematic in consumer markets, where buyers are unlikely to shop around carefully and thus only *ex post* mechanisms such as litigation would be able to correct market imperfections.[5]

Under this skeptical view, choice of law clauses also remove *ex post* corrective mechanisms by enabling sellers to avoid state consumer-protection laws, which are designed, in part, precisely to address market failures stemming from consumers' inability to read or understand the fine print. As one commentator notes (based on anecdotal evidence) that "we now see the aggressive use of choice of law clauses in consumer and small business settings to a degree unimagined in the late 20th Century and this development threatens to undermine the consumer law States have developed in the last 50 years."[6] Thus, consumers are likely to be price insensitive to these clauses and do not consider them in their purchasing decisions, thus failing to demand any price reduction that is potentially associated with these clauses.[7]

Although this more academic debate is ongoing, there has been growing activity on the reform front. One of the most contested amendments proposed for Article 1 of the Uniform Commercial Code (UCC) has to do with the choice of law rules. Pre-revision section 1–105 allows contracting parties to select the law of a specific jurisdiction only if the transaction bears a "reasonable relationship" to the jurisdiction.[8] This requirement limits parties' choice to only a handful of states, such as the state where the parties are headquartered or reside, or where performance takes place. In contrast, revised section 1–103 makes a distinction between consumer and nonconsumer parties. For the latter, it drops the "reasonable relationship" requirement and affords parties greater autonomy by allowing them to choose the law of *any* jurisdiction to govern their transaction.[9] For transactions involving consumers, revised section 1–103 maintains the "reasonable relationship" requirement and compounds it with a restriction that the chosen regime cannot deprive consumers of mandatory consumer protections afforded by the consumer’s state of residence.

In the past few years since the revised Article 1 was approved by American Law Institute (ALI) and National Conference of Commissioners on Uniform State Law (NCCUSL), twenty-two states adopted the majority of its provisions. However, each retained the constrained approach of section 1–105 instead of adopting section 1–103. To this date, only the U.S. Virgin Islands has adopted Revised Article 1 in full.[10] As legislatures continue to consider different versions of Revised Article 1, it is clear that the issue of DRCs is deemed one of the major topics of importance.

The approach of section 1–103 of Revised Article 1 was partly driven by earlier efforts to increase choice of law flexibility in transactions involving computer information, such as software, in which the physical location of the transaction is irrelevant.[11] Rejected by every state except Maryland and Virginia, Uniform Computer Information Transactions Act (UCITA) has very permissive choice of law and forum sections and allows parties to select *any* law contractually regardless of their relationship to the enacting states.[12] Aside from its permissive choice of law and forum rules, UCITA has been widely criticized as weakening consumer protections and favoring software publishers. Commentators are particularly concerned by Maryland and Virginia’s adoption of UCITA, noting that UCITA’s liberal choice of law and forum rules “create new forum shopping opportunities.” Most important, despite most states’ rejection of UCITA, this statute can still become a standard if enacting states attract enough sellers to their jurisdiction.

Despite the charged academic debates and the regulatory flux of electronic commerce, there is little evidence on how sellers actually use DRCs in their standard-form contracts and, in particular, whether there is any evidence of systematic abuse. Many of the claims in the debate are based on anecdotal impressions of commentators or exposure to a few extreme cases that were litigated. None of these varied claims have been substantiated by a more systematic examination of a broad sample of contracts.[13]

This chapter addresses the DRC debate in the context of End User Software License Agreements (EULAs) – the standard-form contracts used in software transactions online. I analyze a sample of 597 software EULAs. For each EULA, I record detailed information regarding the DRC provisions, such as whether the seller includes choice of law, choice of forum, and/or arbitration clauses, and note the chosen state whose laws or fora were selected to govern the dispute. I explore who uses what type of DRC and whether there is any indication that they are used in a way that abuses consumers’ rights.

My main descriptive findings are as follows. Seventy-five percent of EULAs contain a choice of law clause in their standard-form contracts. Forum selection is much rarer than choice of law, with only 28 percent of EULAs containing such a clause, hence providing little support for the hypothesis that their widespread use is depriving buyers of their day in court. The use of arbitration is even rarer, with only 6 percent of EULAs containing such a clause. Moreover, not a single EULA includes a class-action waiver. Although such low numbers might be surprising to commentators on both sides of the debate, these data should be reassuring to those who have expressed fears that a widespread use of forum selection and arbitration clauses are effectively eliminating buyers' options to seek redress *ex post.* And sellers are equally likely to include DRCs in EULAs for consumer-oriented products as in those of products that are directed to larger business. This result questions the reasoning behind section 1–103's differential treatment of business- and consumer-oriented transactions.

I also look for any hints that sellers are using DRCs "strategically." I find that sellers located in more seller-friendly states, such as the UCITA states of Maryland and Virginia, are actually *less* likely to have choice of law clauses than sellers located in more consumer-receptive jurisdictions, such as California and Massachusetts. Eighty-six percent of the contracts that contain a choice of law clause stipulate the laws of the state where the seller is headquartered. In addition, despite UCITA's liberal choice of law and forum rules and relatively seller-friendly rules, we do not see a stampede of sellers locating in UCITA jurisdictions.

There is also no evidence in my sample that the modest fraction of sellers that uses choice of forum clauses goes out of its way to select a forum that may be inconvenient for buyers. Choice of forum clauses always stipulate the same state as choice of law clauses, which in turn is typically the headquarters state. Of course, sellers could be selecting a local forum to obtain beneficial treatment from courts, but because the median firm with a choice of forum clause has only thirty-five employees, firms here are not large enough to have real political clout. The more likely explanation is that firms simply select the most convenient forum, which is the local forum.

Finally, among the small fraction of EULAs that contain arbitration clauses, about 30 percent (and 50% of those that pertain to consumer-oriented products) stipulate California law and venue. This is inconsistent with the suggestion that sellers are trying to select pro-seller laws to govern their substantive claims because California affords many protections to consumers in arbitration. Also, the vast majority of arbitration clauses select the American Arbitration Association to govern the dispute, a widely recognized neutral organization with supplemental procedures for disputes involving consumers. The distribution across arbitration organizations is similar for business-oriented products.

I. The Sample

I use a large subsample of the EULAs that I put together in a previous study.[14] That study looked at 647 EULAs from 598 distinct companies. Typically, the EULA of one representative product is studied for each company but, for forty-nine companies, I gather EULAs for both the "business" and "consumer" versions of the same product. All software products for which EULAs were gathered in that sample are sold online through a corporate Web site to U.S. buyers.

In this chapter, I narrow down the sample to companies for which I was able to document that the company was incorporated in the United States or else had a major U.S. subsidiary. This led to a sample of 597 EULAs from 552 companies. For each EULA, I record whether it includes a choice of law clause and, if so, the state whose law is chosen. I follow the same process for choice of forum clauses. Finally, I record whether the EULA contains an arbitration clause, the arbitration forum, and the name of the organization that will arbitrate the dispute.[15] Because a company's choice of a particular law or venue may be closely related to its location or state of incorporation, especially if the choice is not "strategic," I note the state of incorporation as well as the state of headquarters.[16] To determine whether sellers impose more stringent DRCs on unsophisticated buyers, I note whether the product seems directed to the general public or to business users.[17]

I also collect several other market, product, and company characteristics for use as control variables. The summary statistics are similar to those reported in my previous studies, so I only mention them briefly. Average revenue is $537 million but median revenue is only $2.4 million, indicating that the average is driven by very large companies such as Microsoft and Adobe. Ninety-two percent of the companies in the sample are corporations, 5 percent are limited liability companies, and the remaining companies are sole proprietorships or partnerships. Publicly traded companies make up 16 percent of the sample. A little under half of the products in the sample, 43 percent, are oriented toward consumers (or small home businesses) rather than businesses. The average price of consumer-oriented products is $137 and the median price is $65, whereas the average price of business-oriented products is $1,297 and the median price is $499.

II. The Presence of DRCs in Software EULAs

A. *How Pervasive Are Choice of Law, Forum, and Arbitration Clauses?*

Some of the most novel findings of the paper are simple descriptive statistics. The right column in Table 4.1 shows that a majority, or 75 percent of the

Table 4.1. *Dispute resolution provisions: summary statistics*

	Mean (s.d.)	Revenue weighted mean (s.d.)
Choice of Law Clause	.75	.91
	(.43)	(.29)
Choice of Forum Clause	.28	.42
	(.45)	(.49)
Arbitration Clause	.06	.01
	(.23)	(.12)

Note: Means, revenue weighted means, and standard deviations for choice of law, forum, and arbitration provisions in a sample of 597 software EULAs.

EULAs in the sample, include choice of law clauses. In contrast, only 28 percent of EULAs includes forum selection clauses, and only 6 percent of the EULAs include arbitration clauses. Are these results surprising? We expect Internet sellers to include choice of law clauses to minimize the costs of having to comply with the laws and regulations of multiple jurisdictions. Given that such clauses are generally enforceable, it is harder to understand why 25 percent of sellers in the sample choose to remain exposed to the risk of having to comply with inconsistent laws. This is especially puzzling considering that sellers (no matter how small) can easily copy the dispute resolution provisions from more sophisticated EULAs, thus reducing the drafting costs of these clauses to a very low level. Even if the chances of being sued are small, one significant lawsuit could wipe out a small seller.

These results may be influenced by the presence of many small companies in the sample with relatively simpler licenses. Because larger companies tend to sell more software, the left column in Table 4.1 shows the revenue weighted average for presence of DRCs to provide a sense of the type of EULA that a given buyer is actually likely to encounter in the market. Under this measure, the proportion of EULAs with choice of law clauses increases to 91 percent, the proportion with forum selection clauses rise moderately to 42 percent, and the proportion with arbitration clauses shrinks dramatically to 1 percent. The presence of choice of law clauses now seems more consistent with expectations.

Even under this revised measure, the question remains why forum selection and arbitration clauses are so rare, given that otherwise sellers who mass-market their products over the Internet are exposed to the risk of getting sued virtually anywhere a plaintiff resides. It is also surprising that sellers include choice of law clauses but fail to include choice of forum clauses. These results are not inconsistent with those of Eisenberg and Miller who, in a recent study of choice of law and forum selection clauses in 412 intensely negotiated merger and acquisition contracts by sophisticated commercial parties, find that only 53 percent contain forum selection clauses.[18] Sparse use of these clauses is common among large and small parties alike. Perhaps sellers involved in mass-market transactions do not include choice of forum or arbitration in their contracts because they perceive their enforcement to be uncertain. Absent unconscionability, however, forum selection and arbitration clauses have generally been enforced (including those contained in shrinkwrap and clickwrap software license agreements).[19]

The sparse use of arbitration seems particularly surprising if this form of adjudication is indeed faster, cheaper, and more predictable than traditional adjudication. Alternatively, this might reflect the nature of software disputes, in which it is common for one party to seek injunctive relief. Parties seeking equitable remedies, as is common in disputes involving issues of intellectual property or confidentiality, might prefer that a court rather than an arbitrator be the one to grant such remedies.

Not a single EULA out of 597 includes a class-action waiver. Again, sellers might not use class-action waivers because of concerns about their enforceability or because of the bad publicity such waivers might generate. Although much analysis remains to be done, these results immediately cast doubt on casual claims that sellers' rampant use of choice of forum and arbitration clauses deprive buyers of their day in court, or that sellers are shielding themselves from liability by making it impossible for buyers to aggregate low-value claims.

B. *Relationships among DRCs and Market, Product, Buyer, and Seller Characteristics*

This section explores the previous results in further detail. Table 4.2 breaks down the sample into twelve main software sectors as classified by Amazon.com; for example, "Business and Office" includes products used for check printing, marketing, word processing, and office management. The table breaks these categories further into consumer- and business-oriented products. Within each group, the table notes the number of EULAs that include choice of law, forum, or arbitration clauses.

For example, the sample includes 185 EULAs from products in the "Business and Office" sector. Of these, 137 (74%) include choice of law clauses, 52 (28%) include forum selection clauses, and 7 (4%) include arbitration clauses. Sixty-three of the EULAs in this category are for consumer-oriented products, of which forty-six (73%) include choice of law clauses, nineteen (30%) include forum selection clauses, and three (5%) include arbitration clauses. The remaining 122 EULAs are for business-oriented products, 91 (75%) of

Table 4.2. *Prevalence of dispute resolution provisions*

	All				Consumer				Business			
Sector	N EULAs	N w/ choice of law clause	N w/ choice of forum clause	N w/ arbit. clause	N EULAs	N w/ choice of law clause	N w/ choice of forum clause	N w/ arbit. clause	N EULAs	N w/ choice of law clause	N w/ choice of forum clause	N w/ arbit. clause
Business & Office	185	137	52	7	63	46	19	3	122	91	33	4
(% of total sector)		(74)	(28)	(4)		(73)	(30)	(5)		(75)	(27)	(3)
Education	68	41	12	1	42	24	9	0	26	17	3	1
(% of total sector)		(60)	(18)	(1)		(57)	(21)	(0)		(65)	(11)	(4)
Graphics	50	37	15	4	21	16	8	2	29	21	7	2
(% of total sector)		(74)	(30)	(8)		(76)	(31)	(10)		(72)	(24)	(7)
Home & Hobbies	26	15	3	1	20	11	2	1	6	4	1	0
(% of total sector)		(58)	(12)	(4)		(55)	(10)	(5)		(67)	(17)	(0)
Linux	7	4	3	2	3	2	1	2	4	2	2	0
(% of total sector)		(57)	(42)	(29)		(67)	(33)	(67)		(50)	(50)	(0)
Networking	53	43	15	4	12	10	6	1	41	33	9	3
(% of total sector)		(81)	(28)	(8)		(83)	(50)	(8)		(80)	(22)	(7)
Operating Systems	5	5	2	0	3	3	1	0	2	2	1	0
(% of total sector)		(100)	(40)	(0)		(100)	(33)	(0)		(100)	(50)	(0)
Personal Finance	39	32	14	7	6	4	2	1	33	28	12	6
(% of total sector)		(82)	(36)	(18)		(67)	(33)	(17)		(84)	(36)	(18)
Programming	7	3	1	1	6	3	1	1	1	0	0	0
(% of total sector)		(43)	(14)	(14)		(50)	(17)	(17)		(0)	(0)	(0)
Utilities	67	57	21	1	35	30	10	1	32	27	11	0
(% of total sector)		(85)	(31)	(1)		(86)	(29)	(3)		(84)	(34)	(0)
Video & Music	36	30	13	2	31	25	10	2	5	5	3	0
(% of total sector)		(83)	(36)	(5)		(81)	(31)	(6)		(100)	(60)	(0)
Web Development	54	44	18	4	17	14	8	1	37	30	10	3
(% of total sector)		(81)	(33)	(7)		(82)	(47)	(6)		(81)	(27)	(8)
All Markets	**597**	**448**	**169**	**34**	**259**	**188**	**77**	**15**	**338**	**260**	**92**	**19**
(%)		**(75)**	**(28)**	**(6)**		**(73)**	**(30)**	**(6)**		**(77)**	**(27)**	**(6)**
F-test		**2.53*****	**1.127**	**2.42*****		**1.55**	**1.025**	**2.63*****		**1.177**	**1.01**	**1.37**

Note: Number of EULAs in the sample and number of EULAs with choice of law, choice of forum, or arbitration clauses, as described in Table 4.1, by sector and user type. Software sectors are based on groups of related Amazon.com product categories. Consumer products are those oriented toward the general public or small-business users, whereas business products are those oriented toward medium- or large-size business users. ***Indicates statistical significance at the 1% level.

which include choice of law clauses, 33 (27%) include choice of forum clauses, and 4 (3%) include arbitration clauses.

The propensity to use different types of DRCs is similar across sectors – in each sector, EULAs are more likely to include choice of law than choice of forum or arbitration clauses. Slight differences arise, however, as evidenced by the F-tests, which reject the equality of incidence of choice of law and arbitration clauses across sectors. Products in the "Home and Hobbies" and "Education" sectors tend to have fewer DRCs than sectors such as "Business and Office." Surprisingly, in product categories that are generally directed to buyers who are less likely to be repeat players or careful shoppers, the incidence of DRCs is not higher. Another point worth noting is the heterogeneity within sectors. If other product characteristics are held constant, this heterogeneity suggests that it would be possible for concerned buyers to comparison shop for their preferred DRCs.

Again, in contrast to the consumer-abuse hypothesis, Table 4.2 shows that the incidence of DRCs is similar for consumer- and business-oriented products. EULAs of business-oriented products are more likely to include choice of law clauses and less likely to include forum selection clauses, but the differences are very small and not statistically significant (unreported). Because forty-five companies in my sample sell both business and consumer versions of the same product, I also can test whether sellers offer more restrictive contracts to unsophisticated consumers than to savvy business buyers and also control for company and product characteristics. I find that sellers use virtually the same clauses for both business and consumer versions (unreported). Thus, even sellers who could in principle easily discriminate among buyer types do not, in fact, offer more onerous DRCs to less sophisticated consumers. These results are consistent with what I found in previous studies, that EULAs of consumer products did not have more restrictive terms (in dimensions other than dispute resolution) than those of business products, and that sellers of consumer software were equally likely to use "pay now, terms later" contracts with both types of buyers.[20]

Table 4.3 develops this analysis by studying the company, product, and market characteristics that are associated with a particular dispute resolution clause. In models (1) through (4), the dependent variable is *Choice of Law Specified*, a dummy variable that takes the value of 1 if the EULA includes a choice of law clause and 0 otherwise.[21] Product price is the only product characteristic that increases the chance that the EULA will include a choice of law clause, with a 100 percent increase in price increasing the probability of a choice of law clause by 4 percent to 5 percent. This result is robust to the inclusion to state-, market-, and sector-fixed effects. Although I am agnostic about causality,

Table 4.3. *Regressions: choice of law, forum, and arbitration and product and company characteristics*

	Dep. var.: choice of law specified				Dep. var.: choice of forum specified				Dep. var.: arbitration clause specified			
	(1)	(2)	(3)	(4)	(5)	(6)	(7)	(8)	(9)	(10)	(11)	(12)
Ln Price	.04***	.05***	.05***	.04**	−.01	−.01	.00	−.01	.00	.00	.01	.00
	(.02)	(.02)	(.02)	(.02)	(.02)	(.02)	(.02)	(.02)	(.0)	(.01)	(.01)	(.00)
Consumer	.02	.04	.04	.01	0	.01	.01	−.01	.01	.02	.03	.00
	(.05)	(.05)	(.05)	(.05)	(.05)	(.05)	(.05)	(.05)	(.02)	(.03)	(.03)	(.00)
Multiuser	−.07	−.06	−.06	−.05	−.02	−.01	.00	.00	.00	.00	.00	.00
	(.06)	(.06)	(.08)	(.07)	(.07)	(.07)	(.10)	(.07)	(.03)	(.04)	(.04)	(.03)
Developer	.01	−.04	−.01	.01	.07	.03	.05	.1	.08*	.02	.04	.08*
	(.07)	(.08)	(.10)	(.07)	(.07)	(.08)	(.10)	(.08)	(.04)	(.04)	(.05)	(.04)
Ln Revenue	.02**	.02**	.01	.02***	.03***	.03***	.02**	.03***	.01**	.01***	.01**	.01**
	(.01)	(.01)	(.01)	(.01)	(.01)	(.01)	(.01)	(.01)	(.00)	(.00)	(.01)	(.01)
Ln Age	−.13***	−.12***	−.13***	−.12***	−.18***	−.18***	−.22***	−.17***	−.07***	−.06***	−.06***	−.07***
	(.03)	(.03)	(.04)	(.0)	(.03)	(.04)	(.04)	(.04)	(.02)	(.02)	(.02)	(.03)
Public	.09	.06	.07	.09	.12*	.11*	.09	.11*	−.04	−.04	−.01	−.04
	(.06)	(.06)	(.07)	(.06)	(.06)	(.06)	(.07)	(.06)	(.03)	(.03)	(.04)	(.03)
Fixed Effects	No	Sector**	Market*	State*	No	Sector	Market**	State	No	Sector**	Market	State
N	597	597	597	597	597	597	597	597	597	597	597	597
Adj. R^2	.06	.07	.09	.07	.07	.06	.11	.06	.03	.04	.05	−.01

Note: Linear probability regression results. In the left panel, the dependent variable is a dummy indicating a EULA that has a choice of law clause. In the middle panel, the dependent variable is a dummy indicating a EULA that has a choice of forum clause. In the right panel, the dependent variable is a dummy indicating a EULA that has an arbitration clause. Product characteristics include the natural log of the price of the product for which the EULA is collected and dummies indicating consumer-oriented products, multiuser products, and developer products (the default is single-user license). Company characteristics include the size of the company as proxied by the natural log of revenue, the natural log of the age of the company since incorporating as of 2005, and a dummy for publicly traded companies. Fixed effects may include Amazon.com software sectors (e.g., Business & Office), Amazon.com software markets (e.g., Business & Office > Business Accounting > Accounting), and state where the company whose EULA is collected is either incorporated or headquartered. Standard errors are in parentheses; ***, **, and * indicate statistical significance at the 1%, 5%, and 10% level, respectively. Significance of F-Tests for fixed effects are indicated by asterisks.

lacking an instrument for product price, this positive association is not, at face value, consistent with the theoretical prediction that sellers must offer lower prices in order to accept terms favorable to sellers. Instead, perhaps an explanation is that buyers of more expensive products are more likely to sue in the event of a dispute, and thus sellers of more expensive products (who face more lawsuits) are more likely to reduce their higher expected legal costs by subjecting their transactions to a unique law. Another possible explanation for this result might have to do with the fact that an overwhelming number (40%) of choice of law clauses select the laws of California or Massachusetts, two states known for their pro-consumer laws.[22] Choice of law clauses are priced, perhaps, to reflect the benefit they accord *consumers*. More realistically, though, choice of law clauses are not first-order determinants of product price, and it is hard to imagine that most buyers factor EULAs' inclusion of a choice of law clause in their purchase decision.[23]

As to company characteristics that are associated with a choice of law clause, the results show that larger companies and, controlling for size, younger companies are more likely to include these clauses. The size relationship may have to do with the fact that larger companies are more likely to obtain legal advice from counsel who may take more precautions to limit legal exposure and, in particular, may wish to select the law with which they are most familiar.[24] EULAs of larger companies are especially likely to be more restrictive in disclaiming liability restricting use of the license. This also suggests that smaller sellers are not simply copying the EULAs of larger companies. The age relationship is somewhat curious but quite strong. Perhaps older companies may have more established relationships with or better reputations among their customers and thus be less likely to get involved in formal legal disputes. Or, a less elaborate explanation is that many younger software companies were set up exclusively with a plan to market software online across state boundaries; for many older companies in the sample, by contrast, selling software online represents an expansion of product lines, and their legal departments may not have kept up.

In models (5) through (8), I examine the factors that affect the likelihood that a EULA will include a forum selection clause. The dependent variable is *Choice of Forum Specified*, a dummy variable indicating the existence of a forum selection clause. In models (9) through (12), the dependent variable is *Arbitration Clause Specified*, another dummy variable. The results are generally similar to those for choice of law clauses. Larger companies are significantly more likely to include these DRCs, as are younger companies. By contrast, product price plays no role for either of these clauses, in contrast to the results for choice of law clauses. Interestingly, public companies are, all else equal, more likely to include choice of forum clauses. "Developer" licenses are somewhat more likely to include arbitration clauses.

These results – that buyer type is not related to the frequency of DRCs – contrast with anecdotal claims that sellers are more likely to impose restrictive DRCs (such as mandatory arbitration) to the general public or less sophisticated buyers. Still, despite this evidence, one might still be concerned that consumers are being discriminated against in another way, that they are not getting price reductions in exchange for accepting restrictions, while businesses are. However, as discussed earlier, note that DRCs are not compensated for with lower prices on average across buyer types; indeed, the only significant relationship between price and the presence of DRCs (involving choice of law provisions) is *positive*, not negative. Nonetheless, I have tested for the possibility that the trade-off between DRCs and price is more favorable for business buyers, that is, more negative for them and more positive for consumer buyers. I create an interaction variable of the log of price and the consumer buyer dummy, include it alongside the previous variables, and examine its coefficient. Unreported results show no significant coefficients of either sign. Thus, there is no empirical evidence of a different trade-off between DRCs and price for business and consumer buyers.

III. Looking for Evidence of Strategic Use of DRCs

A. *Are Choices of Law More Likely in Seller-Friendly States?*

The last column of each panel of Table 4.3 shows that the location of the headquarters of the company is not a primary determinant of the presence of a DRC because the state-fixed effects are at best marginally significant. Nonetheless, it may be the case that sellers are discernibly more likely to select DRCs in seller-friendly states such as Delaware, Maryland, New York, and Virginia and less likely to select them in more consumer-friendly states such as California, Illinois (at the state level), Iowa, Massachusetts, and North Carolina.[25] (Assume for the moment that when sellers select a particular law, they select the law of their headquarters state. We will relax this later.)

To investigate this possibility in detail, Table 4.4 breaks the sample down by headquarters state and reports the incidence of DRCs by state. As reported previously, 75 percent of EULAs contain a choice of law clause; hence, of the states with at least one EULA in the sample, 75 percent of those EULAS contain a choice of law clause. Now examine the incidence of choice of law clauses in seller-friendly states. The percentage of EULAs with such clauses in Delaware, Maryland, New York, and Virginia is 100, 61.5, 60.8, and 80, respectively. Two

Table 4.4. *Dispute resolution provisions: by state*

	All				Consumer				Business			
HQ state	N EULA	N w/ Ch. of law clause (%)	N w/ Ch. of forum clause (%)	N w/ arbit. clause (%)	N EULA	N w/ Ch. of law clause (%)	N w/ Ch. of forum clause (%)	N w/ arbit. clause (%)	N EULA	N w/ Ch. of law clause (%)	N w/ Ch. of forum clause (%)	N w/ arbit. clause (%)
AL	1	1	1	0	1	1	1	0	0	0	0	0
		(100)	(100)	.		(100)	(100)	.		.	.	.
AK	1	0	0	0	0	0	0	0	1	0	0	0
		.	.	.		.	.	.		.	.	.
AZ	9	6	4	0	1	1	0	0	8	5	4	0
		(67)	(44)	.		(100)	.	.		(63)	(50)	.
AR	0	0	0	0	0	0	0	0	0	0	0	0
		.	.	.		.	.	.		.	.	.
CA	169	133	57	10	80	59	27	7	89	74	30	3
		(79)	(34)	(6)		(74)	(34)	(9)		(83)	(34)	(3)
CO	17	11	6	2	4	3	0	0	13	8	6	2
		(65)	(36)	(12)		(75)	.	.		(62)	(46)	(15)
CT	4	2	1	0	1	1	1	0	3	1	0	0
		(50)	(25)	.		(100)	(100)	.		(33)	.	.
DE	2	2	1	0	0	0	0	0	2	2	1	0
		(100)	(50)	.		.	.	.		(100)	(50)	.
FL	25	21	11	3	11	9	6	2	14	12	5	1
		(84)	(44)	(12)		(82)	(55)	(18)		(86)	(36)	(7)
GA	8	7	2	2	3	3	0	1	5	4	2	1
		(88)	(25)	(25)		(100)	.	(33)		(80)	(40)	(20)
HI	1	0	0	0	1	0	0	0	0	0	0	0
		.	.	.		.	.	.		.	.	.
ID	4	3	1	0	3	2	1	0	1	1	0	0
		(75)	(25)	.		(67)	(33)	.		(100)	.	.
IL	18	16	6	1	11	10	4	1	7	6	2	0
		(89.8)	(33)	(6)		(91)	(36)	(9)		(86)	(29)	.

(continued)

Table 4.4. *(continued)*

	All				Consumer				Business			
HQ state	N EULA	N w/ Ch. of law clause (%)	N w/ Ch. of forum clause (%)	N w/ arbit. clause (%)	N EULA	N w/ Ch. of law clause (%)	N w/ Ch. of forum clause (%)	N w/ arbit. clause (%)	N EULA	N w/ Ch. of law clause (%)	N w/ Ch. of forum clause (%)	N w/ arbit. clause (%)
IN	1	1 (100)	1 (100)	0 .	0	0 .	0 .	0 .	1	1 (100)	1 (100)	0 .
IA	3	2 (67)	1 (33)	0 .	3	2 (67)	1 (33)	0 .	0	0 .	0 .	0 .
KS	2	0 .	0 .	0 .	2	0 .	0 .	0 .	0	0 .	0 .	0 .
KY	1	1 (100)	0 .	0 .	1	1 (100)	0 .	0 .	0	0 .	0 .	0 .
LA	1	0 .	0 .	0 .	0	0 .	0 .	0 .	1	0 .	0 .	0 .
ME	4	2 (50)	1 (20)	0 .	3	2 (67)	1 (33)	0 .	1	0 .	0 .	0 .
MD	13	8 (62)	3 (23)	0 .	7	5 (71)	2 (29)	0 .	6	3 (50)	1 (17)	0 .
MA	73	59 (81)	17 (23)	5 (7)	28	23 (82)	5 (18)	0 .	45	36 (80)	12 (27)	5 (11)
MI	15	12 (80)	4 (27)	0 .	4	3 (75)	2 (50)	0 .	11	9 (82)	2 (18)	0 .
MN	9	7 (78)	3 (33)	1 (11)	7	5 (71)	1 (14)	1 (14)	2	2 (100)	2 (100)	0 .
MS	1	0 .	0 .	0 .	0	0 .	0 .	0 .	1	0 .	0 .	0 .
MO	4	3 (75)	1 (20)	1 (20)	4	3 (75)	1 (25)	1 (25)	0	0 .	0 .	0 .
MT	3	3 (100)	3 (100)	0 .	2	2 (100)	2 (100)	0 .	1	1 (100)	1 (100)	0 .

NE	3	2 (67)	0 .	0 .	1	0 .	0 .	0 .	2	2 (100)	0 .	0 .
NV	5	4 (80)	2 (40)	0 .	2	2 (100)	1 (50)	0 .	3	2 (67)	0 .	0 .
NH	9	9 (100)	4 (44)	1 (11)	4	4 (100)	2 (50)	0 .	5	5 (100)	2 (40)	1 (20)
NJ	12	8 (67)	2 (17)	0 .	6	2 (30)	0 .	0 .	6	6 (100)	2 (33)	0 .
NM	3	2 (67)	1 (33)	0 .	3	2 (67)	1 (33)	0 .	0	0 .	0 .	0 .
NY	23	14 (61)	8 (35)	0 .	13	9 (70)	5 (39)	0 .	10	5 (50)	3 (30)	0 .
NC	17	12 (71)	4 (24)	1 (6)	6	3 (50)	1 (17)	0 .	11	9 (82)	3 (27)	1 (9)
ND	1	0 .	0 .	0 .	0	0 .	0 .	0 .	1	0 .	0 .	0 .
OH	10	9 (90)	0 .	1 (10)	3	3 (100)	0 .	1 (33)	7	6 (86)	0 .	0 .
OK	2	1 (50)	0 .	0 .	1	0 .	0 .	0 .	1	1 (100)	0 .	0 .
OR	19	13 (68)	5 (26)	2 (11)	7	5 (71)	4 (57)	0 .	12	8 (67)	1 (8)	2 (17)
PA	12	7 (58)	2 (17)	0 .	3	1 (33)	0 .	0 .	9	6 (67)	2 (22)	0 .
RI	3	3 (100)	2 (67)	0 .	1	1 (100)	0 .	0 .	2	2 (100)	2 (100)	0 .
SC	0	0 .	0 .	0 .	0	0 .	0 .	0 .	0	0 .	0 .	0 .
SD	0	0 .	0 .	0 .	0	0 .	0 .	0 .	0	0 .	0 .	0 .

(continued)

Table 4.4. *(continued)*

HQ state	All N EULA	All N w/ Ch. of law clause (%)	All N w/ Ch. of forum clause (%)	All N w/ arbit. clause (%)	Consumer N EULA	Consumer N w/ Ch. of law clause (%)	Consumer N w/ Ch. of forum clause (%)	Consumer N w/ arbit. clause (%)	Business N EULA	Business N w/ Ch. of law clause (%)	Business N w/ Ch. of forum clause (%)	Business N w/ arbit. clause (%)
TN	3	0	0	0	2	0	0	0	1	0	0	0
		.	.	.		.	.	.		.	.	.
TX	25	18	2	1	6	4	0	0	19	14	2	1
		(72)	(8)	(4)		(67)	.	.		(74)	(11)	(5)
UT	11	7	1	1	7	3	1	0	5	4	0	1
		(64)	(9)	(9)		(43)	(14)	.		(80)	.	(20)
VT	1	0	0	0	1	0	0	0	0	0	0	0
		.	.	.		.	.	.		.	.	.
VA	15	12	3	1	5	4	1	1	10	8	1	0
		(80)	(20)	(7)		(80)	(20)	(20)		(80)	(10)	.
WV	0	0	0	0	0	0	0	0	0	0	0	0
		.	.	.		.	.	.		.	.	.
WA	28	23	8	1	12	10	5	0	16	13	3	1
		(82)	(29)	(4)		(83)	(42)	.		(81)	(19)	(6)
WI	4	3	1	0	0	0	0	0	4	3	1	0
		(75)	(2)	.		.	.	.		(75)	(25)	.
WY	1	0	0	0	0	0	0	0	1	0	0	0
		.	.	.	.	.	.	.	.	.	.	.
Other	1	1	0	0	0	0	0	0	1	1	0	0
		(100)	.	.	.	.	.	.		(100)	.	.
AllEULA	**597**	**448**	**169**	**34**	**259**	**188**	**77**	**15**	**338**	**260**	**92**	**19**
(%)		(75)	**(28)**	**(6)**		**(73)**	**(30)**	**(6)**		**(77)**	**(27)**	**(6)**
Avg. State	**13**	**10**	**4**	**.7**	**6**	**4**	**2**	**.3**	**7**	**6**	**2**	**.4**

Note: Number of EULAs in the sample and number of EULAs with choice of law, choice of forum, or arbitration clauses, as described in Table 4.1, by state where the company is headquartered and user type. Consumer products are those oriented toward the general public or small-business users, whereas business products are those oriented toward medium- or large-size business users.

states are above average and two states below. The observation-weighted average percentage of EULAs in those states that contain choice of law clauses (i.e., downweighting Delaware relative to the other states because it only pertains to two EULAs) is 65.4.

Compare this to the incidence of choice of law provisions in the more consumer-friendly states of California, Illinois, Iowa, Massachusetts, and North Carolina. There, the percentages of EULAs including choice of law clauses are 78.7, 88.8, 66.7, 80.8, and 70.6, respectively. Thus, three out of five states' companies have an above-average proportion of choice of law clauses. The observation-weighted average percentage is 73.2. Thus, sellers located in more seller-friendly states are actually *less* likely to have choice of law clauses than sellers located in less consumer-receptive jurisdictions.

B. *Do Sellers Actively Establish Relationships in Seller-Friendly States?*

A key assumption in this analysis is that when a corporation selects a choice of law, it selects the law of its own state. Of course, the easiest way for sellers to establish the UCC's section 1–105 "reasonable relationship" requirement under the current approach is to establish their business in the state by whose laws they wish their transactions to be governed. Alternatively, sellers can satisfy this requirement just by incorporating in a given state.[26] Table 4.5 examines this possibility by looking at the relationship between seller location and choice of law for the subsample of EULAs with a choice of law clause. The most salient feature of the table is the strong concentration of firms along the diagonal, indicating that most EULAs in this subsample (86%) do indeed select the laws of the states where the seller is located, consistent with the premise of the previous subsection.

One way for sellers to behave strategically is to locate in states with seller-friendly laws, such as Delaware, Maryland, New York, and Virginia, as described earlier. This behavior has been observed, for example, in credit-card companies that generally choose to locate in Delaware or South Dakota to take advantage of their favorable laws. Do software publishers tend to locate in seller-friendly states? Table 4.5 shows that 275 (or 61%) of EULAs with choice of law clauses are from sellers located in California, Illinois, Iowa, Massachusetts, and North Carolina. In contrast, only fifty (or 11%) of EULAs are from sellers in the relatively seller-friendly states of Delaware, Maryland, New York, and Virginia. Although state size has a great influence on these numbers (California is the largest state in the United States and, thus, will have more businesses located in it), I control for state size in an unreported regression to test whether sellers are more or less likely to locate in seller-friendly states. I find that, controlling for

Table 4.5. *Location and choice of law*

HQ State	Choice of Law																																							
St.	AL	AZ	CA	CO	CT	DE	DC	FL	GA	ID	IL	IN	IA	KY	ME	MD	MA	MI	MN	MO	MT	NE	NV	NH	NJ	NM	NY	NC	OH	OK	OR	PA	RI	TX	UT	VA	WA	WI	Oth.	All
AL	1																																							1
AZ		4																													1				1					6
CA			115			1			1								3															2			1	1	1		8	133
CO				9																																			2	11
CT					2																																			2
DE						2																																		2
DC																																								0
FL			2					17																															2	21
GA									6																														1	7
ID										3																														3
IL											14								1	1																				16
IN												1																												1
IA													2																											2
KY												1																												1
ME															2																									2
MD						1										7																								8
MA			3	1		1											52																		1				1	59
MI											1							10																					1	12
MN																			6					1																7
MO																				3																				3
MT				2																	1																			3
NE																						2																		2
NV																	1						2																1	4
NH									1						1		1							5															1	9
NJ																									8															8
NM																										2														2
NY																											14													14
NC																												12												12
OH							1																						8											9
OK																														1										1
OR																															11						1		1	13
PA						1																										6								7
RI																																	3							3
TX			1	1																														14						18
UT																								1											6					7
VA			1																																	9			2	12
WA						1											1																				21			23
WI			1																																			2		3
Oth.								1																																1
All	1	4	123	13	2	7	1	18	8	3	15	2	2	0	3	7	58	10	7	4	1	2	2	6	8	2	14	12	9	1	12	8	3	14	9	10	23	2	20	448

Note: The left column lists the states where the companies whose EULAs are collected are headquartered. The top row lists the states (and the District of Columbia) whose law is selected in a EULA's choice of law clause. The category "Oth." refers to the law of a country other than the United States or headquarters location outside the United States.

size, software sellers are still *more* likely to locate in California and Massachusetts (and Washington). There is no such evidence for seller location in seller-friendly states.

Perhaps it is the deviations from the diagonal that contain some support for strategic use of choice of law. However, there is no obvious deviation toward the "seller-friendly" states and away from the "buyer-friendly" ones examined in the previous subsection. In particular, given that UCITA is particularly seller-friendly for software publishers, it is interesting to focus just on Maryland and Virginia. However, of the sixty-two EULAs that do not select the laws of the sellers' home state, only one selects Virginia, and none selects Maryland. A useful perspective on these results involves a comparison between firm location and state of incorporation. As has been widely documented (and as I have confirmed in this sample), sellers that do not incorporate in their home state are most likely to incorporate in Delaware. That is, for corporate law purposes, many firms appear to make careful decisions and perhaps incur costs to choose the state of incorporation. In contrast, there is no evidence here to suggest that they go similarly out of their way to establish out-of-state relationships for consumer law purposes.[27]

C. *Choice of Forum*

Finding little evidence of strategic use of choice of law clauses, we turn to choice of forum clauses. Recall that forum selection is much rarer than choice of law, with only 28 percent of EULAs containing such a clause, and hence the potential for systematic abuse is lower. In this subset, perhaps choice of forum could be used strategically in that sellers go out of their way to select a forum that is inconvenient for buyers. However, there is no evidence of this in my sample, as *choice of forum clauses (when they are used) are always exactly equal to choice of law*, which in turn is almost always the headquarters state. Still, choice of forum could be considered strategic to the extent that it requires out-of-state buyers to litigate in a particular forum, which may be distant from the buyer.

One other way in which choice of forum could be used strategically is suggested by Bebchuk and Cohen. They point out that one reason for sellers to incorporate in-state is to obtain beneficial treatment by courts.[28] Unfortunately, the analogous hypothesis for choice of forum clauses is difficult to distinguish from the simpler hypothesis that sellers simply choose the forum that is most convenient. The fact that the median of the 156 firms in my sample with a choice of forum clause has only 35 employees, however, suggests that the majority of firms here are simply not large enough to have meaningful political clout.

D. *Arbitration*

Finally, sellers can take advantage of buyers by choosing to arbitrate claims. The main concern about arbitration is its very use, which deprives consumers of the possibility of a jury trial. Regardless of whether arbitration is viewed as abusive or as a less costly alternative to litigation, arbitration is very rare in my sample, so it will receive only brief attention here.

For the small sample of sellers that use arbitration, one concern is that sellers will select pro-seller laws to govern the substantive claim. This is not the case in my sample, however, because sellers who select arbitration invariably select the law of the state in which they are headquartered. The same is true for arbitration location. In fact, about 50 percent of arbitration clauses in the EULAs of consumer-oriented products select California law and California venue. As is well known, California affords many protections to consumers in arbitration.[29]

Finally, sellers could be somewhat strategic in their choice of procedural arbitration rules, for instance, by selecting an organization that charges high fees to consumers or that have seller-friendly procedural rules. I find that 74 percent (twenty-five out of thirty-four) of the arbitration clauses in consumer-oriented EULAs select the American Arbitration Association, a widely recognized neutral organization with supplementary procedures for consumer disputes involving a standard-form contract drafted by a larger business.[30] A little over 10 percent of consumer contracts do not stipulate an arbitration organization, and the remaining fraction selects the *National Arbitration Forum* (NAF) or JAMS to govern the arbitration. Of these two, consumer advocates have expressed concern only about NAF's high fees. The sample is too small to test whether the distribution across organizations is similar for business-oriented products.

Conclusion

Sellers often reduce the uncertainty about which laws and regulations will apply to their transaction by including choice of law, forum, or arbitration clauses in standard-form contracts. This practice has sparked heated debate among legal academics and legislators. A serious concern is that sellers take advantage of consumers' lack of bargaining power or attention to fine print by including choice of law clauses that deprive consumers of state consumer-protection laws, forum selection clauses that make it too costly for consumers to pursue their claims in court, and individualized arbitration clauses that prevent class actions.

Relying on one of the first large-sample analyses of the actual use of DRCs, this analysis finds little evidence to substantiate this concern. DRCs are not used to a greater extent against consumers; they are not used strategically to inconvenience buyers or to import pro-seller contract law regimes; and they most often refer to the state where the seller is headquartered. In fact, what commentators often perceive as the most effective antibuyer DRCs – forum selection clauses and arbitration clauses – are used very little in the context of software license agreements.

FIVE

The Unconventional Uses of Transaction Costs

David Gilo and Ariel Porat

Editor's Note: *This chapter explores various ways in which benefits and burdens hidden in boilerplate affect more than the direct parties involved. Because the language of boilerplate terms is only selectively accessible, drafters can exploit this to discriminate among partners, to signal hidden aspects of the deal, to effectively "communicate" with nontransacting parties, and more. In all these cases, transaction costs are used strategically to gain advantages. Some of the uses are welfare-enhancing and others are not. The chapter explores ways in which social intervention can be designed to address anticompetitive effects of boilerplate.*

Standard-form contracts offered to consumers contain numerous terms and clauses, most of which are ancillary to the main terms of the transaction. We call these ancillary terms "boilerplate provisions." Because most consumers do not read boilerplate provisions, or find them hard to understand, courts are suspicious of harsh boilerplate provisions and sometimes strike them down. Many law-and-economics scholars agree that striking down harsh clauses included in boilerplate language is justified when there is asymmetry of information between the supplier and consumers with respect to the harsh clause, which precludes consumers from fully understanding the effects of the clause on their legal rights. In such cases, there is a risk that the supplier will extract payment from the consumer without the latter being aware of the fact that the payment does not reflect the reduction of value due to the harsh clause.

In this chapter, we argue that boilerplate provisions and standard-form contracts with the transaction costs that they generate are used – or could be used – by suppliers for purposes other than for extracting payments from consumers through harsh clauses. Some of these uses are efficient and some are inefficient. What all these uses have in common is that their virtue to the supplier lies in the transaction costs imposed upon consumers, from which the supplier expects to gain. However, in contrast to the familiar use of boilerplate provisions as creating asymmetry of information between the supplier and consumers, we discuss cases in which the asymmetry of information is not necessarily between the supplier and consumers but rather between different kinds of consumers or between consumers and nonconsumers. We also discuss cases in which the supplier could gain from the transaction costs imposed on consumers even absent any kind of information asymmetries.

We identify four main categories of cases, characterized by the different goals suppliers might try to achieve by imposing transaction costs on consumers. *In the first category of cases*, the supplier uses boilerplate provisions and other contractual terms for segmentation of consumers. By creating transaction costs that some consumers are willing to bear while others are not, suppliers could screen out unwanted consumers, discriminate in prices by conferring benefits only on consumers who incur the transaction costs, hide benefits conferred on one group of consumers from the eyes of another group, and receive information about consumers' preferences. *In the second category of cases*, the supplier uses boilerplate provisions for stabilization of cartels, obstruction of competition among suppliers, and as an anticompetitive signaling device. Suppliers achieve these goals by using boilerplate language to make their contracts complex and by hiding beneficial terms in boilerplate provisions, making them available only to consumers who are ready to incur transaction costs. *In the third category of cases*, the supplier imposes transaction costs in order to create a facade of a contract that is different than its true nature, thereby escaping legal or public scrutiny. *In the fourth and last category of cases*, the supplier uses standard-form contracts to create self-inflicted transaction costs that credibly signal that the contract, or some of its terms, is not negotiable. This signal is conveyed to consumers as well as to competitors, for different purposes.

The various uses of boilerplate language and standard-form contracts to generate transaction costs raise the question of whether these uses are desirable from a social perspective. We discuss some policy implications and demonstrate how certain doctrines and principles of antitrust law, consumer law, contracts, and torts could be applied to cope with the harsh effects of beneficial boilerplate terms that we identify.

I. Segmentation of Consumers

A. *Screening Consumers Out*

At times, the supplier is not interested in transacting with all consumers but only with certain segments that are more profitable. She could screen out unwanted consumers by inflicting high transaction costs on them, thereby making the transaction prohibitively costly for them. For example, an Israeli landlord who offers apartments for rent and wants to exclude ethnic Arabs can draft all contracts in Hebrew, thus raising transaction costs for non-Hebrew speakers and deterring Arabs from transacting with him. Or, a supplier who wishes to attract repeat or large buyers (for whom it is cost-effective to incur set-up costs and to reach sale volume targets) can raise transaction costs for all consumers by complicating the boilerplate language or the contracting stage as a whole. Only consumers who expect high enough gains or who could economize on the transaction costs would incur them, and typically those would be the repeat or large consumers. For various reasons, which we elaborate on elsewhere, suppliers are expected sometimes to prefer using transaction costs to using a subscription fee, even though transaction costs constitute a net loss to both sides of the contract, whereas a subscription fee raises the supplier's revenue.[1]

In other cases, the supplier is concerned about "risky" consumers who would not fulfill their part of the deal or otherwise burden the supplier. Ideally, the supplier could charge them higher prices or collect damages from them when they fail to perform their part of the contract. Practically, when it is hard to directly observe consumer types, requiring consumers to pass the test of high transaction costs could often be a better choice. For example, short-term employment contracts and rental contracts require applicants to fill out long forms that differ from each other for each and every workplace or lease.[2]

Note that using transaction costs and standard-form contracts to screen out unwanted consumers could be sustainable even when the supplier faces intense competition from other suppliers. First, in some cases, as in the example of using contracts in Hebrew to exclude Arabs, many consumers the supplier wishes to retain do not bear considerable transaction costs and, therefore, competing suppliers could not steal such consumers on account of such transaction costs. Second, even in cases in which consumers the supplier wishes to retain do bear some transaction costs, they can potentially enjoy the fact that other consumers are excluded. Accordingly, they may well prefer the supplier to competitors who do not screen out unwanted consumers via transaction costs.

B. *Price Discrimination*

A supplier of uniform goods and services may find it beneficial to discriminate in prices in order to extract more surplus from consumers. But price discrimination could be prohibited by law or hard to implement because it requires information about consumers' willingness to pay. Suppliers would therefore try to use approximations for consumers' willingness to pay. They do so in many familiar ways. Airlines charge consumers higher prices for short stays, knowing that most short-journey travelers are businesspeople who are willing to pay higher prices. Or, many vendors distribute free coupons, entitling their holders to discounts, knowing that most of those who spend time collecting coupons have a lower willingness to pay.

Boilerplate provisions can serve a similar sorting function, facilitating price discrimination. For example, a seller of a relatively cheap product might offer in a boilerplate provision a special discount if consumers fill out a certain form and mail it back to the supplier. Only consumers who bear the transaction costs will get the special discount, and those are typically the ones whose willingness to pay is lower and would not have bought the product at the posted price absent the beneficial term. Had the beneficial term been more salient, many other consumers would also have received the discount, and the supplier's overall profits would have diminished.

Of course, this proxy of consumers' willingness to pay is an imperfect one. In particular, some consumers who do not incur the transaction costs would not be willing to pay the posted price absent the discount. Conversely, some consumers who incur the transaction costs would buy the product even absent the discount but nevertheless incur them because they gain more than others from doing so or are more sophisticated and well-informed consumers.

A common example is hiding a best-price-guarantee in the boilerplate. Another example is the case of selling goods with an option to return the product, even after a considerable period, and receive a refund if later the consumer changes his mind for any reason. A similar practice is common in subscription sales. For example, Internet service providers often have a boilerplate provision granting customers an option to cancel within a certain period of time and get their money back.[3] Many customers are not aware of this option, hidden in the fine print, and do not execute it. But it is those who are more hesitant about signing up that would tend to incur the transaction costs and explore the boilerplate. They will be the ones disproportionately utilizing the benefit.

Conferring benefits only on those who know how to appreciate them is the mirror image of the familiar use of harsh boilerplate terms set by the supplier in order to extract surplus from consumers, without them being aware of it. There, the supplier incorporates a boilerplate term hoping that most consumers will not be able to estimate their negative effect. In the beneficial-terms case, however, those who do not appreciate the beneficial terms and therefore do not receive them cannot argue that their expectations were frustrated: They got exactly what they expected to get. This is in contrast to the familiar use of harsh boilerplate terms, in which the main concern is that the consumer expected a different contract than the one she actually got.

A related technique that could be used by suppliers is that of hiding benefits in boilerplate and drawing a customer's attention to these benefits when the consumer is hesitant about whether to purchase the product. Such a technique can be preferable to offering such consumers a direct discount because it avoids reputational sanctions or retaliation by frustrated consumers who have not enjoyed the benefits offered to other consumers. For example, this technique can be used to draw new customers by offering them better deals than those granted to old consumers. Instead of explicitly limiting the applicability of beneficial terms to new consumers and offending old faithful consumers, the supplier could hide the beneficial term in boilerplate and exercise it selectively only to a subset of consumers.

Another strategy that could lead to price discrimination is to raise transaction costs by complicating the contract offered to consumers, without using beneficial terms at all. Cellular phone contracts are a good example. Consumers face a menu of packages, each different with regard to rate per minute, monthly fee, night rate, and so forth, in a way that it is difficult for a consumer to calculate which package is better. Those who would incur the transaction costs and get the better deals are probably those who use their cellular phones more and therefore have more to gain from thoroughly exploring all of the available options. They also could be the more sophisticated consumers, who can easily understand the differences among the various options and choose the one most suitable to their needs. Here, the supplier is using complicated boilerplate in order to offer better deals to high-volume or sophisticated users, who would often be more sensitive to the price they are required to pay.

Yet another boilerplate-based strategy to achieve price discrimination is to induce the consumer to rely and depend on the supplier for ongoing assistance. Dependency often results in the purchase of more services and products. For example, suppliers of computer accessories and programs can distribute manuals that are inaccessible to unsophisticated users.[4] If the unsophisticated (or inexperienced) consumers are less sensitive to the price or less aware of the additional price they would have to pay for the supplier's assistance, the supplier could extract payments from these consumers that she would not have been able to extract but for the transaction costs she artificially created. At the same time, the supplier manages to retain sophisticated consumers with a lower willingness to pay.

C. *Hiding Benefits Granted to Selected Consumers*

Sometimes there are privileged consumers who are entitled to benefits beyond what most consumers expect. The supplier would often like to understate these benefits, by placing them in boilerplate language, in order to avoid frustrating the consumers who do not receive them.

An illustrative example is benefits granted by airlines to frequent flyers. In the forms that establish the relationships between the airlines and the passengers, the privileges for frequent flyers are understated. However, the airlines directly mail frequent flyers all the relevant details concerning the privileges to which they are entitled.

D. *Collecting Information about Consumers' Preferences*

Suppliers would often like consumers to reveal not only their willingness to pay, as discussed in previous sections of this chapter, but other preferences as well. This information helps suppliers market their products and services to new consumers and to update strategies vis-à-vis their existing consumers. Occasionally, boilerplate language and the imposition of transaction costs could help extract this information from consumers. For example, a cellular phone provider could offer additional services for free but make them available through a process that requires consumers to read and learn instructions placed in boilerplate language or to fill out long and time-consuming forms. Had the cellular phone company not conditioned the availability of the various services on incurring the transaction costs, most consumers would order these services and the cellular phone company would know very little about their true preferences. Using the transaction-costs strategy could occasionally be more effective than charging consumers for the services they order because the latter strategy could be more costly to administer, more deterring for many consumers, or raise consumers' suspicion with regard to the supplier's motives.

II. Prevention of Competition and Cartel Stabilization

Explicit collusion between competitors is prohibited by antitrust law. But firms often try to sustain higher-than-competitive prices even absent explicit coordination, through what is known as tacit collusion. Tacit collusion is possible when firms independently find it unprofitable to deviate from a collusive price. A growing body of the antitrust literature is devoted to identifying practices that facilitate the sustainability of tacit collusion.[5]

A. *Making It Difficult to Compare among Rivals*

The complexity of boilerplate is a method that can help firms promote anticompetitive goals, in at least three ways:

1. Facilitation of Collusion. If most firms in a market offer noncompetitive terms, and their contracts with consumers are complex, the profits one of them could make by offering more competitive terms are small because many consumers would find it difficult to assess whether the complex terms offered by their current supplier are better than the competing offer. Stealing a substantial number of customers would require an extreme and salient benefit, which is less profitable. Note that, unlike consumers, the firms themselves would not find it hard to assess whether their rival has deviated from a collusive equilibrium because they are sophisticated and have a lot at stake. Hence, complexity facilitates ongoing (tacit or explicit) collusion between rivals.[6]

2. Raising Prices even Absent Collusion. Complexity of boilerplate also typically raises the prices that would prevail absent collusion. As is well known, in markets with only a few firms, even absent ongoing collusion, prices will often exceed marginal costs. Common reasons for this are product differentiation (i.e., consumers do not see the competing products as perfect substitutes) and capacity constraints (i.e., firms are not able to lower prices all the way down to marginal costs, due to their capacity constraints). Consumers' difficulties in fully understanding the value they get from a supplier, and their consequent difficulties in comparing suppliers, can enable suppliers in such industries, even absent collusion, to raise prices even further above marginal costs. Indeed, various economic models find that elevated search costs, which consumers need to bear in order to compare between competing suppliers, have the effect of raising prices in oligopolies, even absent ongoing collusion.[7]

3. Entry Deterrence. Complexity of contracts also can serve as a barrier to entry of new firms into the market. A new entrant would find it hard to steal customers away from the incumbent firms because their customers would find it hard to verify that the entrant is offering them a better deal.

B. *How Can Beneficial Boilerplate Terms Harm Competition?*

Let us begin by showing that collusion over harsh boilerplate terms can be less sustainable than collusion with beneficial competitive boilerplate terms, in which competitive benefits are offered only to readers. With collusion over harsh boilerplate terms, suppliers can steal two kinds of consumers by "deviating" from collusion (i.e., by highlighting that their rivals' contracts have harsh terms and removing the harsh terms in their own contracts): readers of boilerplate terms, who are aware of the harsh terms, and nonreaders of boilerplate terms, who find out about them only when the deviating supplier highlights their existence. Moreover, both groups of consumers might develop antagonism about their previous supplier who until then tried to abuse them via harsh boilerplate terms. This type of collusion is also vulnerable to a court striking down the harsh terms of one supplier, thereby forcing him to "deviate" from this type of collusion.

By contrast, when suppliers collude over the salient part of their contract (typically, by charging a collusive price) and offer competitive benefits only to readers of the boilerplate terms, deviating from collusion (by offering the competitive benefits not only to readers of the boilerplate provision, but to all customers) becomes less profitable. First, when suppliers collude over price but hide competitive beneficial terms in their boilerplate, deviation from collusion has the potential of stealing only nonreaders of the boilerplate provision because readers of the boilerplate provision already enjoy competitive terms.[8] Second, even the nonreaders of the boilerplate provision would not necessarily switch to the deviating supplier because their original supplier could retain them by pointing out that the special discount was in their contract (in a boilerplate) all along. Third, firms often deviate from collusion in order to exclude their rivals from the market. But, as we show elsewhere,[9] a supplier can use beneficial boilerplate terms to credibly signal to his rivals that he is too efficient to be successfully excluded. Accordingly, when benefits are hidden in boilerplate, there are fewer reasons for deviating from collusion. Thus far, we have shown that collusion over price coupled with competitive beneficial boilerplate terms could be more sustainable than collusion over harsh boilerplate terms because deviation from the former type of collusion is less profitable than deviation from the latter type of collusion. But suppose we observe that suppliers hid competitive beneficial boilerplate terms in their contracts. Can we say that this practice facilitates collusion compared to the case in which boilerplate terms are not used at all? The answer is yes. Suppliers' profits when deviating from collusion without any boilerplate provisions are larger than their profits when deviating from collusion with competitive beneficial boilerplate terms. As in the case of collusion over harsh boilerplate terms discussed previously, without any boilerplate provisions, the deviating supplier can steal all types of consumers – readers and nonreaders of boilerplate provisions alike. By contrast, when suppliers place competitive benefits in their boilerplate terms, a deviating supplier can steal only nonreaders. Even nonreaders would remain with their current supplier if their current supplier immediately makes it apparent to them that they could have enjoyed the benefits hidden in their contract all along. Furthermore, as explained earlier, to the extent a supplier wishes to deviate from collusion in order to exclude its rival, it is less likely to do so when suppliers hide benefits in boilerplate provisions.[10]

Even if a single firm in an industry adopts beneficial boilerplate terms, collusion could be facilitated. Beneficial boilerplate terms adopted by a single supplier make his rivals less eager to cut prices because their profits from deviating from collusion diminish. It also makes this supplier less eager to cut prices because his collusive profits become larger.

Finally, beneficial boilerplate terms also could deter entry of new rivals. A potential entrant is signaled how far an incumbent firm could go in fighting to keep its customers. Planting this "dormant" weapon – beneficial boilerplate that needs to be exercised with regard to all customers only when entry actually occurs – is cheaper for the incumbent than other signals of its propensity to fight back, which require the expenditure of higher costs.

III. Creating False Appearances

When courts assess a harsh clause in a standard-form contract, they consider the fairness of the contract in its entirety and not only the particular clause.[11] Accordingly, a supplier who wishes to minimize the chances that a certain term would be struck down would try to offset it with beneficial terms, which would help convince the court that the contract in its entirety is fair. This strategy could prove useful not only vis-à-vis courts but also vis-à-vis the press, consumer organizations, or competitors who try to criticize the supplier for harsh clauses in its standard-form contract.

Such offsetting beneficial terms, however, are costly to the supplier. It would prefer to keep the oppressive terms intact and not have to bear the full cost of the offsetting beneficial terms. The supplier could achieve this by placing the beneficial terms in boilerplate language, so that only those who read and fully understand them would actually enjoy them. The supplier can influence the number of customers that actually enjoy the beneficial terms by controlling the complexity of their apprehension and "hiding" them deeper in boilerplate language.

Moreover, at times a supplier who grants some parties certain special benefits might be interested in hiding these benefits from third parties. For example, a university that has a standard contract with faculty who are inventors does not want faculty members who do not have a chance of being inventors, and the public at large, to observe the extreme benefits granted to the inventors. To achieve this goal, the university could use language that is full of jargon and that is obscure and difficult to understand.

IV. A Credible Signal for Not Negotiating

In many cases, a supplier would like to signal his customers or his competitors that certain terms in the contract are not negotiable. Standard-form terms are a way for a supplier to impose transaction costs on himself in the event that the contract is negotiated, thereby credibly committing not to negotiate his contracts. Nonnegotiability of contracts could serve various purposes. We focus here on three purposes that have received less attention.

A. *Signaling Improved Incentives*

Nonnegotiability of contractual terms could signal that the supplier's improved incentives, brought about by maintaining these terms in all or most of the supplier's contracts, remain intact.[12] For example, a car manufacturer may want to signal consumers the car's quality by offering a long-term warranty. But, in order for the warranty to credibly signal the car's quality, the customer has to know that the warranty applies to all or most customers and cannot be waived easily. After getting the signal and recognizing the car's high quality, any given customer may try to waive the warranty in exchange for a refund. But, if many customers do so, the supplier's improved incentives would no longer exist. Accordingly, the supplier needs to credibly commit not to negotiate the warranty.

One way to do so is to commit contractually not to negotiate. This would usually not be an effective commitment device, however, because customers would find it hard to monitor the supplier's relations with all its other customers. An alternative commitment device is to use boilerplate provisions or standard-form contracts to make negotiation over the warranty particularly difficult and complicated. For example, the boilerplate provisions could provide that the warranty cannot be waived without prior approval by the CEO or the board, or without following a cumbersome process. If customers know that all contracts contain this boilerplate, they would worry less about waivers.

Alternatively, actual contacts with buyers could be made by the supplier's agents, and these agents could have no discretion to negotiate the contract. Typically, such a supplier will operate with standard-form contracts, the terms of which are rigid and not negotiable. Blocking negotiation by the supplier's agents could be achieved either by an explicit rule forbidding negotiation or by filling the boilerplate language with professional or legal jargon and employing agents that are not capable or lack sufficient information or skills to understand or negotiate the standard terms.

State laws often enable suppliers to submit their standard contracts to a certain agency or to the state's attorney general for approval.[13] Such submission of a supplier's standard contracts enhances their rigidity and negotiation-proofness. This is because any subsequent change of the contract's terms would require resubmission to the state agency for new approval in order to enjoy the legal defenses inherent in such approval. Also, a very convincing way for a supplier to signal consumers that negotiating the contract is impossible is by making the transaction through the Internet, where, obviously, no live agent conducts any type of negotiation.[14]

B. *Signaling Buyers about Uniformity of Terms*

Another case in which a supplier would want to impose on itself and its customers costs of negotiating terms is when the supplier wishes to signal to its customers that prices, or other terms, are uniform for all customers. If a buyer were to suspect that the supplier is granting special benefits to other buyers, he might hesitate to enter the contract or insist on better terms.[15] One way that the supplier can promise not to grant discriminatory benefits is to commit contractually not to discriminate. However, such a commitment is difficult to enforce, and complicated monitoring mechanisms would have to be constructed. Such mechanisms also could be relatively easily circumvented by the supplier by offering subtle or disguised benefits.

A possibly more credible way for the supplier to commit not to discriminate is by developing uniform contracts and boilerplate provisions that are difficult for the supplier to negotiate.[16] For example, a boilerplate that says:

> "NO LICENSOR, DISTRIBUTOR, DEALER, RETAILER, RESELLER, SALES PERSON, OR EMPLOYEE IS AUTHORIZED TO MODIFY THIS AGREEMENT OR TO MAKE ANY REPRESENTATION OR PROMISE THAT IS DIFFERENT FROM, OR IN ADDITION TO, THE TERMS OF THIS AGREEMENT"

helps the seller credibly commit not to negotiate.[17]

C. *Signaling Competitors about Uniformity of Terms*

Firms often like to commit to being less aggressive and less eager to cut prices in order to induce rivals to compete less aggressively as well. They can do so by making their terms of sale rigid and costly to change. When changing terms of sale vis-à-vis particular buyers involves high transaction costs, a supplier that wants to offer more competitive terms than its rivals would have to change its standard-form contract with regard to all buyers. But such a competitive move would be less profitable to the supplier because it is more detectable to its rivals and they would respond more quickly.[18] This could improve the prospects of tacit collusion in the supplier's industry.

V. The Legal Implications of Hiding Benefits in the Boilerplate

Identifying the various uses of boilerplate language and artificial transaction costs imposed on buyers raises the question of whether these uses are desirable from a social point of view. If the answer is negative, a second question arises: Should the law intervene and, if so, by what means? The analysis in Sections I–IV reveals that there are two specific practices that may raise legal concerns that have been ignored by the current literature and by courts. The first is the practice of artificially complicating the transaction in ways that benefit suppliers at the expense of buyers, and the second is the practice of hiding benefits in the boilerplate. In what follows, we focus on the policy implications of the latter.

A. *Price Discrimination*

We argued that hidden benefits could be used to price discriminate between readers and nonreaders of the boilerplate. This practice raises objections from both a social welfare perspective and from the perspective of consumers who are adversely affected by the discrimination. We discuss these two perspectives separately.

Social Welfare Perspective. Recall that discrimination via beneficial boilerplate terms causes readers to pay less (or receive more) and causes nonreaders to pay more (or receive less) than in the case with uniform pricing. Accordingly, in order to assess whether such discrimination is welfare-reducing, the court needs to examine whether discrimination raised or reduced the total number of units sold by the supplier. But because various other factors affect the number of units sold, this would be practically impossible. Accordingly, we believe that intervention should hinge not merely on the discriminatory nature of beneficial boilerplate terms but rather on their other two uses: harming competition and creating the appearance of a fair contract.

The Discriminated Consumer Perspective. One possible claim a nonreader could invoke against the supplier is that the supplier failed to disclose to him that other consumers got a better deal than the one he got. In particular, the nonreader could claim that this undisclosed fact is a material part of the bargain, and because the supplier failed to disclose it, the consumer is entitled to rescind the contract or even sue for damages or enforce the beneficial terms in his favor.

There are numerous consumer-protection statutes that impose duties of disclosure. However, most of these statutes oblige suppliers to disclose exclusionary clauses, limitations on explicit or implicit warranties, and many other terms that could constitute "a (bad) surprise" to a consumer who does not or cannot read boilerplate provisions carefully enough.[19] Such statutes are not relevant to our case because we are dealing here with "good" surprises. Other statutes, prevailing in several states, impose a duty on suppliers to draft consumers' contracts in plain language.[20] Such statutes could be of relevance here, as long as the transaction costs consumers need to incur in order to reveal the benefits in boilerplate provisions stem from difficulties in understanding the wording of the contract.

The common law also imposes on a supplier a duty of disclosure in appropriate cases. In certain special cases, the consumer may have reasonable expectations – stemming from his special or long-term relationship with the supplier or from a promise or representation made by the supplier – that he would disclose any material fact of the bargain to the consumer.[21] In such special cases, regardless of the welfare analysis we conducted previously, there could be grounds under contract law for the consumer to rescind the contract due to nondisclosure of the hidden benefits[22] and even, in appropriate cases, to sue for damages or to enforce the beneficial terms on his behalf.[23]

B. *Using Beneficial Boilerplate Terms to Harm Competition*

We argued in Section II that beneficial boilerplate terms, even if adopted by only one supplier, could harm competition by making tacit or explicit collusion more sustainable. Note that when the practice is banned, if collusion breaks down, nonreaders and readers of the boilerplate provisions alike enjoy competitive terms. This means that the collusion-facilitating characteristic of beneficial boilerplate terms is unambiguously harmful. Similar are the anticompetitive harms from beneficial boilerplate provisions that encourage anticompetitive accommodation by rivals or deter entry.

Accordingly, although the mere discriminatory characteristics of beneficial boilerplate terms do not justify intervention, when beneficial boilerplate terms are adopted by suppliers in an oligopolistic setting, the case for legal intervention is strengthened. Naturally, the most appropriate legal tools to deal with such effects are the antitrust laws. We examine a host of possible antitrust tools elsewhere.[24] Within contract law doctrine, a possible approach would be to allow nonreaders of boilerplate language to attack the supplier for violating disclosure requirements. We noted earlier that such an approach would usually be unwarranted if the plaintiff's sole claim was that he was the victim of price discrimination. In cases in which the practice facilitates cartels, raises prices, or deters entry, however, intervention through disclosure rules becomes warranted. Another contract law doctrine that could be invoked when boilerplate is shown to harm competition is to declare such contracts unenforceable for public policy considerations, as done with other types of anticompetitive agreements.

To be sure, we are not advocating here a per se prohibition of beneficial boilerplate terms adopted by oligopolistic suppliers. Suppliers should be allowed to claim, in a particular case, that the practice involves welfare-enhancing attributes that outweigh the potential anticompetitive harm. The court would then face the nontrivial task of balancing between the probable anticompetitive threat and the welfare-enhancing benefits. Such balancing is extremely familiar to courts in antitrust cases involving conduct that is not illegal per se but still raises considerable anticompetitive concerns.

C. *Creating the Appearance of a Fair Contract*

We argued in Section III that beneficial boilerplate terms raise policy concerns even absent an oligopolistic setting, when they are used by the supplier to create a false appearance of a fair contract, that is, when the benefits are not enjoyed by most consumers. Courts that review standard-form contracts should be aware of this. Therefore, when courts consider a standard-form contract, they should look not only at the appearance of the contract and at its theoretical potential to be fair but also at its fairness in fact, given the transaction costs imposed on consumers who may want to enjoy its beneficial terms.

Conclusion

Unlike much of previous literature, this chapter did not focus on the asymmetric information between the supplier and consumers created by boilerplate language that includes harsh terms. We focused on other benefits the supplier can derive from the transaction costs that boilerplate language and standard-form contracts create. Because the costs of reading and understanding boilerplate are borne differently by different consumers, suppliers can set these costs to screen out unwanted consumers, price discriminate, stabilize cartels, elicit consumer preferences, and hide benefits granted to certain consumers. Boilerplate also serves to self-impose transaction costs by the supplier in order to signal to buyers or to its competitors that negotiation of the contract would be very costly. Other uses of boilerplate create asymmetry of information between the supplier and its consumers, as in the classic discussions of standard forms, but they differ in that they do not extract surplus from uninformed consumers directly.

Rather, they operate indirectly, as a cartel-facilitating tool, an anticompetitive signaling device, or a tool for creating the appearance of a fair contract.

Some of the uses of boilerplate language and transaction costs that we identify are desirable (such as signaling not to negotiate a warranty) and some are not (such as facilitating ethnic discrimination, artificially complicating the contract in order to harm competition, and creating a false appearance of a fair contract). Most of the uses, however, are in between these two polarities, and their desirability depends on the particular circumstances of the case (such as some cases of screening out small buyers, some cases of price discrimination, and some cases of collecting information about consumer preferences).

We identified two practices that especially raise policy concerns. The first is the practice of artificially complicating the transaction, and the second is the practice of hiding benefits in the boilerplate. These concerns are new to the legal scholarship and case law and should be addressed by courts in appropriate cases. Section V of this chapter approached the question of whether and when the use of beneficial boilerplate terms is desirable from a social perspective, and if not, we ask how the law should discourage them.

It is hard to verify whether suppliers are really trying to achieve most or all of the different goals discussed in this chapter. But even if suppliers are completely ignorant of these goals and uses, it is still important to be aware of the *consequences*, even if unintended, of using boilerplate language and artificially raising transaction costs. The aim of this chapter was to illuminate these consequences.

PART TWO

SHOULD BOILERPLATE BE REGULATED?

The next five chapters explore ways in which the boilerplate aspect of contracts can be regulated. These chapters look at the role of legislators and regulators, rather than the role of courts, in fixing systematic problems with boilerplate. They explore techniques that include disclosure regulation, regulatory pre-approval of form language, and direct regulation of mandatory terms. The also examine ways in which regulation may backfire or produce undesirable terms, and why some of the perceived reasons for regulation are misguided. Finally, one of the chapters explores the role of private regulation of boilerplate, through nonprofits.

SIX

Online Boilerplate: Would Mandatory Web Site Disclosure of e-Standard Terms Backfire?

Robert A. Hillman

Editor's Note: *In this chapter, Robert A. Hillman explores the merits of mandatory online disclosure of terms. Online disclosure can accord transactors the opportunity to read terms and respond to concerns about boilerplate either packed in the box or posted in nonconspicuous fashion on Web sites. Hillman's concern is that this increased opportunity to read might backfire. Actual readership of terms would not increase by much, but the opportunity-to-read might shield vendors from claims of procedural unconscionability.*

Should the law mandate that Web sites disclose e-standard terms? This is a potential solution advocated by some to market failures that occur when consumers contract over the Internet. This chapter analyzes whether such mandatory Web site disclosure of e-standard terms is a potential legal backfire – whether it would produce results opposite from those intended.

By mandatory Web site disclosure, I do not mean a "clickwrap" presentation of terms, in which a consumer must click "I agree" or the like on a screen presenting the terms prior to the completion of a transaction in progress.[1] Mandatory Web site disclosure would require a business to maintain an Internet presence and to post its terms prior to any particular transaction so that a consumer could read and compare terms without making a purchase at all.

The problem is not that mandatory Web site disclosure would increase the cost of doing business, which would be passed on to consumers in the form of higher prices. Businesses have been unable to demonstrate that displaying their terms on their Web sites would be costly.[2] Nor should drafting rules that implement the law be too difficult. Businesses could be required to display their terms on their homepage or on another page reachable directly through a clearly identified hyperlink. Furthermore, businesses could be required to prove the availability of their terms by furnishing relatively inexpensive archival records of their Web sites. Mandatory Web site disclosure may backfire, however, because it may not increase reading or shopping for terms or motivate businesses to draft reasonable ones but instead may make heretofore suspect terms more likely enforceable.

Section I argues that despite the relative luxury of time and the lack of sales pressure, consumers generally do not read their e-standard forms presented during a transaction beyond price and the description of the goods and rarely shop for terms.[3] As a result, market pressure may be insufficient to deter some businesses from overreaching. Section II shows that mandatory Web site disclosure as a remedy for market failure is worthy of a focused analysis because its surface attractiveness means that lawmakers are likely to adopt it. It is appealing because, in theory, it would increase the numbers of readers of and shoppers for standard terms who would have time to contemplate and compare terms. Furthermore, mandatory Web site disclosure would help motivate businesses to write fair terms in order to avoid losing customers to competitors with better terms or to avoid adverse publicity from watchdog groups that can monitor Web sites and spread the word about unreasonable terms quickly and easily over the Internet. Finally, mandatory Web site disclosure would not be too expensive or administratively infeasible.

Section III addresses whether mandatory Web site disclosure can succeed. Despite its appeal, I worry that it may not achieve its objectives or, worse, may backfire. My preliminary empirical work on e-consumer reading of standard forms, as well as studies of e-shopping behavior, suggests that advance disclosure of terms likely will fail to increase reading or shopping for terms.[4] This should be no surprise. Despite the opportunity to read, most e-consumers may still have ample rational reasons for not reading and cognitive processes that deter reading and processing terms.[5] In addition, e-consumers, drawn to the speed and novelty of the Internet, are unlikely to have the patience or discipline to compare terms regardless of when the terms become available. Furthermore, watchdog groups may not positively motivate businesses because they may lack influence and because businesses may conclude that the benefits of particular terms outweigh any potential costs in adverse publicity.

In light of the potential failure of mandatory Web site disclosure to increase reading and to discipline businesses, the only effects of the proposal may be to insulate businesses from claims of procedural unconscionability and to create a safe harbor for businesses to draft suspect terms. My goal is not to claim that mandatory Web site disclosure will certainly backfire so that the proposal should be taken off the table. In fact, I conclude that mandatory Web site disclosure ultimately may be the most viable alternative. I simply want to elaborate on the reasons that the possibility of backfire should be taken seriously before moving in the direction of mandatory Web site disclosure.

I. The e-Standard-Form Environment

A. *Do Consumers Read Their e-Standard Forms?*

Although the e-world makes it easier for consumers to read contract terms, which I have discussed elsewhere,[6] there are several pitfalls, consisting of either rational, cognitive, or social reasons for consumers' failure to read terms or to consider them in their decisions. Some of the rational reasons coincide with paper-world barriers to reading, such as boilerplate's lack of lucidity, consumers' lack of bargaining power and choices, and the relative likelihood that nothing will go wrong. In addition, the e-environment adds to the futility of reading because of the lack of a live contracting partner and the time and effort necessary to locate terms that e-businesses can easily hide. In short, e-consumers may rationally compare the costs and benefits of reading terms and find a net benefit in spending their time on another activity.

Cognitive reasons for failing to read and process terms also coincide with those in the paper world. These include consumers' propensity to equate "low probability" risks with "zero probability" risks[7] and their tendencies to digest a limited quantity of information and to rely instead on hunches and processes that simplify decision making. For these reasons, terms that apply when things go wrong, such as dispute resolution and forum selection, especially may not be salient to consumers.[8]

On the surface, the e-environment appears to favor e-consumers by eliminating social pressures such as hovering sales agents and impatient people in line. However, Professor Rachlinski and I pointed out that the e-environment substitutes other hurdles to reading and processing terms. E-consumers may not attach appropriate significance to a mouse click and therefore may fail to appreciate the seriousness of their actions.[9] Furthermore, computers and the Internet appear to cast a spell over many consumers, making them impatient, even impetuous. We used the term "click-happy" to describe the activity of many consumers contemplating e-standard forms.

In light of these factors, Rachlinski and I predicted that e-consumers were just as unlikely to read and shop for standard terms as their paper-world counterparts, who, by and large, ignore their standard forms and fail to shop for favorable terms.[10] Preliminary empirical evidence from my forthcoming survey of ninety-two contracts students bears out this prediction.[11] Beyond price and product description, only 4 percent of the sample read their e-purchase contracts "as a general matter." Furthermore, 44 percent of the respondents reported affirmatively that, other than price and product description, they *do not read* their e-purchase contracts under any circumstances. One third of the respondents may be spurred on to read when the value of the contract is high, and one third may read when the vendor is unknown. About 17 percent read some selected terms, mainly warranties, product information, disclosures, and warnings. Impatience accounts most often for the failure of respondents to read their forms, reinforcing the image of the "click-happy" consumer.[12] Finally, only 7 percent of respondents shop for advantageous terms (beyond price and description of the goods) despite the advantage of shopping on the Internet.[13]

B. *Can Market Pressure Discipline e-Businesses?*

Despite the apparent failure of most e-consumers to read their standard forms and to shop for terms, standard-form contracting is good for businesses and consumers alike, provided that market or other forces deter businesses from overreaching. The pros and cons of standard forms are well known. The bottom line is that standard forms reduce the cost of doing business because the drafter, familiar with its products and services, can best determine the risks it can efficiently bear and the risks better allocated to the consumer. Furthermore, businesses that use standard forms do not have to bear the cost of bargaining over terms. Drafters can reduce prices because of these savings.

Many scholars have discussed whether market forces discipline the drafters of standard forms. Notwithstanding the common failure of most consumers to read standard forms, analysts have suggested that in competitive markets a small number of readers, whom businesses cannot afford to lose, may be sufficient to deter overreaching.[14] Competition for market share in the e-environment may therefore deter businesses from drafting onerous terms or even motivate them to write terms favorable to consumers. Because e-consumers can easily spread the word about the nature of the terms, the Internet should increase this incentive.[15]

However, market pressure may be insufficient to discipline businesses.[16] In insufficiently competitive industries, businesses can afford to lose the small cadre of readers and dictate onerous terms to the nonreaders.[17] Furthermore, in more competitive climates, businesses may be able to identify readers and offer them more favorable terms. E-technology facilitates such segregation by enabling businesses to gather data on consumer behavior on the Internet.[18] In addition, e-commerce offers businesses new and inexpensive strategies for manipulating consumers to minimize standard-term shopping. Businesses can experiment with modes of presentation, including methods of accessing the standard terms, graphics, and font sizes, to determine which presentations most effectively deter reading.[19]

In the article reporting my survey, I evaluated various proposals for intervention in the e-market on the assumption that market failures exist and that the benefits of regulation exceed its costs.[20] The proposals include enforcing clickwrap but not browsewrap contracts, adopting more specific rules about presentation and agreement to terms, requiring a cooling-off period, and adopting substantive mandatory terms. Suffice it to say here that enforcing only clickwrap terms may not be enough because, for the reasons already mentioned, consumers are unlikely to read and digest the terms presented on a screen during a transaction. Furthermore, other methods of attracting attention to the terms, such as requiring bold text or clicking after each term on the screen (or both), might increase reading, but analogous strategies in the paper world have had mixed results, probably in part because consumers, worn down by the contracting process, are unlikely to be riveted to attention by such formalities.[21] In addition, contracting could become prohibitively expensive for e-businesses if consumers could retract their consent during a cooling-off period and for little gain because consumers are as unlikely to read terms after a transaction as during one. Finally, prescribing mandatory terms that extend regulation beyond the tested limits of unconscionability and related litmus tests of reasonable contracting, such as the doctrines of duress and misrepresentation, runs into serious autonomy objections and a legitimate concern over whether third-party regulators can effectively identify the class of terms that are the product of market failures.

Perhaps the most practical and promising suggestion is to require precontract mandatory Web site disclosure of terms. The next two sections of this chapter analyze this proposal.

II. The Potential Benefits of Mandatory Web Site Disclosure

This section shows that a very promising theoretical case for mandatory Web site disclosure can be made. Nonetheless, in Section III, I confess to serious reservations about whether mandatory Web site disclosure can be successful.

In theory, mandatory Web site disclosure would increase the number of readers of standard forms and shoppers for terms to a level that businesses could not ignore. Furthermore, mandatory Web site disclosure would allow consumers to educate themselves by perusing and comparing terms far removed from the excitement and anticipation of an imminent purchase. Businesses in competitive markets would vie for a larger market share by writing terms attractive to consumers. Market segregation of readers would be unsuccessful because of the volume of readers. Businesses in less competitive industries would seek to draft attractive terms to appeal to the high volume of readers as well. Consumers could shop in these markets with some confidence that prices adequately reflect the quality of the terms.[22]

Even if mandatory Web site disclosure did not increase consumer reading very much, in theory it still might motivate businesses to write fair terms. Businesses would worry, for example, that disclosure would facilitate watchdog-group exposure of unsavory terms. Such exposure could ruin a business's reputation, which is especially critical on the Web where consumer trust is the key to success, and thereby diminish the business's market share. For example, the Electronic Frontier Foundation lists "dangerous terms" on its Web site, such as those that bar criticism of products, permit monitoring of a transferee's computer, or allow modification of agreements without notice or consent.[23]

By increasing the opportunity to read e-standard forms, contract law would also reinforce autonomy reasons for enforcing contracts. Consumers who have an opportunity to read and compare terms can better choose for themselves whether and with whom to contract. Mandatory Web site disclosure would therefore reinforce Llewellyn's conception of consumers' blanket *assent* to reasonable standard terms. Llewellyn wrote that so long as a consumer has access to standard terms, her signature constitutes an implied delegation to the drafter of the duty to draft fair and efficient boilerplate terms, even if the consumer does not read them.[24] The delegation is not unlike a consumer's delegation to a seller of the duty to select the component parts of goods. Under Llewellyn's theory, consumers who agree to a standard-form transaction after mandatory Web site disclosure would have a more difficult time complaining of hollow assent. The end result would be that freedom of contract would have some meaning within the realm of e-standard-form transactions.

Relatedly, even if disclosure fails to increase reading, it still may have symbolic value by demonstrating lawmakers' efforts to make business-consumer transactions fairer. Disclosure would show that lawmakers are not content treating consumer assent to standard forms as what Lon Fuller called an "apologetic or merciful [legal] fiction[]."[25] Fuller thought that the presumption that "everyone knows the law," for example, is a useful fiction to "apologize" for the troubling reality that people who are punished often do not even realize that they are breaking the law. Disclosure laws in the context of e-standard-form contracts would mean that lawmakers were making an effort to turn assent into something more meaningful.

Finally, mandatory Web site disclosure would eliminate painful decisions, like drawing lines between those consumer nonreaders who are entitled to relief from standard terms and those who should be subject to the duty to read. After all, consumers bring a whole range of emotions, attitudes, and resources to their shopping experience. The law cannot easily sort out those Internet shoppers who should fend for themselves from those who, because of emotional or cognitive processes, may have failed to internalize adverse terms.[26]

The obvious costs of mandatory Web site disclosure should not be too high because displaying standard forms on a Web site should be inexpensive. In fact, to date, businesses have failed to mount an effective argument against the requirement.[27] Nor should lawmakers have insurmountable problems drafting rules that successfully implement disclosure. The rules of mandatory Web site disclosure must be clear and detailed if e-businesses are to be discouraged from devising methods of deterring reading. Easily accessible terms written in plain English on a Web site's homepage or on a clearly identified hyperlink may add to the phalanx of readers, but legalese that can be reached only after several mouse clicks likely would not.[28] Mandatory Web site disclosure rules must therefore account for such strategies by requiring businesses to display terms on their homepages or on another page only a few clicks away. Furthermore, the rules should bar scroll-down windows that disappear or are too small.

Enforcement costs would include the cost of proving that a business failed to display its terms prior to the transaction in a manner prescribed by the law or at all. Mandatory Web site disclosure rules could allocate the burden of proof to businesses to prove the content of their Web sites, which would motivate them to keep accurate evidence of the content. Many e-businesses currently keep archival records of their Web site content, including when it was introduced, modified, and removed. They also maintain server logs, which indicate when and if a Web page was modified. Under a regime of mandatory Web site disclosure, all e-businesses would have to follow suit. Of course, businesses willing to engage in fraud may be able to alter their records, but this problem should not be too different from the challenge of weeding out fraud in the paper-contracting world. Evidence to corroborate a business's proof could include, for example, the testimony of other visitors to the Web site during the contested period. E-businesses can find these visitors by consulting their Web logs. In the e-world, we can also expect rapid technological advances combined with entrepreneurial activity to produce new methods of establishing credible evidence of Web site content over time. For example, if contract law adopts mandatory Web site disclosure, do not be surprised to see new Web businesses spring up to archive the standard forms of e-businesses.

III. Will Mandatory Web Site Disclosure Backfire?

A. *Will Mandatory Web Site Disclosure Alleviate Market Failures?*

Disclosure does not mandate the content of terms. Rather, it is intended to influence businesses to write reasonable terms on the theory that more consumers will read and shop for terms or that watchdog groups will publicize adverse terms. The problem is that people do not always act the way lawmakers predict and, therefore, laws designed to achieve purposes by influencing people's conduct can go astray, or even backfire. There are several reasons to worry that mandatory disclosure may backfire.

1. Disclosure as a Method of Increasing Reading. Mandatory Web site disclosure may fail to increase reading and shopping for terms. Most of the rational, cognitive, and emotional reasons that consumers do not read terms still apply regardless of when businesses display the terms. Businesses can still hide behind legalese and consumers, who do not have bargaining power, will continue to process information selectively and to believe that nothing will go wrong. In fact, by increasing the information available to consumers, the early display of terms may add to the problem of information overload. Furthermore, without the immediacy of an actual transaction, consumers may find plowing through legalese more tedious and worthless than ever.

Perhaps most important, if consumers are truly "click happy," they are unlikely to settle down simply because of advance disclosure of terms. Understanding people's Internet shopping processes adds to the pessimism. Analysis of such shopping is still relatively novel, but early reports are not promising. One study identifies two major types of shoppers on the Internet.[29] One type, the "convenience" shopper, has a particular purchase in mind and rationally uses the Internet to reduce search costs, such as by using a search engine to gather information on a product and compare prices and by reading product reviews online. The "recreational" shopper, by contrast, shops for the sheer enjoyment of the experience and, stimulated by the interactive nature of the Internet, often purchases impulsively. Recreational shoppers "may be driven by *need to purchase* rather than *need for a product*" and that recreation may be "more important than convenience for online shoppers."[30] Even shoppers who begin their shopping experience rationally to reduce the costs of their transaction may ultimately engage in impulse buying. The Internet environment apparently contributes to impulse purchasing because of its anonymity (people purchasing impulsively prefer privacy), availability twenty-four hours a day, and other "recreational shopping features," such as "e-mail alerts of new products ... [and] special offers."[31]

In short, the online environment may contribute to impulsivity and even addictive purchasing among consumers. For consumers who succumb, Internet shopping may consist in large part of "consumers who utilize interactive features [to] enter a seamless sequence of responses, a 'flow' state in which their sense of time and reality becomes distorted and their self-control is diminished."[32] These findings "challenge [the] explanations of the online shopping experience that emphasize economic convenience and the operation of an efficient electronic marketplace.... [O]nline buying could be out of control and...not...judged against rational standards of consumer efficiency."[33]

By contrast, some characteristics of online shopping may contribute to shopping rationality. Convenient access to prices, search engines that easily take consumers to competitors' sites, shopping carts, product reviews, and the absence of a hands-on bonding experience with a product moderate consumer impulsivity.[34] In fact, business publications paint a rosy picture of the Internet's empowerment of consumers who are "taking control of the way [they] learn[] and hear[] about products."[35]

More study is necessary before we can reach any conclusions about the ultimate influence of the Internet on shopping behavior, but if the Internet marketplace consists in large part of impulse purchasers or people who turn into impulse purchasers, it is obviously not the kind of environment that is conducive to reading and shopping for terms prior to a transaction. If consumers throw caution to the wind in the very decision to partake in a transaction, this suggests only a small possibility that such consumers would studiously read and shop for terms prior to the transaction. Ironically, the very lack of time pressure that might be thought to increase reading may do the opposite. Theorists of the Internet shopping process surmise that the lack of time pressure ironically may increase impulse purchasing as consumers get caught up in the enjoyment of surfing for unnecessary items.[36] At the least, additional time allows consumers more interaction with a site, which, in turn, may enhance a consumer's favorable attitude toward and confidence in the site.[37] Such beliefs may reduce the perceived need to read terms.

To this point, I have said nothing about the reality that people review their standard forms on their screens instead of by reading hard copy. Will this increase or decrease reading? Reading from the screen can be difficult on the eyes, not to mention can create orthopedic emergencies.[38] In short, reading is probably not enhanced by the absence of hard copy. People can print out terms, but from what has been said already about impatience and the like, the likelihood seems small that people will take the time to do so. In short, the lack of a hard copy probably contributes to consumers' lack of reading of their standard forms.

2. Watchdog Groups. As discussed, mandatory Web site disclosure might create incentives for businesses to write reasonable terms because watchdog groups can spread the word about unreasonable terms. The problem is that although the fear of watchdog groups may create incentives to avoid drafting *outrageous* terms (that would be stricken today under unconscionability or related law anyway), this concern may be insufficient to deter businesses from drafting *marginal* terms that may not create significant reputational concerns but would harm consumers just the same. For example, a business that is wary of watchdog groups may shy away from a term that requires a consumer to reimburse the business's attorneys' fees and costs regardless of the outcome of a dispute or to arbitrate in a nonneutral setting,[39] but such terms may be unenforceable on unconscionability grounds anyway. By contrast, a firm may decide that the benefits of a forum-selection clause that is inconvenient for the consumer or a term allowing an Internet site to "collect[] certain non-personally identifiable information about a consumer's web surfing and computer usage"[40] outweighs the costs of whatever bad press they may produce. And, as I discuss more fully later, such terms may be enforceable if disclosed on a business's Web site because of the absence of procedural unconscionability.

The efficacy of watchdog groups also depends on whether consumers and news services access the groups' Web sites and whether visitors to these sites publicize the information. This will depend in turn on the reputations of the watchdogs, as well as the reliability and timeliness of their information. Currently, apparently because of insufficient resources and questionable consumer interest, many watchdog groups monitor only large software developers. The success of watchdog groups has yet to be proven.

B. *Legal Ramifications of Mandatory Web Site Disclosure When Consumers Do Not Read and Shop*

An ominous possibility is that mandatory Web site disclosure will backfire and create a safe haven for businesses that are seeking to write marginal but not outrageous terms. Terms once potentially stricken on unconscionability or related grounds might be enforceable because of their reasonable disclosure.

Most cases entertaining an unconscionability or related claim, including those involving e-commerce, look for both procedural and substantive unconscionability.[41] Procedural unconscionability involves the manner in which the contract was made and regulates situations resembling, among other things, duress, misrepresentation, or, most important here, an unfair presentation of the terms.[42] Although contract law generally does not evaluate the adequacy of an exchange, substantive unconscionability focuses on whether the exchange is grossly imbalanced. Many courts apply a sliding scale to the unconscionability inquiry whereby "the more substantively oppressive the contract term, the less evidence of procedural unconscionability is required to come to the conclusion that the term is unenforceable, and vice versa."[43]

If courts rarely strike a contract or term based solely on one or the other kind of unconscionability but rather use a sliding scale of procedural and substantive unconscionability, what will be the outcome of mandatory Web site disclosure? Perhaps marginal terms, insufficiently outlandish to motivate a court to strike them on substantive unconscionability grounds alone, will be enforceable because of their early disclosure on the Web site. For example, consider the term mentioned earlier allowing a software vendor to "collect[] certain non-personally identifiable information about [a consumer's] Web surfing and computer usage."[44] If such authorization to "follow around" the consumer is fully disclosed on the vendor's Web page, I doubt that a court would strike it on substantive unconscionability grounds alone.

The result of mandatory Web site disclosure would constitute a legal backfire. Mandatory Web site disclosure would narrow consumer rights rather than expand them. Lawmakers must understand that their predictions about how people will respond to a law can miss the mark and must realize that a disclosure strategy may inadvertently place consumers in a worse position than the status quo and even forestall other attempts at reform.[45]

Conclusion

Despite all that has been said, mandatory Web site disclosure may still be the best strategy for dealing with the problem of e-standard forms. As mentioned, other solutions present significant problems of their own. Furthermore, mandatory Web site disclosure is cheap, substantiates the claim of consumer assent, and constitutes a symbolic victory for those advocating greater fairness in e-standard-form contracting.

Of course, mandatory Web site disclosure is attractive for these reasons only if my fear of a legal backfire proves exaggerated because the benefits of disclosure outweigh the costs of the enforcement of some questionable terms. And perhaps I am being unduly pessimistic about the possibility that disclosure will backfire. After all, if disclosure were a good strategy for businesses to avoid unconscionability claims and of little concern because consumers do not read their standard forms, one would expect to see lots of precontract disclosure of e-standard forms already. Businesses tempted to draft unfair terms must therefore believe that disclosure benefits consumers. But I am not convinced by this argument. Business decision makers may themselves fail to make rational decisions for much the same reasons as consumers. For example, businesses may be unduly risk averse concerning the outcome of disclosure and therefore prefer to hide their marginal terms, even though disclosing them actually would work to their advantage.

Ultimately, optimism about disclosure may depend on one's time frame for measuring the law's effects. Even if disclosure backfires in the short term, perhaps eventually the word will get out about a business's unsavory terms. Consider the experience of cigarette manufacturers who, in response to legislation, put warning labels on their packages. For a considerable period of time, these labels helped manufacturers "'fend[] off smokers' suits'" based on smokers' assumption of the risk. As a result, "'[w]hat was intended as a burden on tobacco became a shield instead.'"[46] In the long run, however, the package warnings, along with the many revelations about cigarette manufacturers' attempts to hide other adverse facts about their products, led to a massive change in public opinion and, ultimately, to serious legal sanctions against the cigarette companies. Perhaps mandatory Web site disclosure will also have a long-term beneficial effect.

SEVEN

Preapproved Boilerplate*

Clayton P. Gillette

Editor's Note: *This chapter explores the case in favor of preapproved boilerplate – standard forms that, if approved by the government, would accord their users immunity from invalidation doctrines such as unconscionability. Although a safe harbor can be a useful device in this context, Gillette is skeptical whether the bureaucratic approval process can yield better monitoring of contracts than judicial and market mechanisms.*

One of the prominent themes of current contract law scholarship is the concern that sellers will be able to exploit buyers, especially consumer buyers, by inserting into standard-form contracts terms that systematically favor the former.[1] Many commentators believe that sellers insert oppressive terms and that buyers are often surprised to learn that they bear risks to which they did not explicitly assent, of which they were not aware, and to which they allegedly would not have agreed.[2] Others, myself included, have expressed some doubt about the plausibility of these claims and the prevalence of the problem, pointing instead to market and reputation mechanisms that constrain sellers' overreaching.[3]

However powerful market and reputation mechanisms are, there remains significant space within which seller exploitation is theoretically plausible and events in which it in fact occurs. Buyers may ignore terms that are not salient, that pose minimal risks, or about which they have insufficient information, and it is plausible that sellers could systematically exploit this oversight. Where potential losses to any given consumer are small, the likelihood of either reputational or legal redress may be so remote that sellers essentially face little downside risk from efforts to exploit.

Judicial redress is currently the primary method of dealing with cases of exploitation. But the usefulness of this method is limited because of the difficulty for courts to balance the interests of consumers and businesses and

* This chapter is an abridged version of the article "Preapproved Contracts for Internet Commerce," 42 Houston Law Review 975 (2005).

because the amounts at issue in any case may be too insubstantial to warrant the litigation costs. Indeed, where litigation has occurred, courts have responded with inconsistent results, thus reducing commercial certainty about what is permissible.

The inadequacy of *ex-post* methods of redress raise the question of whether some form of *ex-ante* intervention can improve the social control over bad contracts. Other contributors to this volume explore this avenue. Robert Hillman, for example, examines the desirability of mandatory online disclosure of contracts.[4] Ronald Mann argues for regulation of mandatory terms in credit card agreements.[5] In this chapter, I explore a different procedure: *ex ante* approval of contracts. Under this proposal – or, more correctly, a thought experiment – sellers could propose contracts to an administrative agency that would evaluate the propriety of the contracts' terms. The agency would be modeled on (or folded into) an agency such as the Federal Trade Commission or the Consumer Product Safety Commission. Its task would be to examine the language of the standard-form contract and obtain comments from interested parties prior to issuing final decisions to approve or disapprove a proffered contract. Sellers do not have to submit their contracts for approval, nor are they required to use a contract already approved. The advantage of using the approval option is that contracts that were administratively approved would qualify for safe-harbor treatment – clauses contained therein would not be assailable in court on the grounds of unconscionability or other forms of overreaching.

The idea of an approval process is not untested. The Israeli Standard Contracts Law of 1982 explicitly allows sellers to submit a standard-form contract for approval from a Standard Contract Tribunal.[6] Approval constitutes certification that the contract does not contain any terms that are unduly disadvantageous to consumer buyers and renders the contract immune from judicial invalidation for a period. Similarly, the European Union's Directive on Unfair Terms in Consumer Contracts ("Directive")[7] similarly bears some of the features of a preapproval system. The Directive requires member states, as a matter of national law, to declare unenforceable any unfair terms used in a contract concluded between a consumer and buyer or seller. An "unfair term" under the Directive is one that "causes a significant imbalance in the parties' rights and obligations arising under the contract, to the detriment of the consumer." Although the Directive does not create a system to evaluate individual contracts prior to their use in consumer markets, it does contain an Annex that contains a "non-exhaustive list of the terms which may be regarded as unfair."[8] As a result, the Directive has the effect of denying in advance approval of any contract containing one or more of the prohibited terms.

In theory, the preapproval option appears attractive from the perspective of both buyers and sellers. For sellers, it provides legal certainty about the effects of their terms and reduces the risk of litigation, judicial inconsistency in the evaluation of contract terms, and the invalidation of contract terms without a commensurate reduction in the price of the underlying good. From the buyer's perspective, administrative approval permits an objective third party to peruse contract terms and evaluate the relative risks associated with the good.

Nevertheless, I conclude that the administrative approval option is more problematic than this first glance indicates. In the balance of this chapter, I pursue the potential and the limitations of the preapproval process.

I. Safe Harbors

A. *Incentives for Creating Safe Harbors*

Administrative approval of contractual terms for one seller would presumably immunize all users of the terms from judicial evaluation and invalidation for use of the approved terms. Approval of terms, therefore, amounts to a safe harbor for all who sell goods of the same type as those offered by the seller that obtained the approval and who use the accepted terms. As a consequence, one would expect that once a seller obtains approval for a term, other sellers will employ identical or similar terms in order to receive the benefits of immunity. Counterintuitively, this creation of a safe harbor may reduce use of the approval process and perhaps explain some of its limited utilization to date.

The process of obtaining approval is likely to prove costly to the party obtaining it. Approval involves monetary costs of submission and defense of the proposed contract. In addition, a seller faces some risk of reputational damage if a submission is rejected by the administrative agency. Because approved contracts of necessity become publicly available after administrative endorsement (publicity of their approval, after all, is their purpose) and can be mimicked by competing sellers who did not contribute to the process of obtaining approval, sellers may refrain from submitting proposals in order to free ride off the efforts of competitors without incurring any of the commensurate costs or downside risks.

It might be possible to avoid free riding, however, if a trade organization submitted a contract on behalf of its members.[9] But it is not entirely clear that centralized submissions would be appropriate in all industries. Contractual clauses may also be a basis for competition within a trade. Credit card contracts, for instance, often vary in such terms as interest rate, annual fee, late fees, and overlimit fees. One would expect, therefore, that while a trade association might seek preapproval for a particular term that would benefit all members, such as an arbitration clause, only individual firms would submit relatively complete contracts.[10] Free riding might be reduced in this situation, but only if sellers are willing to limit their competition to the nonstandardized terms.

The extent to which this reduction in free riding occurs should depend significantly on the motivation that leads sellers to seek the safe harbor of administrative approval. Sellers will be attracted to the prospect of preapproval in either of two situations. First, sellers would be likely to use the safe harbor if failure to do so created a risk of significant liability. Because punitive damages are typically not awarded in contracts cases, however, the risk of not using the preapproval process may be too insubstantial to warrant the costs of obtaining preapproval. Second, sellers may be encouraged to use the preapproval procedure when it confers a competitive advantage not otherwise available. An approved seller can advertise something like "This contract has been certified as appropriate for consumers by the Federal Trade Commission." Nonsubmitting sellers would be unable to provide a mimicking assurance.

B. *Approved Contracts as Safe Harbors*

Safe harbors make sense when they take the form of relatively precise rules. Contractual language, albeit administratively approved, that is sufficiently ambiguous to require subsequent interpretation will not provide the seller with the immunity from judicial intervention that warrants incurring the costs of seeking preapproval in the first place. For instance, an administrative mandate that approves, without further specification, contracts that provide a "reasonable remedy" for the buyer would offer little solace to the seller; courts would still have to determine whether a remedy proposed for a particular case satisfied the administratively approved criterion.

By this metric, the terms that have become controversial in standard-form contracts suggest a mixed response. Some of these clauses are quite precise. Think of a forum selection clause that requires claims against the seller to be brought in a particular jurisdiction. On its face, such a clause leaves little room for interpretation. In addition, because the forum selected is likely to be a jurisdiction where the seller is located or that has law with which the seller is familiar and that the seller finds hospitable to its interests, there is a low likelihood that the seller would want to alter the selected jurisdiction frequently. Thus, sellers would enjoy sufficient benefits from obtaining preapproval of a forum selection clause to justify incurring the related costs.

But although the language may be precise, a contract may not be approved if it is intended to be used in a great variance of situations. For example, a forum clause selecting Virginia may be reasonable when the seller sells computers to firms but not when it sells to individuals, for whom the cost of travel to the forum often exceeds the stakes.[11] A flat rule concerning the validity of a forum selection clause in that context would be more suspect because it would be less clear that all buyers would, if informed and able to bargain, have the same reaction to the proposed term. Of course, even if an agency were faced with a set of buyers who were similarly situated with respect to the potential adverse effects of the proposed clause, the agency would not necessarily approve the proposal. Instead, the agency would presumably want to investigate whether any ostensibly pro-seller effects were offset either by pro-buyer terms elsewhere in the contract or by a pricing scheme that reflected the risks taken by buyers. That, after all, is the alleged comparative advantage offered by administrative intervention.

Variance across state laws regarding enforceability of some terms can further undermine the uniformity obtained by a safe harbor and diminish the desirability of seeking preapproval for the initial clause. For example, some states strike down choice-of-law clauses that name a jurisdiction that does not permit class actions in the type of case that the consumer desires to bring against the seller. These states consider the limitation on class actions to be unconscionable because individual litigation is largely impractical.[12] Even if a federal agency validates the choice of law clause, a local may refuse to apply all aspects of the selected jurisdiction's law. If so, a buyer might still challenge such a clause where it allegedly required a court to apply law that offends the public policy of the forum state. The resulting uncertainty about that outcome could be sufficient to reduce the benefits of obtaining preapproval.

Other controversial terms appear even less susceptible to the conditions of safe harbors. Although much of the debate about rolling contracts, for instance, focuses on the minutiae of contract formation, the underlying issue reflects different conceptions of the salience of terms presented at different times of the transaction. But those conceptions rely heavily on context. The implications of a presentation of postdelivery terms may vary significantly depending on whether the buyer is a consumer opening a gift on Christmas morning or a vendor of a multiuser system purchasing standard software. A rule that either approves or disapproves the incorporation of postdelivery terms into contracts on a wholesale basis ignores that context. A standard that attempts to specify the factors that might render such a term acceptable or unacceptably onerous ultimately degrades the utility of the preapproval because subsequent litigation will still be necessary to determine how the factors cut in a particular case.

C. *Lock-In*

Approval of contracts might pose a threat of unfortunate lock-in. When new conditions justify a revision in the contract, would the contracting parties adjust governmentally approved terms? A lock-in of a well-accepted contractual might occur because widespread use permits the development of settled meanings and norms within the community of contracting parties. Once the contractual term is employed, it will generate the benefits associated with widespread contracts – boilerplate – generally. Courts will interpret the meaning of the clause, potentially reducing ambiguity about its meaning (as opposed to its enforceability).[13] Parties to contracts will develop a set of widely known and consistent practices around the clause. Those who fail to use the term will be seen as outliers and will send implicit signals of uncertain meaning, including the plausible signal that they are too idiosyncratic to be desirable trading partners. Most important, perhaps, using the approved form immunizes it from invalidation through judicial challenge. The result is that sellers will fail to utilize more efficient terms that are not found in the approved contract.

Market mechanisms are, of course, susceptible to similar pressures. Nevertheless, contract terms that evolve through a series of market transactions may be less apt to suffer these effects because it is more difficult for a single term to attain the salience necessary for potential contracting parties to coordinate. The approval process generates salience because the approved contract would be readily available to potential users, whereas the government's imprimatur would provide both legitimacy and a signal that the contract was one that was appropriate for use.

Nevertheless, lock-in may not be as great a danger because switching costs from one preapproved term to another are also low under such a regime. The fact that one contract has been approved does not preclude other sellers from submitting alternative forms. If a subsequent form provides more efficient risk allocations, other sellers could adopt it without fear of incurring liability. The agency's signal of quality control dilutes any incentives to stick with an existing contractual form simply because it represented the current industry standard. The proposer of the new form will still incur the direct costs and risks related to the submission. Potential users will still incur some learning costs related to the scope and meaning of the new form and will lose the experiential benefits related to the existing form. But the primary benefit of using the old approved form – avoiding legal uncertainty about validity of terms – would carry over to the approved revised form.

II. Institutional Issues: Competence and Capture

A. *The Capacity to Calculate*

The possibility that an administrative process is more amenable than a litigation process to considering a contract as a whole poses at least a theoretical advantage. Contracts constitute bundles of entitlements and risk allocations, so that the propriety of any one clause will necessarily depend on trade-offs among the various clauses and the price. The success of a preapproval process, therefore, depends on the institutional capacity of the agency to consider the proposed contract as a whole as well as the effect of a particular clause within it. Indeed, the assumption that an approval process can avoid lock-in depends on the ability of the agency to make such evaluations because the acceptability of subsequent forms requires a willingness to consider the consequences of small changes from previously approved contracts. Sellers presumably would be willing to participate in such a process if, but only if, they believed that the agency could determine that ostensibly pro-seller clauses will be approved, as long as the contract as a whole reflects a bargain that does not exploit buyers.

At best, however, administrative ability to execute this task is dubious. It is not enough for agencies to have staffs that can perform econometric studies that measure the price effects of different contractual clauses, although that task itself is daunting. In addition, the agency must have the inclination to evaluate the findings of the expert staff and incorporate those findings into decisions that ultimately generate political implications. Consider, for instance, the classic example of a contractual term of uncertain efficiency and significant consumer effects: The cross-collateral clause in the controversial case of *Williams v. Walker-Thomas Furniture Co.*[14] Wholly apart from the issue of whether the clause was expressed in comprehensible language,[15] one could rehearse all the standard arguments about whether even an intelligible clause to the same effect would be justified (it reduces credit costs) or exploitative (informed buyers would not agree to it). Administrative efforts to resolve these conflicting concerns definitively or to confirm the empirical claims that underlie them are unlikely to be much more successful than the efforts of law professors to navigate and resolve them over the past four decades. Agency expertise might provide a better avenue for resolving these disputes than generalist courts. But the low baseline with which courts begin suggests that the improvement that agencies provide will not necessarily entail a satisfactory resolution of the difficult issues that contract terms imply.

Agencies could minimize the difficulty by responding with less highly tailored inquiries that do not look at the entire contract but rather focus on terms in isolation and disapprove individual terms that appear unduly burdensome. That categorical approach characterizes many administrative reactions to contract clauses that are considered potentially exploitative, such as the FTC's flat prohibition on holder-in-due-course clauses in consumer credit contracts[16] or the mandated reversibility of contracts made during door-to-door sales.[17] The validity of these clauses does not depend on the surrounding circumstances in which they are deployed. A flat rule of that sort, as I have suggested earlier, implies that the circumstances in which the regulated practice occurs do not vary significantly from case to case. Other contract terms and practices, however, will be less susceptible to a categorical approach. The propriety of a forum selection clause, for example, may depend on whether the forum selected is convenient for all parties or appears to have been selected purely for strategic reasons. The deployment of such clauses is likely to be sufficiently contingent on varying circumstances, rendering the categorical approach inadequate.

Nevertheless, the European Union has adopted a categorical approach in its Directive. The Directive defines an unenforceable, "unfair term" as one that "causes a significant imbalance in the parties' rights and obligations arising under the contract, to the detriment of the consumer."[18] Although this definition, by referring to "significant imbalance," would appear to mandate evaluation of the contract as a whole, the Directive contains an Annex that, as noted earlier, lists terms, the inclusion of which require invalidation, regardless of the context in which they are employed.

The problem with such an approach is that it declines to engage in the very analysis for which administrative agencies presumably have a comparative advantage – the ability to review contract terms comprehensively and contextually in order to evaluate the net effects of the contract taken as a whole. Presumably, it is the greater ability to consider the contract as a whole, rather than to defend contract clauses in isolation, that would induce sellers to submit to a preapproval process. Moreover, the ability of administrative agencies to avoid the risks of lock-in are likely to depend on how marginal changes affect the balance of contract terms as a whole rather than individually. Categorical approaches, therefore, are likely to have the effect of reducing submissions and of inducing only submissions that omit banned terms, a result that is likely to retard the very development of contractual clauses that could otherwise cause sellers to compete over terms.

B. *Vulnerability to Capture*

The final concern is that the preapproval process itself will systematically generate results that deviate from the conclusions that would be reached by a publicly interested arbiter of fair contracts. The familiar capture story becomes somewhat complicated in the context of consumer regulation. Obviously, sellers and trade associations that represent them could be repeat players in front of agencies, with a greater stake in the outcome, skewing the decisions of agencies in a manner that was more sympathetic to the very pro-seller clauses that the agency was intended to scrutinize.

From this perspective, we would expect to see very little regulation that purports to favor consumers. But that prediction varies significantly from the landscape that dominates agencies that were created to advance consumer protection. Those agencies – such as the Federal Trade Commission and the Consumer Product Safety Commission – appear to promulgate a significant amount of regulation that, on its face, favors buyers. What makes consumer representation plausible in the regulatory context is the existence of organizational surrogates for individual consumers.[19] Groups such as Public Citizen, Consumers Union, and the AARP have proven to be very effective proponents for their positions.[20] Thus, if both business and consumer interests will be represented, we might initially conclude that administrative decision making constitutes a Madisonian ideal in which debate among different factions ultimately generates a publicly interested result.

But looking more carefully, there is an asymmetry between representatives of consumers and of sellers. On the sellers' side, representative groups such as trade organizations are small, members are more homogeneous and have intense interest in the outcomes, and many of them can monitor the representatives. Thus, there is a good correspondence between member preferences and association activity. On the consumer side, in contrast, few consumers have an incentive to invest the resources necessary to monitor the conduct of the group's representatives. These representatives have personal incentives to prefer activities that demonstrate political entrepreneurship, attract potential funding sponsors, and provide public exposure. Flat prohibitions on particular clauses, generated by testimony from those who have suffered the downside risk of those terms, are likely to be more salient with the group's audience than advocacy of the nuanced, subtle balancing that is inherent in optimal contract design. Officials may choose the former even if consumers as a group would be better served by the latter. As a result, the political influences on the agency might not lead to the optimal balance between the parties.

Consider, for instance, the possibility that the benefits of an arbitration clause include a reduction in the price of the good to reflect savings enjoyed by the seller due to the absence of a threat of class-action litigation. It is plausible that consumers as a group would prefer a reduced price to the right to institute litigation that few consumers would initiate, even if the good turned out to be defective. Nevertheless, a consumer organization, confronted with reports of unsatisfied consumers, may find that opposition to arbitration clauses in all circumstances is more politically attractive, and more prone to generate publicity for the organization, than efforts to explain to consumers that they could receive economic benefits from waiving their right to litigate.

Generally, it is plausible that "proconsumer" interest groups will tend toward support of a particular decision, such as favoring invalidation of clauses that place risks on consumers, because their invocation creates salient events that leaders of the organization can utilize. That resolution may be inconsistent with the analytical advantages of agencies that might cause us to prefer administrative decision making in the first instance. If interest-group representation forecloses or skews the very debate that administrative agencies are enlisted to provide, we should perhaps be more reluctant to enlist them.

I am somewhat hesitant to reach this conclusion, however, because the same bias that pro-consumer groups may exhibit toward ex-post harm over ex-ante statistical cost may produce a more benign result. Sellers that submit contracts for preapproval may favor clauses that systematically shift risks to identifiable defaulting buyers, especially where the risk at issue has low salience to most consumers. Under these conditions, market competition is less likely to correct misallocations that are costly to consumers because consumers will not compare sellers' terms on these issues. Sellers may propose such clauses because they reduce seller costs or because risk allocation at least provides sellers with an option to enforce the clause against individual buyers whom a seller perceives as misbehaving. Self-help in this context allows sellers to avoid consumer misbehavior that is observable but not necessarily verifiable.[21] Buyers who do not misbehave and who expect to benefit from seller largesse even in the face of such a clause presumably would also prefer its inclusion in the contract because it would reduce the risk that they would have to subsidize misbehaving buyers. But, in order to assert their claims, sellers will systematically seek to obtain agency approval of clauses by demonstrating that buyers as a class will benefit and that in so doing, sellers will necessarily elevate statistical buyers over identifiable ones.

But if sellers have incentives systematically to encourage preapproving agencies to favor statistical buyers over identifiable buyers, whereas pro-buyer groups systematically advocate solutions that favor identifiable individuals who bear the risks of such clauses, perhaps we obtain an ideal environment for publicly interested decision making. If there are distributive or paternalistic reasons for favoring an *ex-post* perspective, then perhaps pro-consumer organizations that tend to favor that view – even if motivated by self-interest – would balance tendencies of pro-seller groups that might otherwise ignore that viewpoint by exclusively focusing on *ex-ante* analysis.

Conclusion

Initially, a preapproval system promises to provide a higher level of certainty about the enforceability of clauses in consumer contracts. But further investigation reveals a series of difficulties, which diminish the likelihood that sellers would submit contracts for preapproval. Nevertheless, even as a thought experiment, consideration of a preapproval process tells us something about the alternatives. The apparent biases of an administrative process for categorical approaches to contract terms or for *ex-ante* decision making also cause us to focus on the comparable biases in the other regulatory environments that might be used to reduce exploitation of consumers. Even if administrative processes favor *ex-ante* decision making, for instance, adjudication surely favors the *ex-post*. If courts are incapable of reverse engineering multiterm contracts, markets are also imperfect in translating nonsalient terms into prices that reflect contractual risk allocations. The relevant and, I fear, still unanswered question is whether a preapproval process will improve the desired match between contract terms found in the marketplace and those preferred by informed buyers.

EIGHT

"Contracting" for Credit

Ronald J. Mann

Editor's Note: *In this chapter, Ronald J. Mann argues that boilerplate terms in credit card agreements enable issuers to modify meaningful elements of the transaction retroactively, to the detriment of consumers. These effects, he argues, are not priced upfront and are not suppressed by market efficiency pressures. Mann explores the merits of two types of regulatory solutions. One solution involves a prohibition against some of the most problematic clauses. Another solution is a regulated standard mandatory contract, drafted either by regulators or by the leading credit card networks.*

In 2005, U.S. consumers used credit cards in about 100 purchasing transactions per capita, with an average value of about $70. Many do not pay the full balance when it is due and prefer to pay interest on their debt. These debtors owe, altogether, nearly $500 billion dollars.[1] Individual credit card transactions are small and routine but collectively have led to a rise in consumer borrowing and an increase in bankruptcy filing rates. The crux of the borrowing problem is the relationship between the cardholder and the issuer, which the law relegates almost entirely to the private contractual relationships between those groups. Yet the existing literature has only begun to assess the unique contracting problems that those transactions present.[2]

Two features of the context make credit card contracting more problematic than other consumer credit transactions. The first is that credit cards have their effect in a large number of small transactions, each of which is so insignificant as to make careful consideration and calculating reflection impractical. More fundamentally, the transactions occur over an extended period, during which the business conditions that confront the issuer are likely to change. That means the terms on which the issuer extends credit and seeks repayment will need to change over time. Because it is not cost-effective to engage in a separate contracting ritual for each purchase, the result in practice is a set of terms that are defined by the issuer and changed with surprising frequency (often without meaningful notice to the user).

A striking aspect of credit card contracts is the comparative lack of regulation. In other similarly important consumer financial transactions – like the home mortgage transaction and even the purchase of insurance – regulators or intermediaries have stepped in to standardize terms in a way that focuses competition on the attributes of products that are most readily comprehensible to consumers.

Credit card contracts nevertheless share many of the problematic properties of other standardized contracts. These contracts challenge the notion of informed assent upon which a traditional contract law relies. Many of the terms in the contracts are a result of modification of the original agreement. These modifications are always done in a unilateral fashion. Even where bilateral modification is required due to regulatory constraint or the drafter's failure to reserve the unfettered right to amend, acceptance is established by notice and continued performance. Moreover, the language of credit card agreements, or of the modification notice, is notoriously unreadable, or presented in a way that does not reach the consumer effectively. Thus, most consumers are not aware of the actual terms. Similarly, even a consumer that reads the notice might be unable or disinclined to comply with an available opt-out right. Like other standard-form contracts, credit card agreements are fragmented. They need not contain the full set of terms but may incorporate terms that appear elsewhere, further burdening the consumer who might want to become informed. But perhaps most significant, as with many standard forms, consumers have little incentive to keep up with the terms, recognizing that the terms are not negotiable anyway, and that it would be difficult to rationally assess the true burden that some of the terms hide.

In this chapter, I describe the contracting practices that dominate the modern credit card industry and that create unique problems. I consider some solutions to the problems I identify and eventually propose a new solution: a centrally promulgated set of mandatory standardized terms that would leave businesses free to compete on the key financial terms that consumers are most likely to understand.

I. Credit Card Account Agreements

A. *Context*

It is not clear that a cardholder of reasonable care and intellectual capability can be expected to read or understand the agreement. A typical credit card agreement, for example, might have about eight single-spaced pages of small (seven-point) type, including about eighty separately numbered provisions. Many of the terms in the agreement are comprehensible only for cardholders with specialized knowledge about financial and legal concepts.

The likelihood that the cardholder will have cards from multiple issuers only exacerbates the complexity of the relationships. Although most consumers have only one deposit account, the typical cardholder, and especially the frequent borrower, is likely to have several different cardholder agreements. They also are likely to contain choice-of-law provisions that select the laws of different states. Moreover, unlike the issuers of home mortgages or insurance policies, to take the closest parallels, each credit card issuer is likely to use a standardized agreement that is in form (if not substance) different in several respects from the forms of other major issuers. Maintaining a comprehensive understanding of the status of cardholder agreements is thus a formidable task in a world in which few consumers are likely even to notice, much less retain, the relevant agreements as they arrive in their stack of daily junk mail.

Another point is that it is not always easy for a layperson to determine which papers constitute the agreement for each card. The current Bank of America agreement, for example, has a set of "Additional Disclosures" that appear in the billing statement at the bottom of a sheet labeled "Important Summary of Changes to Your Account." The cardholder who skips the summary after reading the agreement would fail to notice additional terms such as a default provision that permits Bank of America to impose a penalty APR of about 10 percent per annum more than the standard APR.

Finally, as mentioned at the outset, a cardholder also would need to monitor the frequent amendments of each of the agreements. Amendments, although frequent, are not the typical bargained-for modifications of contract theory. Rather, the typical agreement reserves to the issuer the right to amend the agreement at any time, with the issuer promising at best that it will provide notice of the amendments. When it does provide notice, the notice typically is in the form of a new agreement included in a billing statement together with a variety of other promotional materials. The cardholder who uses a rule of thumb to discard all marketing information that comes with bills is likely to fail to notice such amendments. Under existing contract law, assent to such modifications is inferred from continued use of the card after notice of the amendment or failure to close the account and send a prompt written objection to the amendment. Importantly, amendments typically apply to funds already borrowed. For example, a change in the terms of default might substantially increase the interest rate the cardholder will pay on balances outstanding at the time of the amendment.

A legal solution making it more difficulty to modify the contract may not be desirable. Because interest rates and the competitive landscape change rapidly, credit card issuers require a great deal of flexibility to operate. Forcing an issuing bank to adhere to credit terms in a dynamic economic environment with a large numbers of cardholders would not promote an efficient credit relationship. Thus, market conditions require that issuers retain *some* ability to modify the terms of their agreements. This ability to modify is less onerous than might initially seem. Cardholders, too, have the power to modify their commitment. Notice that the agreement does not require them to use the card. If market conditions change in a manner favorable to cardholders, they are free to switch credit cards, effectively modifying the terms of their credit.

B. *Ramifications*

The key question is whether consumers on the ground are making choices with sufficient care and rationality to drive the market to a competitive and optimal set of products and prices. A typical consumer's ability to evaluate separate attributes declines rapidly after the number of relevant attributes exceeds three. Applied to this particular context, Jeffrey Davis has empirically shown, using an agreement much less complicated than a modern credit card agreement, that most consumers do not understand most consumer finance–agreement terms.[3] Davis's findings emphasize in particular the difficulty that consumers face in understanding terms that involve complex concepts that are not common in daily experience. Although the study is relatively informal, its findings do dovetail with the reality of the modern credit card agreement. We cannot think it likely that consumers understand most of these terms, even when they do review the agreements.

Rather, empirical research suggests, the rational approach for the typical cardholder will be to select a card based on the brand, annual fee, grace period, affinity or rewards benefits, and the stated interest rate if the consumer expects to pay interest in the immediate future. Because those terms are contained in the advertising materials, consumers in most cases are unlikely even to look at the contract. Thus, a consumer of typical decision-making capacity would not rationally consider the terms defining or explaining the consequences of late payment or excessive borrowing, even though they generate a substantial share of issuer revenue (in the form of fees and default APRs). If consumers do not consider those terms, there is a concern that issuers will not draft them in a competitive way.

Equally problematic, consumers might not price the risks of card agreements accurately even if they did invest the time and attention necessary to understand and evaluate the relevant financial terms. Tom Jackson has suggested that systematic failures in the cognitive process cause individuals to underestimate the risks that their current consumption imposes on their future well-being.[4] Building on that point, recent behavioral economics literature suggests that consumers give excessive weight to the conspicuous "up-front" aspects of a relationship and inadequate weight to less conspicuous "back-end" terms.[5]

The pricing problem is associated with the cognitive tendencies to (1) underestimate the likelihood of adverse events, and (2) overweigh the probability of common occurrences while underweighing the probability of uncommon occurrences. If financial distress is an uncommon occurrence, consumers may underweigh the likelihood and consequences of financial distress. Another concern is hyperbolic discounting. Generally, this causes consumers to make intertemporal comparisons that are unstable over time – so that future behavior will be systematically inconsistent with present predictions of that behavior. In this context, it can lead to excessive borrowing.

These concerns are exacerbated if card issuers are in a position to exploit them. David Laibson and Xavier Gabaix have identified a strategy that they call "shrouding," in which merchants identify a myopic or satisficing class of customers and exploit the lack of rationality by systematically backloading the less attractive terms into a less prominent time and place in the relationship. Stewart Macaulay's work on credit cards before the Truth in Lending Act (TILA) suggests that card issuers used similar techniques to make cardholders responsible for the losses from stolen cards.[6] Similarly, Bar-Gill argues specifically that credit card companies use pricing features such as teaser rates to take advantage of a quasi-rationally elevated concern for near-term costs as opposed to long-term costs for market products that depend on systematic underestimation of borrowing costs.[7]

Issuers at one time might have been vulnerable to sophisticated cardholders who avoid the payment of interest and fees by using a card with no annual fee and making timely monthly payments. Modern credit card issuers, however, have used at least two tactics to prevent increased customer sophistication from destabilizing their profit models. The first tactic is to develop product features that segment the market into smaller niches. For example, the sophisticated cardholder who wishes not to pay interest and fees is likely to be attracted to an affinity or rewards card issued by MBNA. For that product, the cardholder is likely to pay an annual fee, which the sophisticated user will rationalize (often incorrectly) as costing less than the value of the rewards (frequent flyer miles or the like). This user accords no weight to the value of the information MBNA obtains from the relationship. This new product makes the relationship more profitable on a cardholder-by-cardholder basis than it was in years past, when there might have been a direct cross-subsidization between convenience users and borrowers.

The second tactic is to take advantage of the fact that consumers are likely to have multiple account agreements, all of which are likely subject to frequent unilateral modifications, both of which work together to hinder consumer understanding. If each issuer has a different set of rules, and if the pitfalls hidden in the rules differ for each issuer and from time to time, only the most careful cardholder will avoid *any* level of interest or fees.

This reality poses a basic policy question: How to regulate a contracting market in which a seller faces a heterogeneous set of purchasers, some but not all of whom are sufficiently careful and sophisticated to respond rationally to the terms offered by the seller? Because of heterogeneity, we cannot rely on a relatively small number of sophisticated customers to induce efficient competition. And because many consumers are not sophisticated, they do not respond rationally to the terms offered by the seller.

II. Responding to Problems with Credit Card Agreements

Regulating specific areas away from the general realm of contract law is a familiar response to failure of the contracting process. For example, as the mail-order industry grew in size, the FTC adopted a set of standardized contract terms related to delays to eliminate competition on terms that consumers were unlikely to notice. In the absence of such a rule, retailers might have different terms in their contracts to deal with the possibility of delayed shipments. Even if the FTC delay term is not optimal, it does serve to focus competition in that industry on the price, selection, and quality of delivered products, terms customers are most likely to notice.

In light of the experience of regulation in other areas of transactions, it is striking how little the existing law does to regulate the credit card agreement. Most of the rules that govern credit card transactions are found in the TILA and Regulation Z, which impose several substantive constraints on the practices of credit card issuers.[8] This is primarily a disclosure-based system, but it also prohibits banks from issuing unsolicited credit cards to consumers, deals with unauthorized use, and gives consumers a broad right to cancel payments.

Assuming that some form of economic regulation is called for, the biggest concern is that a theoretically benign intervention by regulators might in fact undermine the business models prevalent in the industry in ways that harm competition in an especially efficient payment and borrowing device. Working from that perspective, the remainder of this chapter considers a series of possible responses.

A. *Running in Place*

Generally, the borrowing problem associated with credit cards arises from two related consumer errors. The first is what I call the instrument-induced risk. This risk occurs when consumers use a credit card as a payment device and do not intend to borrow. Because some evidence suggests that the credit card encourages consumers to spend more than they otherwise would, and perhaps more than they can repay out of monthly incomes, credit card use can lead to unanticipated debt. The second is the convenience risk. Because the transaction costs of credit-card lending are so low, borrowers are more likely to underestimate the risks associated with future revenue streams than they would be in another type of consumer credit transaction. Both of those risks arise against a trifurcated framework that makes the contracting decision less important to most consumers than the spending and borrowing decisions. Thus, both types of mistakes occur after the contracting decision has been made. Because existing analyses have failed to understand that trifurcated framework and its effect on consumer decision making, neither the current regulatory framework nor the leading proposals in the existing literature respond adequately.

For example, the simplest possibility is the response of the common law: *ex post* judicial invalidation of terms as unconscionable, particularly arbitration clauses. I doubt that judicial or regulatory invalidation of those provisions will have any substantial impact. For one thing, arbitration clauses might not contribute to business models that permit excessive cardholder borrowing. Arbitration clauses are at most a detail in the history of the credit card industry, and the rise in borrowing – and attendant rise in consumer bankruptcy – that troubles policy makers was well on its way even before those clauses came into common use. To be sure, arbitration clauses probably deter at least some class actions, but such litigation would merely increase the ability of cardholders to hold issuers to the terms of the agreements the issuers have drafted. They would have little effect on the substance of the relationship.

Would an information-based initiative work better? Provision of information might overcome the cognitive defects emphasized herein and limit improvident and impulsive spending. One such approach would rely on information campaigns designed to respond to the availability-heuristic, making consumers more cognizant of the effects of excessive borrowing by telling consumers about them. Yet the parallel to smoking campaigns illustrates how difficult such a campaign would be. It has taken decades of concerted effort at all levels of the government to bring the growth of smoking among young people to something of a standstill – this for a product without redeeming social value, plainly addictive, and associated with the most catastrophic health consequences. Consumer expenditure and credit, by contrast, are more ambiguous in their effects on our economy: We can hardly expect the government to urge consumers not to spend or to ban advertisements urging consumers to spend as we have banned most cigarette advertising.

Another possibility – the focus of existing statutory responses such as TILA – is additional disclosures at the time of contracting. Yet there is little reason to think that government-drafted summaries of the terms on which issuers do not compete will make those terms any more important to the vast majority of consumers than they currently are. Though there are certainly ways to improve consumer decision making, I see no cost-effective way to use information-based responses to improve the rationality of cardholder behavior at the point of contracting.

B. *Moving Forward*

I turn now to the possibilities of direct regulation of the terms of credit card agreements. Here, I consider two approaches: prohibiting unpriceable terms and promulgating agreements that provide a standard contractual template for the relationship.

1. Prohibit Specific Terms *Ex Ante*. The first solution would be to prohibit the use of certain terms. That approach is common in other jurisdictions. Consider, for example, the European Union's Unfair Terms Directive,[9] which generally prohibits the inclusion of certain types of unfair terms in consumer contracts unless they are the result of individual negotiation. Such prohibitions appear regularly in the context of residential housing contracts.

In the credit card context, there are price terms that consumers might assess more rationally if the contracting process were improved. Provisions that permit retroactive price adjustments interfere with the ability of consumers to assess the risks of default and nonpayment because they allow price adjustments that come into effect after the time of the purchasing decision to which they apply. I call those "unpriceable" terms because few consumers can be expected to evaluate their significance accurately. That impulse would follow naturally from the idea that it is appropriate to ban terms whenever it is likely that all or almost all consumers will not be able to respond accurately to the terms.

Thus, for example, regulators could ban unilateral amendments that apply to prior transactions without allowing consumers a feasible opportunity to opt out. The fifteen-day notice requirement mandated by Regulation Z gives consumers little time to find alternate credit sources. Depending on the requirements of the particular opt-out provision, the absence of another credit source might make compliance with opt-out requirements impractical.

One possible response would be to lengthen notice requirements so that consumers would have additional time to find alternate credit sources. Going further, regulators could explore ways to improve the readability and presentation of change-in-terms notices, broaden consumer opt-out rights, or even ban post hoc application of unilateral amendments entirely.

A similar example is the "universal default" provision. Essentially, universal default terms in credit card agreements permit an issuer to raise the rate it charges one of its borrowers substantially if that borrower commits a default on an unrelated debt to a different lender, even if the borrower has not missed a payment to the credit card issuer in question. It is one thing for an issuer to stop (or raise the rate on) new extensions of credit based on adverse credit information – we expect (and hope) that issuers will do that routinely. It is quite another, however, for creditors to increase the interest rate on debts already incurred, solely because of a late payment to a different creditor. Regulators, upset by the application of universal default provisions, have responded by insisting that credit card issuers provide better disclosure of the provisions in their agreements with customers.

I doubt, however, whether a disclosure regime is the appropriate response. For one thing, it rests on the highly suspect premise that consumers who receive the disclosures will alter their behavior. More fundamentally, it also misses the point. My sense is that the underlying complaint of consumers is that the provisions are fundamentally unfair: "We shouldn't have to pay more to Bank One simply because we were late on a payment to Providian."

This fairness argument has powerful economic foundations. Universal default rules are one of the attributes consumers are least likely to "price" in their contracting and product-selection decisions. This is true because they are a boilerplate attribute that will not be of great significance for most consumers selecting products. It also is true because the cost of the provision is quite difficult to assess up front (depending, as it does, on the interaction between future defaults by the borrower to other lenders and the other lenders' reactions to those defaults). Because consumers are not pricing these terms, its existence in contracts is not evidence of its optimality.

The absence of contracting competition does not prove, however, that the term is inefficient. Universal default provisions are part of the developments in the credit card market that have fostered segmentation and a marked differentiation of rates among cardholders with different risk profiles. It is possible that the provisions operate to shift the net burden of charges by credit card issuers to some extent toward the most distressed borrowers, the ones most likely to default, and away from those least likely to default. The increased collections from those customers might support lower charges for "convenience" users that do not borrow or default. From an economic perspective, the differentiated prices are more accurate. Thus, it is at least possible that a rational and fully informed cardholder would think the benefits of such a clause exceed its costs.

But the role of universal default terms in pricing default risk is more complex. In conventional commercial markets, an act of default by a borrower is a data point that indicates to the lender that the transaction has become riskier than previously anticipated and enables the lender to respond to the increased risk. In the credit card context, however, an event of default is a signal of two cardholder attributes that collectively make the cardholder a profit center for the issuer. First, the cardholder is likely to borrow more in the immediately ensuing months. Second, the cardholder's switching costs have increased because of the difficulty the cardholder will face in repaying the entire outstanding balance in a time of financial distress. Thus, the issuer has an opportunity to increase the fees charged to the cardholder.

Banning universal default clauses poses a dilemma. On the one hand, they make it possible for convenience users to enjoy better overall terms. But, on the other hand, borrowers who do not understand the clauses (or their consequences) when they enter the agreements end up suffering *ex-post* alteration of terms and a significant cost. An intermediate approach might be to forbid issuers to raise interest rates based on application of a universal default clause without providing cardholders a substantial notice period, coupled with an opportunity to challenge the relevant information and an opportunity to shift their outstanding debt to a different issuer.

For me, in the end, the most sensible approach is a total ban on the clauses, which could result in more extensive and detailed default clauses, focusing on events internal to the cardholder–issuer relationship. That seems positive, at least in part because of the likelihood that it would lessen reliance on external sources of information (with questionable reliability) such as credit reports. Moreover, it might be that cardholders eventually could come to understand and react to those terms.

Another likely effect would be a contraction of credit (or increase in price) to the affected borrowers. Again, that response would be beneficial: A system that induces issuers to terminate lending earlier might lower the social costs of financial distress by pressing risky borrowers into an earlier resolution of their financial affairs.

This discussion is not intended to suggest that universal default provisions are the only – or even the most important – provisions in credit card agreements that do not advance the social value of the relationship but rather to illustrate the kinds of provisions that such an approach would ban.

Presumably, the most sensible way to implement such an approach would be for a relatively well-informed regulator to engage in a cooperative examination, with participation by the affected parties, of the relevant terms. The justification is the idea that contracting is inherently lawmaking, and that standardized adhesion contracts in practice operate as "unilateral codes," by which the parties that promulgate them "usurp the law-making function," effectively providing "government by private law."[10]

There are obvious problems with such an approach. Among other things, it is not clear that regulators *will do* a better job than courts in identifying terms to be invalidated. Still, there is at least some reason to believe that an *ex ante* approach – that can be applied evenly across contracts and be incorporated into the price – is preferable because of the likelihood that the opportunity for input from affected businesses will lead regulators to avoid (or quickly repair) truly egregious errors.

2. Mandatory Boilerplate. Term invalidation is probably an incomplete response. Another response would be to standardize credit card agreements. Term invalidation is the conventional approach for remedying contracting problems in other consumer finance markets. Indeed, credit card agreements stand out as one of the rare types of consumer financial transactions that do not proceed on some set of preapproved terms. Home mortgages are executed almost entirely on the standard FNMA form. A glance at the form would convince most of us that – although it suffers from many of the readability problems discussed earlier – it is not a form drafted to exploit consumer myopia or cognitive weakness. Similarly, state regulators largely determine the major terms of insurance policies.

Presumably, a standard account agreement would include mandatory provisions for the legal aspects of the relationship, with specific options on issues where there are substantial business reasons for product differentiation. Thus, we might expect two or three variations on the method for calculating the outstanding balance – one without any grace period, one with a full grace period, and a moderate provision in between. There also would be options for the financial terms on which issuers compete, including the interest rate and the amount of annual, late, and overlimit fees.

Such a proposal would respond directly to the problem of multiplicity of terms and agreements summarized earlier. Thus, as with the FTC Mail-Order

Rule, it would funnel competition among card issuers directly into the attributes for which variation is permitted, predominantly price-related attributes as to which consumer understanding is heightened.

To be sure, it is doubtful that this solution would simplify the relationship sufficiently to make competition – and the resulting consumer choices – optimal. The number of attributes of relevance to a fair assessment of a modern credit card product, even putting the agreement aside, is sufficiently large as to make it implausible to think that most cardholders can aggregate and assess the attributes rationally.

Still, standardization should, over time, advance cardholder understanding considerably. If the terms of credit cardholder agreements were uniform, we would expect that through experience many cardholders would come to understand the basic terms that define the events that lead to late payments, overlimit fees, events of default, and the like. Given the ways in which multiplicity of terms and term cycling exacerbate the role of complexity in the existing market, standardization would help.

Furthermore, the oft-cited objections to using mandatory terms are less compelling in this context. The first is that standardization decreases consumer welfare to the extent that it drives attractive products out of the market. In this context, however, firms do not currently compete to attract customers based on the nonprice terms of these agreements. Indeed, the root of the problem is that there are terms that have a substantial economic effect that are ignored. With no differentiation on nonprice terms, customers eventually might come to understand those terms sufficiently to consider them in assessing the risks and appropriate pricing of their purchasing and borrowing behavior. To the extent that opportunities for delivering products to particular classes of cardholders are limited, I expect that the benefits to the cardholders in the mainstream would far exceed the harms.

A more difficult problem is the likelihood that regulators will draft the terms less capably than card issuers will. The terms will be more obscure, will not improve over time, will include more unintentional ambiguities, or will not produce the optimal allocations of risks among the parties. However, against the background of existing contract practices, those problems are not serious. For one thing, the previous discussion suggests little reason to think that existing terms are drafted with care to be clear and unambiguous or to create an optimal allocation of risks. Moreover, as long as the terms are standardized and within some broad range of reasonableness, differences in their impact can be treated by alterations in the price terms that would be left to card issuer discretion (grace periods, interest rates, amounts of the various fees, and the like).

Still, the problems of government drafting suggest an alternate approach that might be useful: pressure from federal regulators on the networks to promulgate uniform terms. Many of the examples of mandatory forms do not involve direct government regulation. Rather, they involve drafting by intermediaries in a framework that motivates the intermediaries to consider the interests of consumers.

In this context, the obvious candidates for standardized drafting would be Visa and MasterCard. If Visa and MasterCard could be motivated to perceive that the issuance of uniform (and stable) terms on a network-by-network basis was a prudent course to avoid federal intervention and government standardization, we might reach the best of all possible outcomes: a well-drafted and sophisticated allocation of risks, with sufficient stability that customers could adapt to it. For example, if networks were motivated to allocate risks efficiently, they might include a low-cost dispute-resolution process like the one used for consumer-merchant disputes governed by TILA. Or, networks can guarantee that issuers would be responsive to users' complaints and monitored in assessing late fees. Such guarantees would be a powerful marketplace tool.

At first glance, it might seem difficult to motivate Visa and MasterCard to implement such a scheme. The history of federal regulation of payment intermediaries, however, suggests a more optimistic perspective. The leading card networks already advertise their willingness to accept responsibility for unauthorized use even more broadly than TILA requires. More generally, a familiar pattern of policy development on the Internet has involved extensive initiatives by private intermediaries acting in the shadow of threatened regulation. Thus, just as eBay and the credit card networks have been persuaded by state regulators to limit their involvement in activities in ways existing law probably does not require, there is some reason to think that regulatory authorities could persuade Visa and MasterCard that voluntary "Fair Contracting" initiatives might be a prudent course to forestall formal regulatory intervention.

Finally, a still narrower solution might avoid the risks of centralized drafting but still force the production of terms in a way that makes them amenable to evaluation by intermediaries. There is some reason to think that public scrutiny of the terms of cardholder agreements is more effective than person-by-person negotiation with cardholders. Public attention to cardholder agreements recently led to proposals for standardization of the time by which consumers must send payments to avoid late fees – a bright-line rule, for example, that lenders must treat payments received by mail at 3 p.m. or 5 p.m. as made on the date of actual receipt.

The Internet makes broad dissemination of standard terms easier than it would have been when TILA was enacted. Thus, credit card issuers could be required to post the major nonprice terms of their agreements in a uniform format on either their own sites or publicly available Internet sites (such as a site hosted by the FTC, the Federal Reserve, or the OCC). The simplest approach probably would be to post them on the FTC's user-friendly website, so that intermediaries reliably could find all of the terms in a single place. If the FTC required issuers to provide a URL for an address at which the issuer had posted the terms, it would not matter where the terms technically were posted because the FTC site could provide a catalog of links to the individual postings. The benefit of requiring the terms to be posted directly at the FTC, however, is that it would facilitate downloading the terms in a readily analyzable format such as a spreadsheet.

Regulators also could require that any set of terms remain in effect for a certain minimum period (such as ninety days) to facilitate the activity of intermediaries that might examine the postings and provide public assessments of the various terms. Initiatives to educate consumers about the meaning of unpriceable terms or to persuade responsible issuers to avoid unpriceable terms can have a positive effect only if it is possible for consumers to pick among issuers based on the terms. Public disclosure of the terms is perhaps the simplest way to jump-start such a regime.

Conclusion

Like boilerplate terms in many other consumer transactions, credit card agreements do not provide the assurance that voluntary contracting would yield optimal outcomes. The failure of contract suggests that a regulatory solution can improve matters. One possibility is a selective regulatory invalidation of particularly bad terms in cardholder agreements, such as those that apply to debts incurred in connection with previous transactions. A more effective response, however, would parallel the approach that already exists in most other substantial consumer financial transactions – a regulatory mandatory standard agreement.

NINE

The Role of Nonprofits in the Production of Boilerplate

Kevin E. Davis

Editor's Note: *Recognizing that the production of standard forms raises public good problems, Kevin E. Davis explores in this chapter the role of nonprofit organizations in the drafting and dissemination of contracts. He identifies reasons why the terms they draft might differ from those drafted by law firms and other profit-oriented entities and whether these differences have implications for state intervention in contracts.*

Drafting contracts – by which I really mean the documents that embody contracts – requires investments of time, experience, and ingenuity. Those investments may yield significant returns because the quality of contractual terms can be an important determinant of the gains that parties realize from trade. This in turn suggests that from an economic perspective, it is important to understand how contractual terms and, in particular, widely used "boilerplate" terms are produced. Recent academic literature on this topic has focused on production of boilerplate by either for-profit actors – whether for their own use or for use by their clients – or the state.[1] The dominant theme is that for-profit actors typically have suboptimal incentives to invest in production of contractual terms because they often cannot capture all of the benefits that flow from those investments. As for the state, the main concern is that it lacks the competence to formulate contracts that are suited to the diverse needs of private commercial actors. This chapter takes a different tack and focuses on the substantial role played by entities organized as nonprofits – a broad category that includes charitable organizations as well as distinctly noncharitable organizations such as trade associations – in the production of boilerplate and the reasons to believe that it makes a difference whether boilerplate is produced by a nonprofit as opposed to a for-profit.[2]

I. Nonprofits that Produce Boilerplate

There are a number of different types of sources of boilerplate. Sometimes terms that eventually become boilerplate originate in contracts that are drafted by parties for their own use with little or no assistance from anyone else. On other occasions, terms are drafted by for-profit actors – typically legal professionals – for use by other parties. These terms become boilerplate either because they are widely copied or because they are used repeatedly by the drafter or its client. Still other examples of boilerplate are drafted from the outset for widespread use and are marketed by for-profit firms as "forms" or "model contracts."

Although a great deal remains to be written about the production of boilerplate under these circumstances, the focus of this chapter is on another situation: the production of boilerplate by nonprofits for use by others. It is possible to get a sense of the magnitude of nonprofits' role in the production of boilerplate in the United States by examining the range of nonprofit organizations engaged in producing contractual terms intended for widespread use.

A. *Trade Associations*

In the United States, there are several industries in which trade associations are heavily involved in producing contracts. For instance, many trade associations representing various professions involved in the construction industry produce contracts. The best known of these may be the American Institute of Architects (AIA), which has been distributing contracts since 1888 and now offers more than ninety distinct contracts and documents.

B. *Bar Associations*

The American Bar Association produces (ABA) a range of model contracts jointly with the ALI. According to the joint venture's Web site, the best-selling contracts include various types of real estate leases and an asset purchase agreement. Unlike many of the trade associations discussed earlier, the ABA does not seem to have any institutional structures in place to update its contracts. Rather, the contracts seem to be produced on an ad hoc basis on the initiative of specific committees within the organization.

C. *Other Nonprofits*

There are a few miscellaneous types of nonprofits in addition to trade associations and bar associations that produce contracts.[3] An intriguing recent development has been the emergence of nonprofits dedicated to drafting and disseminating contracts whose terms reflect commitments to values other than creating purely economic benefits for users. Prominent examples of these sorts of organizations are Creative Commons and the Free Software Foundation. These and other organizations freely distribute copyright licenses that are, in their view, consistent with the goal of providing greater access to copyrighted materials than default legal rules would otherwise allow. In addition to providing its own copyright licenses, the Free Software Foundation maintains a webpage analyzing the extent to which various other license agreements are consistent with its commitment to "free software." Similarly, the Open Source Initiative analyzes licenses for consistency with its definition of "open source."

II. Differences between Production of Boilerplate by Nonprofits and For-Profits

There are a number of reasons why it might make a difference whether boilerplate is produced by nonprofits such as trade associations as opposed to for-profits such as private law firms or established providers of legal information such as LexisNexis or Westlaw. These differences include the *objectives* that nonprofits and for-profits pursue when drafting contracts, the *perceptions* that potential users have of their products, their *costs of production*, and their *tax treatment*. It is worth noting at the outset, however, that for analytical purposes, the following discussion oversimplifies reality by drawing broad generalizations about and drawing sharp distinctions between nonprofits and for-profits. Reality is somewhat more complicated. For instance, in many ways for-profits such as customer-owned cooperatives and for-profit corporations controlled by altruistic shareholders are more like nonprofits than for-profits.

A. *Objectives*

Externalities Associated with Drafting Contracts. Nonprofits and for-profits might have different objectives in producing boilerplate for use by others. In particular, although for-profits might only take into account the net financial returns that they realize, nonprofits might take into account a broader range of factors, including factors that a for-profit would regard as "externalities." There are a number of such factors.

To begin with, there are the net benefits that accrue to the customers to whom the drafter sells boilerplate terms. So, for instance, depending on how much it cares about the welfare of its customers, a drafter with market power may or may not exploit that power by raising the price of contracts that it sells. Similarly, the drafter may or may not take into account the extent to which adopting standardized contractual terms makes it easier for, on the one hand, the members of an anticompetitive cartel to detect defection from agreed prices or, on the other hand, for consumers to shop around. A drafter's attitude toward its customers will also determine whether it chooses to make unobservable investments in drafting and updating boilerplate. In many situations, the profit-maximizing course of action will be to avoid truly unobservable investments in drafting and updating simply because customers will be unwilling to trust the drafter enough to pay for benefits that they cannot see.

Leaving aside customers, a drafter also could take into account the benefits or costs its decisions create for users who are not customers and so will not provide compensation to or demand compensation from the drafter. For instance, if, as is often the case, the drafter deals with only one of the parties to the contract in which the terms are ultimately embodied, the customer may pay the drafter to adopt terms that are biased against other parties in ways that are difficult to observe. Taking the point even further, a drafter might take into account the costs and benefits its actions generate for third parties who gain access to copies of the contract indirectly. This phenomenon, whose prevalence will depend in part on the constraints imposed by communications technology and copyright law, is potentially significant because the third parties might benefit considerably from obtaining access to the fruits of a drafter's efforts.

Finally, a drafter also could take into account the effects of its decisions on third parties who will not necessarily have access to copies of the terms that it drafts, but who either already use, or will use, terms that serve similar purposes. Each time a person uses a particular contractual term, it benefits other users of the same term by increasing the rate at which judicial precedents clarifying the meaning of that term can be expected to accumulate and increasing the incentive for actors such as potential counterparties, lawyers, and financiers to invest in becoming familiar with the term. The corollary, though, is that by selecting a particular term, a drafter can reduce the value of alternative terms to third parties. If those third parties find it costly to switch to the new terms – for instance, because it is costly to read them and analyze their import (electronic document comparison technology has been helpful here) – then introducing the boilerplate may serve to make them worse off than before.

Of course, the magnitude of the externalities associated with drafting a contract will vary according to the circumstances. For instance, in industries characterized by high levels of industrial concentration among drafters – whether they are parties to the contract or agents such as law firms – then the costs imposed on customers as a result of pricing above cost might be substantial. By contrast, under these circumstances, other externalities might be quite small: The larger is a drafter's share of the market for a given contract, the fewer third parties there will be.

Nonprofits' Responses to Externalities. Are nonprofits more sensitive than for-profits to the externalities associated with drafting contracts? The answer depends on what we are willing to assume about how nonprofits as opposed to for-profits make decisions.

Suppose we assume that for-profits always ignore externalities and strive to maximize financial returns whereas nonprofits always faithfully pursue formally stated missions that do not involve maximizing financial returns. These assumptions imply that nonprofits are likely to respond differently to the presence of at least certain types of externalities, with the exact nature of the divergence depending on the nature of the nonprofit's mission, which is likely to depend in turn upon the composition of its membership.[4] For instance, if the membership of a trade association comprises a large and representative portion of the potential users of a particular type of contract, then faithful pursuit of the association's mission is likely to be roughly equivalent to maximization of all of those users' net benefits. Such an association might sell boilerplate at or below its cost of production, even if it could maximize its financial returns by setting a higher price. It also may strive to produce boilerplate that is of high quality, unbiased, widely disseminated, and either similar to terms used by other actors or unlikely to cause those actors to incur undue switching cost. By contrast, if the members of an association comprise only a small portion of the potential users of a contract, then they will not have an incentive to make large investments whose benefits redound principally to nonmembers. Similar issues arise where the membership of a trade association is unrepresentative in the sense that the interests of its members systematically diverge from the interests of other users of a contract that it produces. For example, the views of the members of an association of manufacturers of consumer goods may well diverge from those of the other parties (i.e., consumers or suppliers) to the contracts that it drafts. In these situations, the association has an incentive, among other things, to include unobservable but biased terms in the contracts it drafts.

Trying to predict how nonprofits and for-profits will respond to externalities becomes even more complicated if we change our behavioral assumptions and take into account the fact that neither for-profit nor nonprofit organizations will necessarily be faithful to their formally defined roles. For example, staff attorneys who wish to ensure that they retain their jobs might revise contracts frequently and ignore the switching costs entailed for the organization's members. They also might take the easy route through their days by undertaking purely cosmetic revisions rather than making substantial efforts to develop new terms. Similarly, there may be volunteers who join contract-drafting committees solely for the sake of raising their professional profile and contribute little to the process once appointed.

Some might argue that these sorts of agency costs are particularly significant in the nonprofit world because nonprofits have no residual financial claimants with an incentive to hold agents of the organization accountable for deviations from their missions. By contrast, factors such as the fear of competition (from either for-profits or nonprofits), professional pride, or the need to attract continued financial support from members or donors might override the effects of the absence of accountability to residual financial claimants. Other possibilities are that nonprofits will attempt to maximize profits from the sale of contracts because their senior managers personally benefit from higher profits or because they use the profits to subsidize other activities. This last set of factors would cause nonprofits to respond to externalities in exactly the same way as for-profits.

B. *Perceptions*

Regardless of whether nonprofits actually pursue different objectives from for-profits when drafting contracts for use by others, they may be *perceived* to be dedicated to pursuing different objectives. This difference in perceptions may give nonprofits an advantage over for-profits in assuring prospective users of the value of whatever terms they actually draft. More specifically, nonprofits that are perceived to pursue objectives other than simply maximizing the financial returns associated with drafting contracts might be better placed than for-profits to assure prospective users about the value of the terms they draft or endorse. The ability to assure prospective users of the value of contractual terms is important because it may be difficult for those prospective users to assess the value on their own.[5] If prospective users believe that nonprofits have an incentive to make unobservable investments in increasing and maintaining the value of contracts they produce, then nonprofits ought to find it relatively easy to provide credible assurances of the value of their contracts.

Of course, the practical significance of these potential differences between nonprofits and for-profits is unclear. First, for reasons identified previously, prospective users may perceive nonprofits to be no more likely than for-profits to take their interests into account. This seems likely to be a particularly significant concern for trade associations with unrepresentative membership structures (although many of them attempt to overcome this problem by collaborating with other associations in the production of boilerplate). The difference in credibility between nonprofits and for-profits may also be limited because for-profits might use techniques such as warranties and bonds to bolster their credibility (although the scope for using warranties is limited by the fact that, along most dimensions, the quality of contracts is difficult to verify).

C. *Costs of Production*

Nonprofits may also differ from for-profits in the sense that they face different costs of production. One reason that this might be the case is because nonprofits may have superior access to volunteer labor. In fact, trade associations and other nonprofits appear to rely quite heavily on volunteers when they draft boilerplate. However, there may be factors that offset this advantage.

Access to Volunteers. Having the option of tapping volunteers to assist in drafting contracts may be quite advantageous. One reason is that, as noted earlier, it is difficult to assess how well a contract has been drafted. This is true not only for potential users of contracts but also for organizations that employ agents to draft contracts. Under these circumstances, agents have an incentive to shirk their responsibilities. Naturally, external incentive mechanisms such as bonuses, warranties, and bonds (reputational or otherwise) can mitigate this problem. To the extent that these fail, however, it will be helpful if an internal factor such as altruism, professional pride, or the desire to exercise and improve skills motivates agents to exert themselves. This will frequently be the case for volunteers.

A second reason why access to volunteers might be important in drafting contracts is because it may be useful to have large numbers of people assist, at least in small ways, in the drafting process. The principal reason for this is that an extraordinarily large number of combinations of contingencies can arise in the course of the performance of even a moderately complex contract. It is very difficult for any single person, or even small group of people, to foresee all of those contingencies and accurately analyze whether the contract will be interpreted to provide appropriate guidance in each scenario. However, a large group of readers may be well suited to undertake this analysis collectively, even if each member of the group only devotes a relatively small amount of time to the task. The reason is that if the group is sufficiently diverse, each member will bring different experiences to the table and will identify and focus on different sets of contingencies ("Given enough eyeballs, all bugs are shallow"). In addition, allowing readers to play a role in selecting the problems on which they focus may be a useful way to harness the private information that they possess about their own capabilities. Providing monetary compensation to members of such a large group might be prohibitively costly because of both the transaction costs of processing payments and the difficulty of assigning a price to each contribution. If, however, the members of the group provide their services on a voluntary basis, then this sort of collective enterprise becomes a viable mode of production. In fact, it may be superior to production by a smaller group whose members provide their services in exchange for monetary compensation. This is the logic that has been offered to explain the success of open-source software projects and other instances of what Yochai Benkler calls "peer production."[6]

Of course, it is quite possible that access to volunteers does not provide a significant advantage in the production of boilerplate. In the first place, the usefulness of volunteers is likely to depend on how skilled they are; when it comes to drafting contracts, unskilled volunteers may well hinder the process more than they help. Furthermore, it may be possible to replicate the advantages of relying on volunteers by going out of one's way to hire highly motivated employees and, where appropriate, asking large numbers of them to contribute at least small amounts of time to each drafting project. A for-profit organization such as a law firm can easily adopt these practices.

If we assume that access to volunteers is advantageous, it becomes worthwhile to ask: Do nonprofits have better access to volunteers?[7] One would expect the answer to depend in part on the reasons why people do and do not volunteer. One reason for volunteering is altruism. Some altruists may be interested in benefiting the users of a particular class of contracts, for example, "the members of the grain and feed industry" or "users of computer software." However, if altruists volunteer on behalf of a for-profit organization that supplies contracts to these users, some of the benefits of their efforts are likely to flow to the owners of the organization. This suggests that most altruists will be more willing to volunteer to draft contracts on behalf of nonprofits than for-profits.

Whether or not nonprofits have superior access to volunteers also depends on the reasons why people choose *not* to volunteer for certain organizations. Leaving aside altruism, many people volunteer in order to socialize or to exercise and hone their professional skills or to obtain status in the eyes of their peers. There is no obvious reason why these sorts of benefits cannot be obtained by volunteering to draft contracts on behalf of a for-profit enterprise. However, for some people, the direct personal benefits they could receive from volunteering on behalf of a for-profit organization might be outweighed by an aversion to gratuitously conferring benefits on the owners of a for-profit organization (especially if it is a competitor). This aversion might lead even people who are not exactly altruistic to prefer to volunteer for nonprofits.

Other Potential Differences in Production Costs. There are other factors that might influence the relative costs of producing contracts in nonprofit as opposed to for-profit organizations in one way or another. For instance, the absence of residual claimants arguably implies that nonprofits will systematically be run more poorly than for-profits. Another factor to consider is that in certain cases, either nonprofits or for-profits might have privileged access to resources used to produce or distribute contracts. For instance, in certain industries, trade associations may have an advantage in communicating with and distributing contracts to potential users. Alternatively, for-profit legal information services firms might have better access to electronic distribution technology. Or, a for-profit law firm may have better access to experienced drafters. However, it is far from obvious that privileged access to resources will ever be economically significant because firms in one sector can typically obtain access to resources held by firms in another sector through contract. For example, a for-profit organization can purchase access to a trade association's membership list. Similarly, a nonprofit organization can contract with a for-profit software developer to obtain distribution technology or with a law firm to draft contracts.

D. *Tax Treatment*

Nonprofits also differ from for-profits that draft boilerplate for use by others in terms of their tax treatment. Nonprofits are exempt from certain state and local taxes, most notably franchise and property taxes.[8] These exemptions clearly give nonprofits a competitive advantage over for-profits by lowering their relative costs of production.

Many types of nonprofits, including trade associations, also derive an advantage from being exempt from federal income tax.[9] Income from exempt nonprofits' unrelated business activities is subject to a federal tax called the unrelated business income tax (UBIT).[10] However, for many nonprofits, selling or licensing contracts seems unlikely to qualify as an unrelated business activity. Moreover, if the contracts are licensed in exchange for royalties, the royalties are excluded from the definition of unrelated business income.[11] Exemption from income tax gives nonprofits an advantage over for-profits by reducing the nonprofits' cost of raising capital to fund their operations. The narrower is the range of sources of exempt income, the more significant will be the tax-based incentive to produce boilerplate that generates exempt income.

III. Welfare Implications

Many of the differences between nonprofits and for-profits that engage in the production of boilerplate for use by others should, if anything, serve to give nonprofits a competitive advantage. This conjecture is consistent with the fact that if we leave aside boilerplate produced by firms for their own use, nonprofit trade associations appear to dominate the production of many types of boilerplate. There are certain conditions under which this might, from society's perspective, be a desirable state of affairs. First, in producing boilerplate, nonprofits might take into account a larger proportion of the benefits to consumers and third parties than would a similarly situated for-profit. (It is worth emphasizing, however, that what counts as a benefit is an inherently value-laden exercise: Who is to say that software ought to be free?) Second, nonprofits might be accurately perceived to be more credible than for-profits. Third, nonprofits might make better use of the resource represented by skilled potential volunteers.

IV. Legal Implications

The discussion to this point has two implications for decisions about whether and how the state should become involved in the formulation of contractual terms.

The first implication is that in deciding whether state intervention in the production of contracts is required, it is important to consider the drafting capabilities of both for-profit and nonprofit organizations. Most of the academic literature on this topic has focused on for-profit actors and the extent to which factors such as externalities and asymmetric information limit their ability to produce contracts. This narrow focus is potentially misleading. For example, it may be reasonable to conclude that the quality of contracts generated by for-profit actors will be relatively low in industries where none of the users of the contract, or their agents, has a large share of the market. However, it would not be reasonable to conclude that the quality of contracts in these types of industries will typically be low. This is because in many industries in which atomistic contracting prevails, there is at least one trade association that invests in drafting standard-form contracts.

For example, in some regions, a paradigmatic example of an industry characterized by atomistic contracting is the real estate brokerage industry. Conventional analysis might lead one to presume that there is a strong case for state intervention in the production of boilerplate terms in this industry. However, it would be inappropriate to jump to this conclusion without considering the fact that in many areas, state or local realtors' associations draft standard-form contracts that might, for the reasons outlined earlier, be of very high quality.

The idea that nonprofits can play an important role in drafting contracts also has implications for the manner in which the state should intervene in the production of contractual terms. Specifically, it implies that in addition to or instead of attempting to draft contracts itself, the state might attempt to encourage nonprofits to emerge and participate in the process. The encouragement offered could take many forms, ranging from legal doctrines that presume the validity of terms formulated by nonprofits, to privileged access to government officials, to preferential tax treatment. So, for example, in a jurisdiction in which the quality of residential agreements of purchase and sale is perceived to be poor, rather than drafting a set of terms to be implied by law into every agreement of purchase and sale, a government agency could respond by encouraging a group of real estate brokers, or perhaps a group of legal professionals, to form an association with a mandate to draft and maintain a model contract. Or, if such an association already exists but it is doing a poor job, the agency could require that courts undertake heightened scrutiny of the association's contracts unless it improves its practices by, for instance, soliciting assistance from a range of other stakeholders.[12]

Conclusion

The irony here is that some of the most iconic products of a market-oriented society, contracts, often seem to be produced in a realm that is ordinarily presumed to be at least one step removed from a free market. Moreover, this may not be a bad thing, even according to conventional economic criteria. This has potentially significant implications for our understandings of the determinants of the quality of contractual terms, whether and how the state should intervene in the formulation of those terms, and, more generally, the role of trade associations and other nonprofits in a market economy. These topics all warrant further investigation.

TEN

The Boilerplate Puzzle

Douglas G. Baird

Editor's Note: *In this chapter, Douglas G. Baird argues that boilerplate – like mass-produced product components – should not be considered problematic for the reason it usually is, namely, the absence of meaningful bargaining. By looking at three classic contracts case, Baird suggests that boilerplate terms can hide different types of abuses, such as anticompetitive terms, misrepresentation, and provisions that circumvent mandatory protections. It is not the symptom – the standard-form provision – that is troublesome but rather the substance that it sometimes hides.*

The warranty that comes with your laptop computer is one of its many product attributes. The laptop has a screen of a particular size. Its microprocessors work at a particular speed, and the battery lasts a given amount of time between rechargings. The hard drive has a certain capacity and mean time to failure. There is an instruction manual, online technical support (or lack thereof), and software. Then there are the warranties that the seller makes (or does not make) that are also part of the bundle. Just as I know the size of the screen but nothing about the speed of the microprocessor, I know about some of the warranty terms that come with the computer and remain wholly ignorant of others.

With respect to some product attributes, the seller will give buyers a choice of options. For a higher price, I can buy a computer with a bigger screen. But with respect to others, there is no choice. A seller may offer laptop computers with only one type of battery. So too with the attributes that are legal terms. A seller may give me a choice: I can buy a service contract that extends the warranty. Other times, there will be no choice, as when the seller specifies that Delaware law governs any contract dispute between us. Similarly, some product attributes are readily apparent to everyone, such as the size of the screen and the availability of an expensive service contract. Other product attributes, like the speed of the microprocessor and the forum selection clause, are apparent only to those who spend time and energy looking for them.

To say that a product comes with boilerplate is to say that one of its attributes, along with many others, is partially hidden and is one over which there is no choice on the part of the buyer. But why should any of this raise special concern? The legislature can regulate microprocessor speeds or not. The same applies with boilerplate. But why is boilerplate any different? Legal scholars have long assumed that standardized contract terms in fine print are suspect, but it is not at all obvious why they should be, given how readily we accept so much else about products that are standardized and hard to observe. This is the boilerplate puzzle.[1]

Section I of this chapter rehearses ideas that have been well known for more than a quarter of a century.[2] Legal academics too often exaggerate the dangers of boilerplate. The ability to hide terms in fine print creates the potential for advantage-taking, but that potential is modest relative to all the other ways that a seller can take advantage of its buyers. When boilerplate appears troublesome, some other mischief is often afoot. Boilerplate, although not a vice itself, is frequently the symptom of a problem that the law should appropriately address.

In Section II, I show how troublesome boilerplate can emerge from anticompetitive behavior. Legal intervention, however, must aim at the underlying anticompetitive conduct itself, not the boilerplate. *Henningsen v. Bloomfield Motors, Inc.*[3] is the paradigmatic case. In Section III, I argue that intervention in the contract is often based on a substantive policy, not on the boilerplate form. For example, there are some rights for which we require a contractual waiver to be a full and knowing one. U.S. law, for example, has always placed some types of property (such as wedding rings) off limits to creditors. We allow individuals to use such property as collateral for a loan, but we insist that, in such cases, legal formalities are met. Refusing to enforce fine print follows naturally from the decision to create the substantive right in the first instance. I explore this problem, again using a familiar case – *Williams v. Walker-Thomas Furniture Co.*[4]

Section IV shows how the legal rules can dampen or enhance a seller's efforts to distinguish its products from those of others. *Carlill v. Carbolic Smoke Ball Co.*[5] provides an illustration. Rules governing the enforceability of terms in a contract can amplify or dampen the signals that sellers are able to send. By regulating fine print (by requiring, for example, discrete consequences to follow from the use of the word "warranty"), it is easier for sellers in the marketplace to send credible signals and distinguish themselves. Again, the focus should be on how the market as a whole is best regulated in an environment in which discrete arms-length negotiations are impossible.

I. Advantage-Taking and Boilerplate

Buyers often have little choice over the way that a particular seller bundles her product. The inability to choose is a by-product of mass production. Furthermore, the typical buyer cannot rely on her own expertise or her ability to dicker with her seller. But when the market works effectively, she can rely on the presence of other, more sophisticated buyers. As long as there are enough sophisticated buyers aware of the importance of having the right product attributes and the right legal terms, the seller must provide those. Thus, at first approximation, boilerplate is something the typical consumer can safely ignore most of the time. Even if the boilerplate is buried in fine print and written in ancient Greek, as long as the consumer can observe that knowledgeable buyers are satisfied with products that contain this boilerplate, she can be too.

Of course, there may not be enough sophisticated buyers to give a seller the right incentives. There are computers with microprocessors that are too slow and warranties that are too stingy that are sold to people like me every day. But the question is not whether the market is perfect but rather how we should shape legal rules to make markets work more effectively with respect to all product attributes.

Law, of course, has a role to play here. Laws can make it harder or easier for the sophisticated buyer to search. Laws that put sellers in jail if they tell outright lies make searching easier. In fact, legal rules already constrain those who make promises that are disclaimed in the fine print. Rules governing false advertising and fraud prevent such deliberate misconduct.[6] If the law enables the sophisticated buyer to learn about product attributes more easily, sellers will be under greater pressure to build computers that meet such a buyer's expectations. Note, again, that the law against misrepresentation works identically with respect to contract terms and other hidden product attributes.

Other kinds of protection for unsophisticated buyers are worth having because they come at little cost. For example, there are few downsides to making an implied warranty of merchantability hard to waive as long as the warranty provides a baseline that everyone would demand – namely, that the computer passes without objection in the trade and is suitable for the purposes for which it is typically used.

Sellers can shape fine print to suit them and work to the disadvantage of their buyers. Knowing this, however, does not tell us the extent to which preventing sellers from playing games with fine print should be the focus of the regulator.[7] We need to know something about how powerfully the forces of competition push sellers to offer efficient terms and how much they are tempted to engage in advantage-taking. There is no way to answer this question with certainty, but the risk of advantage-taking with respect to boilerplate seems less than with respect to other hidden attributes. An unscrupulous seller is likely to gain more from hidden attributes other than boilerplate. Fine print is an exceedingly poor candidate for potential gains to would-be advantage-takers.

For complex goods such as a computer, it is easier for a seller to shave costs by using low-quality materials than by using fine print. A seller who uses the cheaper (and slower) microprocessor makes additional money on every computer she sells. By contrast, legal terms matter only when something goes wrong. For most goods, the chance of encountering defects that give rise to warranty actions and the like is low.

Sellers who are in business for any length of time must worry about their reputations. Playing games with fine print is a profitable strategy only if it can be done in a way that does not undermine the seller's ability to attract new customers. Moreover, parties have the largest incentive to invest in their reputations in environments in which the other party fears advantage-taking. When customers know they are at the mercy of their sellers, they will buy only from those who can convince them that they stand behind what they sell. Sellers who use too much fine print are shunned.

Boilerplate terms that let the seller off the hook are valuable only to the extent that the buyers would otherwise take the seller to court. If the buyers never learn that their goods are defective, their inability to hold the seller legally liable for the defect is irrelevant. When the buyer learns about the defect and asks the seller to make amends, the seller can often mollify the buyer at little cost. In the rare cases in which the unscrupulous seller is brought to court, we may find that the fine print proves ineffective because considerable discretion is embedded in virtually all legal rules. In other words, sellers are unlikely to invoke fine print and when they do, it often doesn't help them. Hence, those intent on mischief are unlikely to be attracted to this form of advantage-taking. It runs counter to the basic principles of con artistry.

Of course, if it were costless to prevent advantage-taking with boilerplate, we would want to do so. But there are two problems. First, identifying advantage-taking is not simple. Terms that seem unfavorable may, in fact, be part of a sensible bargain.[8] Second, and much more important, legal intervention must be based on something more concrete than blanket assertions about the evils of boilerplate and contracts of adhesion. At the very least, one should pay attention to whether the market is one in which sellers can discriminate between those buyers who are sophisticated and those who are not. Other things equal, regulations targeted at payday lending[9] or door-to-door sales[10] are to be preferred to a broad judicial power to second-guess boilerplate.

II. Collusion and Standardized Terms

In *Henningsen v. Bloomfield Motors, Inc.*,[11] the buyers of a car sued a carmaker for the consequential damages from an accident caused by a defective steering mechanism. The carmaker defended on the ground that the buyers waived any right to sue for consequential damages in fine print. The court ruled in favor of the buyers, holding the waiver ineffective. The court focused on "[t]he gross inequality of bargaining position," and explained:

> The traditional contract is the result of free bargaining of parties who are brought together by the play of the market, and who meet each other on a footing of approximate economic equality. In such a society there is no danger that freedom of contract will be a threat to the social order as a whole. But in present-day commercial life the standardized mass contract has appeared. It is used primarily by enterprises with strong bargaining power and position.[12]

The reasoning that the court uses here is dated, naïve, and hard to take seriously for all the reasons discussed in Section I. Mass markets produced standardized products with standardized terms. Standardization has nothing to do with bargaining power. All carmakers sell cars with four wheels rather than three or five. Anyone who wants to buy a car has to buy one with four wheels, on a take-it-or-leave-it basis. We could mandate the production of three-wheeled or five-wheeled cars, but we should have a better reason than superior bargaining power or armchair notions of car design. The same may be true of a warranty.

It does not seem wildly implausible that a carmaker would want to disclaim liability for consequential damages. The driver will carry insurance. Although it is possible that the steering mechanism was defective, it is also possible that something else caused the accident. In a world in which juries resolve factual disputes, consumers may be better off accepting a disclaimer rather than paying the higher price that covers the cost of paying for accidents caused by the carelessness of others but for which a jury will hold the carmaker liable. Neither the inability of buyers to dicker nor that all carmakers disclaim liability for consequential damages proves such disclaimers are bad.

Although not the focus of the opinion, the court does note that the carmaker used a standard warranty issued by the Automobile Manufacturers Association. Standing alone, this is not problematic either. There are economies of scale in developing contract terms. A trade association can call on the collective expertise of everyone in the business to develop an efficient set of terms. But trade associations also create opportunities for anticompetitive behavior. When each member of the cartel agrees to use the same warranty and to bind its dealers never to go beyond it, they can no longer use a warranty to signal product quality. With less ability to signal quality, they have less incentive to compete over product quality. To be sure, members of the cartel have no reason to choose a standard warranty that is suboptimal, but they do want the warranty to be one that can be easily monitored. Uniform and simple warranties might emerge in such environments. These are not necessarily inefficient, but they are not necessarily efficient either. Even if one might question whether such an agreement would have the anticompetitive effect suggested here, banning such agreements is unproblematic. The problem here was not that the three automakers used the same warranty (the vice the court in *Henningsen* focused upon), but that they *bound themselves* to use the same warranty. It also has nothing to do with lack of sophistication or an inability to bargain. An infinitely sophisticated and savvy car purchaser, completely aware of every term of the warranty, is as subject to cartel behavior as anyone else.

Even if carmakers vigorously competed with respect to warranties, it does not mean that the plaintiff in *Henningsen* would have received the promise she sought – liability for consequential damages. Such liability is regularly and consistently disclaimed, across all products in all markets against all types of buyers of whatever sophistication. A sophisticated buyer with bargaining power does not demand a promise that she values less than it costs the seller.

III. Fine Print and Weak Paternalism

Societies have always restricted the sorts of assets that creditors can seize after they reduce their claims to judgment. Clothes, household furnishings, tools of trade, and wedding rings are off limits. Creditors are denied the ability to reach some assets because individuals are too inclined to make borrowing decisions without taking full account of the long-term consequences. We misjudge the likelihood of future hard times at the time we borrow. We do not fully realize that while the chance of any particular reverse of fortune might be small, the chance that at least one comes to pass is substantial. Moreover, we do not appreciate the value of being able to keep such property in hard times. For centuries, then, our law has assumed that individuals should not be able to put their family Bible, their wedding rings, the clothes on their backs, or basic necessities at risk in ordinary, run-of-the-mill credit transactions.

Once some property is insulated from creditor levy, we have to decide how to treat security interests in such property. Empowering a debtor to grant a security interest in exempt property has the effect of allowing an individual to waive her right to keep it beyond the reach of creditors. There are reasons to allow such waivers. A wedding ring makes for an excellent hostage.[13] The borrower knows that the creditor has little temptation to abscond with it, whereas the lender knows that the borrower will go through great lengths to repay the loan and retrieve the ring. The challenge, however, is allowing individuals to create such security interests without at the same time undercutting the rationale that led to exempting the property from creditor levy in the first place.

It makes no sense to exempt property from creditor levy to protect debtors from their own inability to assess the chances and consequences of default without worrying at the same time about regulating waivers of the right. If debtors are likely to undervalue the importance of household goods, they will also be too quick to grant a security interest in them. At the very least, the law needs to ensure that waivers are done with sufficient reflection and deliberation. The law here, in other words, needs to perform what Lon Fuller called a cautionary function.[14]

Thinking about exempt property in this fashion allows us to make sense of one of the other classic cases involving boilerplate and fine print – *Williams v. Walker-Thomas Furniture.*[15] Williams bought a number of pieces of household furniture from Walker-Thomas for about $1,300. After having paid all but $164 of this amount, she bought a stereo from Walker-Thomas for $514. The contract she signed included a cross-collateralization clause. This provision gave Walker-Thomas a security interest in both the stereo and all the other furniture she bought from it over the years. The case turned on the question of whether this clause in fine print was enforceable. To understand the case, one has to understand the work the clause is doing.

If the household furniture that Walker-Thomas had previously sold Williams were ordinary property subject to creditor levy, the cross-collateralization clause would be meaningless. If Williams fails to pay for the stereo, Walker-Thomas can reduce its claim to judgment, obtain a writ of execution, and require the sheriff to seize all of Williams's nonexempt assets, including the furniture. A security interest gives other rights (e.g., repossession without going to court), but they do not matter here. Walker-Thomas took the security interest in Williams's other household goods because these assets were exempt and could otherwise not be reached in the event of default.

Given the rationale behind the long-standing legislative policy of putting Williams's household goods beyond the reach of creditors, it makes little sense to allow Walker-Thomas to obtain a waiver of the right in fine print. A waiver of such a right must be done in an environment that allows for reflection and deliberation. If Williams is to give up her right to protect exempt property, she should know that she has the right and that she is giving it up. A clause buried in a purchase agreement whose legal consequences are not self-evident (even to many contracts professors who have taught the case for many years) cannot serve that purpose and hence should not be enforced.

One can also take this argument a step further. In a mass market, credit transactions are so routine that it is hard to craft any formal rule that works. The formality must give enough salience to the waiver to ensure that it is done with deliberation. Requiring a cross-collateralization to be disclosed conspicuously or made the subject of explicit negotiation is not enough. Explaining the connection between cross-collateralization clauses and exemption laws is not easy even in the law school classroom. Devising a rule that brings about a fully informed waiver on the floor of an inner-city furniture store is just not possible.

For this reason, it may make sense to ban such clauses altogether. Someone in Williams's position might want to waive her right to exempt property even if she were fully informed. As noted, the household furniture is a good hostage. Her willingness to give up the furniture in the event of default sends a powerful signal that default is unlikely. But we cannot be sure that she will in fact be well informed and, if we cannot be sure, the game may not be worth the candle. We might prefer weak paternalism, but when that avenue is not available, strong paternalism is a sensible course.[16]

This argument against enforcing some kinds of fine-print terms works because of the connection it makes with another substantive legal policy, not because of vague and abstract notions of bargaining power. Giving effect to fine print can undercut other substantive policies embedded in the law as well. Process rights are a case in point. From the beginning, we have always required creditors to cut square corners. If they could not serve their debtors with process and bring them into court, they were out of luck. Such rules can be justified on utilitarian grounds. A court is less likely to make a mistake with both litigants present. But part of the rationale for these rules is decidedly not utilitarian.

The question that needs to be confronted squarely here is how far such arguments should be pressed. The formal rule needed to ensure that a debtor's acceptance of a confession-of-judgment clause is done with sufficient deliberation may be different from the one we put in place for other process rights (such as arbitration clauses or forum selection clauses). The rights implicated are more important with respect to the former, and it may make sense to ban waivers altogether. With respect to the latter, we might conclude that a formal rule that worked would be too costly or that it might be enough merely to require that such clauses be conspicuous.

The law vindicates a number of noninstrumentalist objectives, and doing this is not always consistent with individual perceptions of self-interest. Process rights and privacy rights are embedded in the warp and woof of a society.

Boilerplate terms might compromise process or privacy values and might be regulated on that account, but it is not a rationale that applies broadly across all types of boilerplate. More to the point, boilerplate is neither where such an inquiry should begin nor end.

IV. Fine Print and Signal Dampening

In a mass marketplace in which there is little dickering or negotiating, legal rules should focus not on discrete transactions but rather on ensuring the smooth operation of the market as a whole. As part of making a market work effectively, legal rules should make it easy for buyers to identify different sellers and learn about the attributes of their products. Many legal rules serve this function. The law of trademark and unfair competition is the most conspicuous example. These laws allow a buyer to find a product she likes and tell others about it. Trademark law does nothing to ensure product quality directly, but it works indirectly. With a trademark, sellers with quality products can set themselves apart.

Rules of contract also affect the ability of sellers to set themselves apart. Recall the facts of *Carlill v. Carbolic Smoke Ball Co.*[17] In *Carlill*, the seller ran an advertisement that promised £100 to anyone who used its influenza remedy but nevertheless caught the flu. Carlill used the smoke ball and later caught the flu. When she sued, the seller defended on the ground that the promise was not legally enforceable. The court rejected the company's claim, relying in part on the notion that enforcing such a promise allowed sellers whose products worked to distinguish themselves from sellers whose products did not.[18] Allowing the Carbolic Smoke Ball Companies of this world to escape liability would deprive honest sellers of a way to distinguish themselves. By making such promises enforceable, those with effective cold remedies have an additional way of convincing people that they work.

For our purposes, the aftermath of *Carlill* is the most interesting. After the litigation, the seller ran the same newspaper advertisement and increased the reward to £200, but it added fine print. To be eligible to collect, individuals had to come to the company's offices and sign an application and be subject to the undisclosed conditions set out in the application.[19]

In a circumstance such as this one, the seller is using fine print to undercut the representation that is made conspicuously. The signal sent by the offer of the reward is nullified by the fine print. A buyer in such a world who reads the reward offer or hears about it does not take it seriously unless she also has invested the time to read the fine print. Without reading the fine print, she has no way of telling whether the promise means anything. Not only do quacks get away with sham promises, but those with quality goods no longer are able to use the promise of a reward to easily differentiate themselves from others.

Assume that the seller promises to repair its product free of charge if it fails for any reason for five years. In a world with fine print, it is more difficult for the seller to make this promise credibly. To be sure, the seller cannot deliberately promise one thing in an advertisement and something quite different in the fine print. Rules against fraud prevent this. But even the fine print in *Carlill* (conditioning the warranty on buyers coming to the company's offices and filling out an application before using the ball) does not directly contradict the promise of the reward. And fine print does not need to be nearly as crude as that language in *Carlill* to alter the conspicuous promise fundamentally. Many other terms can have profound effects on the power of the signal that the seller is sending.

The power of a warranty, especially one of any complexity, turns in significant measure on forum selection and choice-of-law provisions. The chosen jurisdiction may measure damages in a different way. It may or may not provide for trial by jury. It may be more or less convenient for the buyer. The fine print may provide for arbitration of disputes. Arbitration might ensure inexpensive and expert decision making. But it also might steer the litigation toward a forum that will be strongly biased in favor of the seller.

Enforcing fine print makes the entire contract harder to understand. It makes it harder for sellers to set themselves apart from each other. A sensible approach to fine print in this context must account for forces that pull in opposite directions. In a market where search costs are low, fine print allows sellers to customize contract terms to everyone's benefit. By enforcing fine print that most never read, we may be enabling sellers to customize terms and offer a package that is far better than one that imposed only a general obligation to conform to generally recognized norms. If there are enough sophisticated buyers in the marketplace and it is easy enough for them to understand what is in the fine print, the forces of competition will drive sellers toward efficient terms. But there is a dark side here as well. Fine print makes it harder for sellers to send clear signals. Sellers who want to send signals have to devise ways of assuring buyers that the promise is not being undercut by what is in the fine print.

Effective legal rules in this environment should make it easy for buyers to shop. At the same time, they should ensure, or at least not significantly undercut, the ability of sellers to customize their terms. The Magnuson-Moss Warranty Act[20] can be justified using this rationale. A seller of consumer products that uses the word "warranty" commits itself to a number of substantive promises, independent of anything that is said in the fine print.[21] Such a rule has obvious costs, of course. A seller who wishes to make fine-tuned promises with respect to the quality of her goods has more trouble doing so. For example, an efficient warranty might involve a copayment on the part of the buyer. If she wants to do this, she must conspicuously state that she is offering only a limited warranty.

But the benefits may offset this cost. If a seller uses the word "warranty," buyers know that the seller will repair or replace any defect without cost to them. This right cannot be taken away in fine print. Blocking the operation of fine print makes it cheaper for sellers to distinguish themselves. Similarly, the Uniform Commercial Code does not provide for disclaimers of express warranties.[22] Any representation that becomes part of the basis of the bargain binds the seller. Moreover, a sophisticated buyer who inspects technical specifications knows that the seller cannot cut back on them in fine print that gives the seller the right to make substitutions or alterations.[23]

One also can argue that limitations on arbitration and forum selection clauses serve the same purpose. A warranty does no good unless one can be confident that the threat to enforce it is credible. A great warranty enforceable only after arbitration in Nepal is not worth much. If we require any change in the forum selection, choice-of-law, or arbitration provisions to be conspicuous or put minimum standards in place, we again make it easier for the sophisticated buyer to know that the warranty she sees has teeth.

This rationale for excluding such clauses from the operation of fine print dovetails with the argument that fine print should not undercut substantive policies embedded elsewhere in the law. An arbitration clause may be problematic along both fronts. Because arbitration clauses are ultimately legally enforceable, we have to worry that an effective arbitration clause undercuts process rights that the law regards as particularly important. Some types of arbitration lack many of the features that are fundamental to our notions of process. In the rules of screenwriter arbitration, for example, the litigants do not even know the names of the three arbiters.[24] The arbiters themselves do not meet. Indeed, they do not even know each other's names.[25] Opting in to such an enforcement regime should not be done in fine print. The argument is not that fine print is special but rather that among hidden product attributes (including fine print), arbitration is special. The speed of a microprocessor does not undercut any substantive legal policies nor dampen any signals in a way that an arbitration clause might.

Conclusion

The boilerplate puzzle has lasted entirely too long. The leading exemplars of the judicial treatment of fine print – *Henningsen* and *Walker-Thomas* – are more than forty years old. The problems they addressed have long since disappeared.

Cartels are unstable, and agreements like the one in *Henningsen* usually have a limited life. It collapsed in 1962 when Chrysler, the defendant in *Henningsen*, broke with the others and started to offer its extended power-train warranty.[26] In today's radically different environment, there is vigorous competition over this product dimension.[27]

The court's rationale in *Walker-Thomas*, one that focused on vague notions of unconscionability, did little to protect those in the position of Mrs. Williams. More to the point, the particular practice at issue in that case – the cross-collateralization clause – is a dead letter. It was banned outright a quarter of a century ago in an uncontroversial regulation issued during the Reagan administration.[28] The problem of protecting Mrs. Williams today has nothing to do with boilerplate but rather with the best way to regulate the multi-billion dollar rent-to-own industry. This business did not even exist at the time of *Walker-Thomas*.[29]

In both *Henningsen* and *Walker-Thomas*, the court's focus on the absence of a dickered bargain blinded it to the aspects of the case that were indeed troublesome. That the judges made these errors is perfectly explicable. At the time these judges went to law school, Arthur Corbin and Fritz Kessler's efforts to understand how the law worked in mass markets, as primitive as they seem today, were state of the art. What remains deeply troubling, however, is the extent to which two such outdated cases continue to define the contours of the debate. In few other fields, even in law, has conventional thought been so fused in amber. Much of the problem is a view of the law that reduces everything to rights that *A* and *B* have against each other. From here, it is but a short step to view any troublesome transaction in which there is boilerplate to be the result of boilerplate and the absence of a fully dickered bargain between two equals. The boilerplate puzzle, in other words, arises from a failure to go beyond the symptom to examine the underlying problem.

PART THREE

INTERPRETATION OF BOILERPLATE

Boilerplate, the next three chapters explain, is different than negotiated contracts in ways that ought to affect how it is interpreted by courts. In important ways, boilerplate resembles other species of legal enactments, which have broader reach than contract, like statutes and property. Borrowing, then, from statutory interpretation and property theory can improve the interpretation and the understanding of this species of contract.

ELEVEN

Contract as Statute

Stephen J. Choi and G. Mitu Gulati

Editor's Note: *When the interpretation of boilerplate clauses is disputed, their meaning ought to be exposed using techniques that resemble statutory interpretation. Boilerplate, the authors of this chapter argue, has many statutory features. Like a statute, it is drafted with a particular intent in mind. Like a statute, it is subsequently used by many parties in varied circumstances. Accordingly, like a statute, it ought to be interpreted with an eye, not to the meaning attached by the current transactors, but to that of the entire industry, as envisioned by the original drafters of the boilerplate language.*

The focus of much of the literature on standard-form contracts has been the problem of power and informational asymmetries among the contracting parties. One party dictates the terms – for example, a big consumer-goods producer may draft a standard-form contract that forms a mandatory part of all consumer purchases – and the other party is a passive recipient of the terms.

Boilerplate contracts, however, are found in many markets where the relationship between the parties is not characterized by power imbalances. Instead, we find sophisticated parties on both sides and a multitude of parties employing contracts with slight variations on the same set of boilerplate terms. For example, large portions of the markets for bonds and derivatives are dominated by boilerplate of this type. Our goal is to suggest that the interpretation of boilerplate contracts among sophisticated parties is a topic in need of attention. We contend that general principles of contract interpretation should not apply to this important subset of commercial contracts and make the case that these contracts are better viewed as akin to statutes.

A handful of courts have taken modified interpretive approaches, recognizing the special nature of boilerplate contracts in markets consisting of sophisticated parties. These courts have recognized that uniformity in the interpretation of this language is important because it enables the underlying financial instruments to be priced and traded. Such courts have adhered strictly to the textual language of the contract, applied deference to prior court interpretations of the same language, displayed a reluctance to imply good-faith duties, and applied judge-made analysis of the economic interests of the parties where the contractual language is undeniably ambiguous.[1]

Courts are right in recognizing the need for uniformity in markets that use boilerplate. We part company with them in terms of strategies that will promote uniformity, such as the preference for textualism and the willingness to defer to prior court interpretations. Rather than have courts attempt the error-prone process of determining what would be in the parties' best interests, we argue that courts should take a more statutory approach to interpreting boilerplate terms. Specifically, courts should look to the intent of the original drafters of the terms, much like courts look to legislative intent in interpreting statutes. In discerning this intent, the court may need to look to the overall history of a term, the process by which the term became a standard (or one of the standards) in the industry, and its context within the greater commercial environment.

This chapter proceeds as follows. In Section I, we discuss two examples of boilerplate terms drawn from the sovereign bond and privately negotiated derivatives markets. In Section II, we explore reasons why markets may have trouble responding to litigation or other interpretive shocks. We set forth in Section III our thesis that judges should interpret commercial boilerplate contracts using an analytical framework closer to statutory analysis than conventional contract analysis.

I. Two Case Studies

A. *The Case of the Pari Passu Clause*[2]

Perhaps the most litigated and most controversial term in the history of sovereign debt is the *pari passu* clause. This term is found in practically every single sovereign debt contract, whether it is a syndicated loan agreement or a bond indenture. A typical formulation of the clause goes as follows: "The obligations of the debtor under this instrument hereunder do rank and will rank *pari passu* in priority of payment with all other External Indebtedness of the debtor."

What does that mean? In the corporate context, there is a meaning on which commentators agree. Those whose debts rank *pari passu* will get paid on an equal priority in the event of an insolvency distribution. The *pari passu* clause serves to contract around the default rule in some jurisdictions that otherwise gives priority to debts that are incurred earlier in time. What does the clause mean when the debtor cannot go bankrupt, as in the case of sovereign lenders?

The leading commentators on sovereign contracts acknowledged that there exists ambiguity as to the meaning of this clause. The presence of ambiguity, in turn, provided an opportunity for rent seeking.

In 2000, in *Elliott Associates v. Peru,*[3] Elliott, a vulture fund, argued that the *pari passu* clause meant that a sovereign could not make preferential payments to any of its creditors whose debt ranked *pari passu* with the debt that they held. Peru had concluded a restructuring with a number of its bondholders and was about to disburse a large payment to its European holders of Brady bonds via Euroclear. A Brussels court ruled, ex parte, in Elliott's favor, granting an injunction against Euroclear. Peru's government, with Alberto Fujimori in his final days in power, was in a precarious state and did not want to be seen as defaulting on its Brady bonds. The end result was that Elliott got paid in full – upward of $55 million on bonds that cost it approximately $11 million.

Once Elliott won against Peru, others tried to replicate the *pari passu* strategy whenever there was a restructuring. In the immediate four-year period after the *Elliott* decision, holdout investors filed suit against sovereigns (the Congo, Nicaragua, and Argentina) in courts located in Belgium, England, and the United States. In some of the cases, the holdouts won and managed to extract significant settlements. More important, the sovereign lawyers have not been able to get any of the courts in these jurisdictions to adopt their interpretation of the *pari passu* clause.

Whatever the merits of the Brussels court's interpretations, one would expect that all contracts *after* the *Elliott* case would pay special attention to the *pari passu* clause and clarify its exact meaning. Economic theory tells us that absent significant negotiation costs, parties will prefer contracts that are clear rather than contracts that present a high likelihood of uncertainty and litigation costs. The questions of (a) the degree to which sovereigns and their creditors modified their contract language in the wake of the *Elliott* case, and (b) the reasons for why individual sovereigns did or did not alter their contractual language formed the basis for a parallel line of research we have pursued examining a dataset of sovereign bond deals from the early 1990s to the early 2000s.

Reading the *pari passu* clauses in the debt contracts of over thirty countries, both in the pre- and post-*Elliott* periods, we found wide variation – upward of a dozen different versions – in the precise wording of the clause. There was no systematic pattern discernible in the data such as more creditworthy countries picking a certain clause and less creditworthy ones picking a different clause. The lack of a pattern is consistent with the view that the differences are more idiosyncratic than due to any purposeful intent to change the *pari passu* clause to favor (or disfavor) holdouts. A court attempting to read meaning into such differences runs a risk of misinterpreting the clause.

Interestingly, we found no changes in the language of contracts subsequent to the *Elliott* decision. Through a set of interviews, we attempted to discern why there was no response. A typical explanation was that any change in the language of the new contracts would run the risk that a court would read the modification of the language to mean that while the new contracts meant something new, the holdouts were correct in their interpretation of the old contracts. But this explanation did not seem plausible. It was more likely that a court would interpret a change in the contract language in response to the interpretive shock as a sign of the market's disapproval for the interpretive shock.

A more meaningful explanation is that it was impossible for standard-form clauses that were present in every single sovereign debt instrument across the globe to change every time there was an aberrant court decision. As a practical matter, the individual lawyer proposing that his client alter a term in response to some interpretive shock faces the possibility that no one else will change their terms. And the market is unlikely to accept a nonstandard term. Furthermore, if the court sees that some parties change their terms and others do not, parties will find it difficult to argue to the court that the market is unambiguous in having an understanding different from that which caused the interpretive shock. In sum, it may be in the individual client's interest to stick with the old term.

The market eventually did provide a coordinated response to the 2000 *Elliott* decision as part of an overall litigation strategy but, importantly, not in drafting a new set of contract terms clarifying the *pari passu* clause. By 2003, when the *pari passu* matter showed up in a New York court in the case involving the Argentine restructuring, the sovereign-debt community organized itself to produce amicus briefs filed by the U.S. Treasury, the New York Federal Reserve, and the Clearinghouse, all opposing the holdout position.

As noted, this concerted attempt to provide a uniform interpretation of the term was done in litigation, not in contract drafting. As of September 2005, we were aware of no serious attempt to coordinate a clarification of the *pari passu* clause in the contracts themselves. The law firm that had been litigating almost all the *pari passu* cases from the sovereign side, Cleary Gottlieb, was also the law firm with the largest volume of business in terms of advising new issuances. So, if any firm understood the kind of problems that the *pari passu* clause was causing and could engineer a coordinated shift in the clause's language, it was Cleary. Yet, even Cleary's clients were not issuing new bonds with clearer language on the *pari passu* matter.

B. *International Swap and Derivatives Association*

The derivatives markets for swaps use boilerplate contracts. Rather than draft a swap contract from scratch, parties turn to both form agreements and standardized definitions provided by the International Swap and Derivatives Association (ISDA). ISDA represents more than 625 member institutions from forty-seven countries, including Goldman Sachs, Morgan Stanley, Deutsche Bank, and other financial institutions as primary members, and Cravath, Swaine & Moore, Dewey Ballantine, and other service providers as associate members. The existence of ISDA allows the swaps market to respond to unexpected court interpretations of contractual ambiguities much differently than the sovereign debt market. Hence, it constitutes our second case study.

Swap contracts can last up to fifteen years. Although parties typically negotiate over economic-related terms (such as the interest-rate terms, the length of the agreement, the fixed versus variable nature of the interest), often noneconomic provisions are not discussed. These include clauses dealing with events constituting default, representation and warranties, and governing law and jurisdiction. Parties leave these noneconomic terms to the ISDA standardized contract known as the ISDA Master Agreement. The Master Agreement contains a series of boilerplate clauses for the noneconomic provisions.

Parties supplement the Master Agreement with the negotiated economic provisions. Typically, parties document the economic terms in a "Confirmation" statement. Parties may include all the definitions for relevant terms within the Confirmation itself. Alternatively, parties may incorporate a separate set of standard definitions by reference into the Confirmation statement. Boilerplate terms provide benefits to market participants, reducing the number of "deal" points on which negotiating parties must contract, thereby reducing contracting costs and speeding up transactions. In the case of swaps and other derivatives, standardization makes possible aftermarket trading in these financial instruments. The boilerplate terms must represent the interests of all the major participants in the market, or else the standard-form will not be broadly adopted. In this market, it is ISDA that drafts a form that meets the needs of the major participants. Individual parties may choose to modify this standard, but the incentives are against modification. Doing so is costly, generates legal uncertainty, and results in instruments that are less tradable on the secondary market (where traders expect the ISDA Master Agreement to govern).

Where an industry already has standard-setting entities, such as law firms with their own boilerplate forms, the gain to establishing a centralized standard-setting entity such as ISDA is reduced. In the sovereign-bond market, for example, where there are but a handful of lawyers with expertise about the meanings of boilerplate terms and, as a result, have a lion's share of the business, these lawyers may have an incentive to resist moves toward a central standard setter.[4] The emergence of bodies such as ISDA eliminates much of the advantage that these elite law firms might have otherwise had as a result of their in-house knowledge. Conversely, resistance to centralized standard-setting organizations may come from the smaller players in the market who fear that the standard setter will get captured by the elites and the result will be private lawmaking that systematically favors the elites.

One difference between drafting through dominant law firms versus a centralized standard setting entity like ISDA is in the response to ambiguities. Recall how sluggish was the redraft of the *pari passu* clause in bond contracts. The opposite is true in the swap contracts, where interpretive shocks are responded to with quickness and punctuality. For example, in a recent set of cases involving Argentine debt, the court needed to decide what triggered the default provision in the swap contracts. Even before the Second Circuit tackled the case in 2004 (the first district court opinion came down in late 2002 and the second one in mid-2003), ISDA moved to revise the definitions clause. An expert group of elite sovereign-debt lawyers was formed, recommended language change to the ISDA, and its recommendations were acted upon within a matter of months.[5] The contrast with the *pari passu* case is striking because at least some of the same expert sovereign-debt lawyers involved in that *pari passu* litigation participated in the ISDA revision process. The same lawyers who took years to respond to litigation or other interpretive shocks in the absence of a centralized standard setter responded quickly when there existed an effective standard-setting body such as ISDA to work through.

II. The Problem with Boilerplate

In sophisticated markets, conventional wisdom holds that the standardized nature of these contracts means that everyone (that is, "the market") understands them. The terms in these contracts are the ones that the market has determined as optimal, hence their widespread adoption. Interpretation (and pricing) is easy because there is only one set of terms, and everyone understands what these terms mean. Even if courts make mistakes in interpretation, as the story goes, the market will contract around those mistakes. We contend that the interpretation of boilerplate terms in these contracts is not as easy as one might think.

A. *Traditional Contract Interpretation*

Courts follow certain precisely defined "canons" of contract interpretation. Under standard canons of contract interpretation, courts first attempt to discern the intent of the parties (the meeting of the minds) from the language of the contract. Second, if actual intent is obscure, courts will turn to the course of dealings and course of performance between the contracting parties in an attempt to indirectly determine intent. Third, courts will look to industry custom and practice. Finally, courts will examine the Uniform Commercial Code for a specifically applicable term, if any. Importantly, the process of contract interpretation flows from evidence specific to the parties outward to more general and contextual sources of contract meaning.

Several costs exist in applying standard contract interpretation techniques to boilerplate that exceed the typical transaction costs for a nonboilerplate contract, as we discuss later.

1. Textual Analysis. The nature of boilerplate terms suggests that looking to the text of the contract alone is problematic. The point of using a boilerplate clause is to invoke, along with the language of the clause, all of the historical context and learning that comes with it. Otherwise, the parties could simply customize a clause that captures their particular understandings. Focusing on solely the text may miss particular nuances of language deriving out of this historical context leading to court errors of interpretation and greater uncertainty for contracting parties. Consider the following two examples of potential court error that may arise from applying solely textual analysis in analyzing the meaning of boilerplate clauses.

a. "Frankenstein" Contracts. The following two clauses appeared in at least a half dozen issuances of sovereign debt by Mexico during the 2003–2005 period. The first clause is the Mexican collective-action clause (CAC) governing changes in payment-related terms. In March 2003, Mexico was the first of the big sovereign borrowers to move from unanimity action clauses (UACs) to CACs. The CAC clause states that 75 percent or more of the creditors (in aggregate principal amount) on a particular bond instrument can agree to modify the payment terms of the instrument. In the contract itself, though, on the page following the page where the new 75-percent-CAC-modification clause appeared was an "Obligation Absolute" clause. The Obligation Absolute clause provided that "no provision of this Note or of the Fiscal Agency Agreement shall alter or impair the obligation, which is absolute and unconditional, to pay principal of and any premium, if any, and interest on this Note."

These two clauses seem both clear and in contradiction with one another. Traditional contract analysis would take the view that it makes little sense that the parties would include these two contradictory provisions. So, proceeding on the assumption that rational parties would not include contradictory provisions, the court would try to reconcile the two provisions. And if that were not possible, the provisions would knock each other out. The end result: confusion and a greater likelihood of court error.

To the extent that contracts with boilerplate pull from different clauses from varying historical sources, a "Frankenstein" contract may result. Taking a boilerplate analysis that looks to the histories of the clauses can help interpret these Frankenstein contracts. In the case of Mexico's bond covenants, a historical analysis would reveal that one of the clauses (Obligation Absolute) was older and a relic of when sovereign-bond contracts used unanimity language similar to that used in domestic corporate bonds. The same analysis would reveal that the other clause (CAC) is of recent vintage and intended to trump the unanimity language.

b. Variations in Language. In our separate *pari passu* case study, we reported that the *pari passu* language for every sovereign was not the same. We saw, for example, that whereas the most standard articulation of the clause was that the sovereign's debt would "rank pari passu in priority" with all other unsubordinated debt of the sovereign, there are clauses, such as that of Italy, that are more specific and say that the sovereign's debt will "rank pari passu in priority and will be payable as such." Applying traditional contract analysis where we assume that the parties intend these small differentials in wording to have significance, we would treat the Italian clause as different from the more standard one. And the commentators who have compared the Italian *pari passu* clause to the others precisely predict this result: The Italian clause is going to be treated differently.

But take a boilerplate analysis. Let us say that the Italian version of the clause is some historical relic from well before the *Elliott Associates v. Peru* case. Lawyers around the world have slightly different phraseology in their contracts, but they are all trying to do the same thing, and that is to invoke the historical understandings of the clause. If the reason for a particular piece of language is to invoke historical understandings, as opposed to setting out a customized statement of intent, then it is not at all clear that the small differences in language, such as that between Italy and the other sovereigns, should be given much weight at all. Italy's lawyers likely were trying to invoke the same history that the lawyers for Belize and Argentina and Peru were invoking, each with their slightly different clauses.

2. Contextual Analysis. The usual alternative to textual formalist analysis is contextual analysis. The context that one looks to in contract interpretation is that surrounding the parties in dispute (course of dealing) and, beyond that, industry custom and trade usage. Here, neither is likely to give one much help due to (a) idiosyncratic contracting parties who do not represent the interests of the group of contracting parties in the industry that may rely on a particular boilerplate term, and (b) the paradox of efficiency for boilerplate terms that may undermine the ability of courts to rely on industry custom.

a. Idiosyncratic Contracting Parties. In the boilerplate context, a focus on the needs of the specific parties before the court may adversely impact the welfare of other contracting parties. An interpretation that increases value for the specific parties may reduce overall value for the majority of other parties using the same term. Even where the specific parties before the court are not systematically different from others, the resources of the specific parties are unlikely to match the resources of the group of all contracting parties. How well a particular position is viewed by the court will depend in part on resources and abilities of the particular party pushing the position. Other interested parties can submit amicus briefs to the court, but their influence will likely be less than that of a litigant before the court. Thus, the decisions of parties to pursue particular claims, concede others, and settle on agreed judgments may be less than perfectly representative of the interests of similarly situated parties.

Focusing on the intent of the specific contracting parties also invites strategic behavior. A party unhappy with how a contract turns out may argue to a court that the contract in fact means something different according to the "private" course of dealings and understandings between the contracting parties. Where few objective indicia exist on this "private" meaning, courts will have difficulty in distinguishing between situations where the parties agreed *ex ante* to vary the contract with situations in which one party *ex post* simply makes such a claim to nullify an unfavorable contract.

b. Industry Custom. Even in the most sophisticated markets, it generally takes time before participants can coordinate and agree to adopt a new standard term. The time during which a term is adopted as the market standard represents the occasion in which there is likely to be maximal knowledge and understanding in the market about what the term was intended to mean. The original adopting parties also will have a sense of which contingencies their terms do not address.

As the standardized terms spread through numerous contracts, later contracting parties will often simply adopt the terms with the implicit assumption that the terms (often coming as a package with other standardized terms) are "efficient." Why else would others use the terms? With the passage of time, the assumption that the terms are efficient – although perhaps justified at the time of the first use of the terms and the initial dispersion of the terms throughout the marketplace – becomes more problematic. Market participants, nonetheless, may cling to the assumption about efficiency for extended periods of time, and attorneys will uncritically include the terms in all their contracts. It bears emphasizing that a key assumption is that this is a world where disputes over the meanings of provisions are rare. Paradoxically, the assumption that the terms are efficient produces an equilibrium in which no one knows what the terms mean, thereby calling into question whether such terms in fact are efficient for the contracting parties.

With clauses whose understandings have been forgotten, neither context about the parties themselves nor current industry custom is likely to be useful. The context that needs to be unearthed is a different beast – it is historical context. Moreover, even if courts are able to determine a current industry custom, it is unclear how much weight to place on this custom. At the time a term is drafted, all affected parties will pay relatively more attention to the meaning of the term. In contrast, after the passage of time, not all affected parties will pay as much attention to the term. Industry participants will simply ignore most boilerplate terms. Any custom that exists, therefore, is unlikely to represent the full array of interests in the industry.

This is different than the problem identified by others, of failure within industry or trade to agree on trade rules. Here, we are interested in what happens *after* industry custom gets reduced to a standard-form provision and when it becomes a default rule.[6] The robust understanding of the standard-form provision that may have taken the market years to develop can then get forgotten. In the *pari passu* case, we find that disagreement over the meaning of that standard-form contract can arise subsequently because the meaning that everyone thinks they understand can then get lost in the sands of time. But the lack of any current industry customary meaning for boilerplate terms due to the passage of time still leaves courts with an important alternative source of interpretive authority. Because a common understanding existed historically, courts may look to the historical context of the term – that is, the point at which disagreements over custom were settled and a standard-form provision arose – to determine the original meaning of the drafters.

3. Guessing at Welfare Maximization. If neither the textual nor the contextual approach yields answers, then a third option is for the court to attempt a welfare-maximizing estimate for what the parties must have wanted from the clause. This is what Judge Winter attempted in the *Sharon Steel* case, in which he recognized that he was dealing with boilerplate terms and the related need to defer to market understandings with these types of terms.[7] Because there was no market understanding readily available to him, though, Winter simply estimated what the two sides might have been looking for in negotiating this clause.

As with textual analysis, the court that attempts to divine a welfare-maximizing solution is misunderstanding the nature of boilerplate. The value of the clause to the parties is in the historical context that it brings with it. The parties may not know what that historical learning is, but they use the clause because they want the benefit of history. In performing the value-maximizing guess, the court is throwing away the historical context and guessing at a solution, leading to a high possibility of error.

B. *Dealing with Court Errors*

Ill-advised attempts on the part of courts to interpret boilerplate terms with standard contract-interpretation techniques may result in a market response. The market can respond in two ways. First, it can reprice the contracts for the new meaning that courts have provided. Second, it can revise the language in existing contracts to communicate to the courts that the understanding that the parties have is different from the one that the courts articulated. In theory, these market responses can ameliorate the costs of court interpretation attempts. But there are reasons to expect that amelioration will be minimal in practice.

1. Pricing Response. In theory, if parties understand a standard provision to mean X, but a court reinterprets it to mean Y, the market price of all contracts will simply adjust to take into account the new meaning. Even if this pricing adjustment does take place, there remains the problem that the parties wanted their contract to mean X, not Y. So, with *pari passu* for example, neither the debtor nor the majority of creditors likely wanted a contract provision that would make it harder for the country to obtain emergency financing from the IMF. In other words, the new interpretation was value-reducing for both sides. Even with the possibility of a price response, uncertainty costs remain. The fact that some local court in Brussels asserts an interpretation does not make it universally accepted. This uncertainty can be priced but, once again, it is a cost that the parties would prefer to avoid. In sum, a pricing response by the market still leaves the parties with significant costs.

2. Language-Clarification Response. If courts misinterpret some customized clause between parties, parties can supposedly correct it because they know what they want their clause to say. If the market functioned well in responding to court interpretations of boilerplate terms, the social cost of remaining with the present contract interpretation doctrine would be low. But with boilerplate clauses, dispersed market participants may lack the ability to coordinate, at least initially, to clarify the language in subsequently adopted terms.

Market participants may also hesitate to correct terms out of a fear that a scattered, nonunified attempt at clarification may increase the likelihood of further unfavorable court rulings. Familiar contract terms, even if interpreted badly by courts, are "sticky." First, there is the benefit of clarity of meaning of terms already interpreted. Second, familiar terms make it possible to conclude a deal with greater speed – an issue that is particularly important in market transactions such as sovereign-bond issues. Slower speed might risk the loss of the entire deal. Furthermore, proposing new language might raise suspicions that the new term hides a "tricky" element. It may signal to the other side that one is perhaps acting opportunistically or is potentially difficult to deal with.[8]

There is also a coordination problem in modifying boilerplate language. An individual party negotiating a contract only internalizes the benefit from the specific contract. The party will ignore the benefit to other contracting parties in various contexts from improving on a boilerplate term. The same lack of coordination may result in a nonuniform response to a court ruling interpreting any given boilerplate term. Rather than put forward a nonuniform response (with unpredictable response on the part of future courts), parties may simply choose not to change a boilerplate term. When coordination does eventually take place, it may take place so long after the initial court interpretive shock to the term that even a coordinated shift in the contract term may fail to convince the court that the market originally had a different understanding. As in the *pari passu* example, sophisticated parties may therefore coordinate instead around litigation strategy, submitting amicus briefs and publishing commentary to affect the public discourse, among other tactics.

An alternative regime that focused first on the historical understandings of a term and accepted evidence from the range of market participants on this understanding would not create the same level of deterrence on market participants seeking to clarify terms in subsequent contracts.

III. A Statutory Theory of Boilerplate Interpretation

Our observation that boilerplate terms are not the product of any actual meeting of the minds but instead are placed into contracts because such terms are used in most form contracts and seem to work leads us to the contention that courts are approaching contract interpretation in exactly the backward fashion. These terms are not representations of the specific intent of the parties to the transaction. They are more like incantations, in which the parties, by invoking the boilerplate language, avail themselves of the historical reasons for the survival of these terms in generations of contracts.

Unlike the focus of much of contract law scholarship on discerning the precise understanding of a particular set of contracting parties, courts should embrace the possibility that a general understanding for boilerplate terms is desirable. Interpretation should be akin to statutory interpretation – courts focus first on unearthing the original intent of the drafters and the historical context in which the terms were initially drafted. Taking a statutory approach to boilerplate enables courts to turn to an alternative, more expert source of interpretive authority, leading to a greater likelihood that the welfare of contracting parties will be maximized. Under such an interpretive approach, industry standard-setting entities are more likely to organize and clarify existing boilerplate terms as well as draft new boilerplate terms for unaddressed contingencies. A statutory approach to contract interpretation also minimizes the influence of any one set of contract parties who happen to litigate over the meaning of a boilerplate term and places greater weight on the industry-wide understanding. Treating boilerplate terms as statutes for purposes of interpretation also will lead to fewer court errors and a greater ability on the part of the market to correct for any errors that do occur.[9]

We set forth a proposal of how courts may implement a contract-as-statute approach to contract interpretation for boilerplate terms in sophisticated contracting situations. We would (A) allow parties to designate a standard-setting entity as the "legislative body" for a particular set of boilerplate provisions in a contract. Where parties do not designate a legislative standard setter, we (B) set forth an alternative set of contract interpretation steps, starting with historical evidence on the meaning of a boilerplate term and moving forward in time toward the market's current understanding of the term. We then discuss (C) how a contract-as-statute approach to interpretation will affect the incentives of standard-setting entities to form in an industry. We conclude that boilerplate terms change the nature of contracts from a single document, representing a single meeting of the minds of the contracting parties, to a compilation of several different sources of authority from varied boilerplate provisions, enacted at different times.

A. *The Designated Legislative Body*

What does it mean to view boilerplate terms more like statutes? First, contracting parties should have the ability to designate a standard-setting entity to provide a definitive source of interpretive authority for the contract. Put differently, the presumption that the state (through its courts) stands at the top of the interpretive hierarchy needs to be altered. Even in the absence of an ideal legislative body capable of incorporating the interests of all relevant industry participants for any given decision, sophisticated contracting parties may find close alternatives. ISDA, for example, provides a close approximation in the swaps and derivatives markets. Courts may use the selection on the part of sophisticated parties of ISDA, or some other entity, as their designated legislative entity as evidence of the parties' revealed belief that selecting the designated legislative entity to interpret future contract ambiguities will result in fewer uncertainties and errors than relying on court-based interpretation.

Such a designation would require courts to adopt the interpretation of the designated standard setter, even if provided after the same court has interpreted the term differently in prior litigation, for terms that are part of contracts negotiated in the past. This "legislative" designation would allow the third party to revise constantly the meaning of boilerplate terms not only for contracts negotiated in the future but also all previously negotiated contracts. The boilerplate section of contracts no longer would reflect a particular snapshot of time but rather form a network of dynamic terms, changing flexibly with the needs of the market or in reaction to ill-advised court interpretations of boilerplate. When a court gets an interpretation of a term incorrect, the designated legislative source could correct the interpretation, affecting not only subsequent but all preexisting contracts, that we argue courts should take as conclusive.

Providing a mechanism for market-based bodies to change the meaning of standardized terms not only for subsequent contracts but also for the pool of preexisting contracts would give several benefits for contracting parties. First, the risk of mistaken court interpretations is lessened. If a court provides an interpretation of a boilerplate term that affects the entire market, private standard-setting bodies may change the term for all preexisting as well as subsequent contracts. Second, an expert industry association would have the ability to fine tune terms, correct prior mistakes in drafting, and respond to changing market conditions. Parties *ex ante* that realize the risk of misinterpretation is reduced may rely more on such boilerplate provisions and reduce any premiums for the reduced level of risk, lowering overall contracting transactions costs.

B. *Interpretation*

What if parties make no such legislative designation in their contracts (as is the case in all boilerplate terms in use today)? Our second insight is that courts, when faced with the interpretation of boilerplate, should attempt to construct how an industry-wide legislative body would have interpreted the boilerplate term, an approach distinct from constructing what the specific contracting parties would have done. Taking an industry-wide view ensures that courts do not place undue weight on the individual contracting parties before them. It also increases the likelihood that other courts taking a similar approach will come to similar results, leading to greater certainty in the marketplace on the meaning of the boilerplate terms.

How should a court construct what an industry-wide legislative body would have provided for in an ambiguous boilerplate provision? The starting point in an analysis of general market understanding should be the historical understandings of a boilerplate clause, discerning the intent of the original drafters of the term. This understanding includes direct evidence of the intent of the drafters, such as memoranda detailing the purpose. The historical record also includes how boilerplate terms fit into the overall structure of the contract envisioned by the original drafters.

Much like the enacting legislative body for a statute, the original drafting parties provide the best source of information on the original meaning of boilerplate contract terms. The original drafting parties will have spent the most time and resources in negotiating the contract term (and thus represent a true "meeting of the minds"). In a market populated with sophisticated parties on all sides, the drafting parties necessarily must balance the interests of all sides for a contract term to gain at least initial widespread acceptance in the industry. The fact that a boilerplate term gains initial acceptance in a market consisting solely of sophisticated parties provides some evidence as to the value of the term for all parties. The drafters will also enjoy an expertise advantage over any court attempting to interpret a term. Courts looking to the historical record will increase the chance that a court interpretation will better match the needs of the marketplace.

To the extent a historical record exists, a doctrine of deferring to this record also encourages consistency across different courts interpreting the same boilerplate provision. Varying parties in different litigation may have idiosyncratic views of what a particular boilerplate term means. Different courts, likewise, may come out with divergent opinions on what maximizes the welfare of any particular set of contracting parties. The historical record provides a common and fixed evidentiary source of the meaning of the term across different litigation. Referring to this source first will minimize the importance of idiosyncratic factors in separate litigation while stressing the common element of the boilerplate terms.

One difficulty with looking to the historical understanding behind a boilerplate term is the potential lack of connection behind the understanding and the particular context of the contracting parties that have chosen to adopt the boilerplate term (often without much thought on the terms). Why should it matter whether the drafters of a term from several decades in the past intended a *pari passu* term to prohibit nonequal payments to creditors? If the current contracting parties had no intention one way or the other about allowing nonequal payments, it is unclear why allowing the historical understanding to prevail will further the intent of the parties. Perversely, the original drafters may not necessarily have the best interests of all contracting parties as their goal, instead adopting terms that systematically favor groups with greater power and influence in the industry. Once a term becomes standard in the industry, such terms may perpetuate themselves despite their one-sided nature.[10] Nonetheless, advantages exist to relying on the historical understanding of boilerplate terms.

Under a regime that makes the historical understanding conclusive, there would be an incentive for the original drafters to create a record in the first place and to disseminate a greater amount of information on the initial intent of the drafters of such terms. Subsequent parties would be more informed about the terms they are adopting.

Moreover, the possibility that the historical understanding may be outdated must be compared with the other possibility, of court error in interpreting a boilerplate contract using standard interpretive techniques. When a court makes an error using standard contract-interpretation techniques, we explained earlier why the error is likely to chill a market response. Where, instead, courts take a historical approach to interpretation, the market is more likely response to a court error in interpretation. Clarifying the language of contract terms does not run the risk that this change will be used to interpret preexisting terms adversely to the parties' interests. The historical approach, as a result, allows market participants to develop new, clearer terms immediately after an interpretive shock.

We concede a cost to our approach. Markets often find it difficult and costly to put new boilerplate terms in place. Restricting courts to original intent – that is, not giving legal recognition to evolving meaning – forces on parties the cost of being stuck with original meaning until resources can be coordinated to produce a marketwide shift. If, however, the result of our proposal is the emergence of a standard setter that can engineer changes in boilerplate at a low cost, the problem is ameliorated. Plus, if the preservation of historical understandings makes it easier for coordination around innovations in language to take place, there is an additional ameliorative effect.

C. *Other Industry-Wide Sources of Authority*

What if the historical record is either absent or ambiguous in meaning? Courts attempting to construct what an industry-wide standard setter would do should next turn to industry views on the meaning of the terms, placing greater weight on groups that aggregate the interests of a greater portion of the industry (and have reputational interests at stake). Courts should look to amicus briefs and other sources from industry groups and others providing evidence on the historical record. Even where an industry-wide group does not exist, but instead a court is faced with disparate views across the industry, our approach will result in a better approximation of what maximizes the welfare of all industry participants compared with simply focusing on the specific contracting parties before a court.

If an industry-wide aggregating body exists, why not presume that the body speaks for all contracting parties in the industry and defer to the group's current understanding of the term without deference to historical understandings? Even where an industry aggregating body such as ISDA exists, turning to historical precedent first provides value. Historical precedence may better comport with what contracting parties at the time thought they were getting in incorporating a boilerplate provision. Stressing historical precedence also places a burden on an aggregating entity to go through the formal process of putting forward new terms to change the historical precedent, creating a "focal" point for those in the industry. Although a group such as ISDA may aggregate the interests of most members of an industry, going through the process of promulgating a new set of terms may heighten the awareness of the industry with respect to the process, ensuring greater participation of the range of industry participants in the redrafting process. More industry participants may take notice if an industry association goes through the process of drafting a new set of model terms than if the association puts out an opinion letter on the interpretation of preexisting terms. Giving deference to the historical context and the intent of the original drafters also gives industry groups an incentive to draft new terms to resolve ambiguities. With the drafting of a new term, the industry group becomes the "original" drafter and, under our proposal, obtains primary deference from courts. Industry groups also will have an incentive to create a detailed record at the time they draft a new term on the meaning of the term to ensure that courts taking a statutory approach to interpreting boilerplate terms have a rich "legislative" history from which to find guidance.

Conclusion

Interpreting contract as a statute invites courts to look at the intent of the original drafters of a particular boilerplate clause. The focus on sources outside of the particular contract and contracting parties provides a new way of looking at the contract as a whole. Rather than one cohesive document, negotiated at one singular point in time, a contract containing boilerplate language is a conglomeration of different pieces. Each piece may have a different history and timing. Courts may take advantage of this differential timing, resolving conflicts between different boilerplate provisions by giving priority to boilerplate terms drafted more recently in time. Our approach moves toward viewing contracts as interconnected parts of a larger overall commercial network that ties market participants to one another.

TWELVE

Modularity in Contracts: Boilerplate and Information Flow

Henry E. Smith

Editor's Note: *In this chapter, Henry E. Smith explores the modularity aspects of boilerplate – how a standard term can be used in many different contracts, plugged in or out without having to modify other aspects of the contract. Smith finds that the modularity property arises from what he calls the "extensiveness" of the information contained in the term, being less context dependent and less informative, thus applicable in more settings. Whereas property rights are the ultimate extensive provisions – having identical structure over all circumstances and incorporating very little ad-hoc information – tailored contracts are at the other extreme, applicable to a single setting and incorporating a great deal of ad-hoc contexts. Within these polar types, boilerplate is intermediate, sharing many of the extensiveness attributes of property rights.*

Contractual boilerplate is a little like property. Such a statement might seem like a category mistake. After all, contractual boilerplate language is part of contracts, which, unlike property, are freely customizable by the parties. Contracts create rights between those parties, not against the world at large. Nor do people who devise new boilerplate terms usually have intellectual property in the provisions themselves.

But in an interesting and overlooked way, boilerplate is the first way station on the road from contract to property. In particular, boilerplate, like all legal communication, is the result of striking a trade-off between communicating intensively in a narrow sphere or communicating in a more stripped-down, formal way in a wider variety of contexts.[1] Contract and property form something close to corner solutions here. Contracting parties are allowed to be as idiosyncratic as they like, but the idiosyncrasies apply simply to their own dealings – usually not to those of third parties. At the other end of the spectrum, property law deals in simple stable signals with a wide currency, but the rules of property eschew a lot of contextual detail. This makes property rights easy to adapt to many contexts and allows those whose expertise is minimal to avoid running afoul of these in rem rights. The simplicity of property rights also helps potential purchasers to inform themselves about the rights in the process of acquiring them.

Boilerplate language in contracts is somewhere in the middle of this spectrum, running from information-rich contract rights limited to a particular deal to simple standardized property rights availing against "the world." Once this aspect of boilerplate is understood, an information-cost theory of property can shed light on how boilerplate is – and is not – used in contracts. By definition, boilerplate is meant to be used in more than one contract, and boilerplate is more self-contained and less specific to a particular contract than might be expected from contract theory. Boilerplate is highly standardized, and when courts interpret boilerplate, they treat it as intentionally standardized and not harboring unusual meanings. In other words, some portability of boilerplate is achieved at the price of less ability to tailor such provisions to particular contexts.

In striking this trade-off between tailoring and portability, boilerplate takes advantage of modularity. Modularity is a device that deals with complexity by decomposing a complex system into pieces (modules), in which communications (or other interdependencies) are intense within the module but sparse and standardized across modules. For example, in a computer program, one can create a print module that can be called on by other parts of the program in standardized ways. When revisions are being made to the print module or to the rest of the program, the interdependencies (which I will also call "interactions") are much easier to foresee. If a better print module comes along, it can be substituted for the existing one, or the success of the print module at hand can lead to its adoption in a wide variety of other programs.

Modularity carries with it characteristic costs and benefits. Modularity is beneficial in that it makes complexity manageable by allowing multiple people to work on a larger problem, often in very specialized ways, without incurring the costs of intense communication. Modularity also creates options in the sense that it allows a system to manage uncertainty; because each module can function and develop in relative isolation, these processes can occur without the need to resolve uncertainty elsewhere in the system.

I introduce the notion of modularity and demonstrate that it plays a pervasive role in managing contractual complexity, particularly through its use in boilerplate provisions. Next, I outline a simple model of modularity in which such formal devices reflect a trade-off between the information-intensiveness and context-dependence of communication, on the one hand, and its adaptability to a wide variety of contexts, on the other. Contractual boilerplate falls between highly tailored contractual provisions and standardized property rights in that it presents externalities that stem from the lack of fit between the language used and some contexts that the drafter will not fully take into account. The information-cost theory helps explain the mild modularity of contracts and why the devices used to manage contractual complexity are reminiscent of those in property law but much less draconian. Boilerplate calls for a more formal and less holistic style of interpretation than do other provisions of contracts. The theory also reinforces and refines the view that contract reading costs contribute to their simplicity.

I. Modularity in Contract

Boilerplate plays a crucial role in bringing the advantages of modularity to contracts as a method of dealing with complexity. Modularity allows complexity to become manageable by interrupting information flow within the system. Forming a modular system involves *partially closing off* some parts of the system and allowing these encapsulated components to interconnect only in certain ways. This allows work to go on in parallel and facilitates certain kinds of innovation and evolution for a simple reason: Adjustment can happen within modules without causing major ripple effects. More sweeping change can call for remodularization, but much can be accomplished without altering the modular setup. Crucially, human understanding of any system is enhanced by breaking it up ("decomposing" it) into modules. Modularity benefits groups of many kinds working together. A burgeoning literature seeks to explain the modular structure of organizations, especially those in the computer industry, as a result of the modular structure of the products they produce.[2]

Similar issues arise surrounding the use of an asset that could be the subject of property rights. One of the problems in deploying the asset is to decide which combination of uses is best. We may not know *ex ante* how many of the uses are compatible with which ones and which those are. One way to handle this type of situation is to delegate the choice of many of these uses to owners who then interact with each other and the state in certain standardized ways, as we actually do in the law of property. To do this, we might divide the world into assets based on natural lines of decomposition and specify modularity between the resulting rights. An asset should embrace known complementary attributes, but we can avoid specifying them directly by hiding them behind a simple right to exclude.[3] This permits actors to proceed largely in ignorance of each other and allows the state not to have to know much about the internal activities and choices of the owners. Dutyholders likewise need not know much about the owner or the internal set of uses but only to stay off and not to commit various kinds of invasions.[4]

Asset-partitioning can be viewed as an example of information-hiding and modularization: Organizational law allows information about the owner's dealings with his creditors to be irrelevant to the enterprise's contractual partners and sometimes makes information about the business's dealings irrelevant to the owner's creditors.[5] Defining pools of assets and segregating them in this way provides for modularity and reduces the complexity and transaction costs involved. It allows for specialization in monitoring assets: Asset partitioning permits creditors to specialize in which persons and assets to monitor.[6] Property itself allows owners to specialize in developing information about their assets.

Although standardization achieves modularity in property rights, what is the role of modularity in contract? Surely, people are not allowed through contract to alter the basic modular setup of property law. But contracts also may be modular, largely because parties design them that way to save on costs among themselves and to manage complexity.

Boilerplate is a key feature of contracts that exploits modularity, and this modularity in turn allows for a greater degree of complexity and specialization than would be possible otherwise. As artifacts – including contracts and other legal relations – become more complex, more specialization is called for. First, at some point, the artifact cannot be made by one person, which requires division of labor. Second, highly complex artifacts cannot be comprehended in all their detail by a single mind, which calls for specialization of information.[7] Modularity promotes both types of specialization, especially the latter. A boilerplate provision can be developed by those versed in an area of law without their having to know in detail about where the boilerplate provision will wind up – and without users of the boilerplate provision having to think through all of the possible scenarios. Nondrafting parties, supported by drafting party incentives and certain interpretive doctrines, can specialize in their own business without having to approach contracts holistically. And, finally, judges can more easily afford to be legal generalists, which is to say they can specialize in legal analysis rather than business custom, when a great deal of contractual language they have to deal with is modular boilerplate.

There is little that is mandatory about all this. If a business organization is a nexus of contracts, then the contracts chosen will be highly modular because the benefits in reduced complexity costs are largely internalized to the contracting parties. If in some respects it is worthwhile to create intense contractual interaction among themselves, they can do so, but not in such a way that information flows increase to third parties, like other property owners, courts, and, to some extent, successors in interest.

But modularity in contracts is more widespread than such a property-centric view would suggest and extends to a realm of contracts relatively untouched by contract theory – the drafting of contracts themselves. One of the cardinal rules of drafting contracts is to be sparing with cross-references. Each cross-reference is a source of interaction between provisions of a contract,[8] and so each cross-reference contributes to complexity. In more extreme cases, the interaction can take the form of potential cycles, which contribute greatly to complexity; some problems involving finding cycles are intractable.[9]

One major source of modularity in contracts is the section on definitions. While recognizing that no definition can be totally context-independent, spelling out definitions increases modularity in at least two ways. One is that the more explicit and formal the definition is, the less the contract interacts with the contracting context – other contractual provisions, the parties' behavior, and the rest of the business environment. The definitions allow *closer approximation* to a plain-meaning or four-corners approach.[10]

Definitions also function as modules themselves. As in a computer program, other parts of the contract can "call on" them without the need to spell things out each time (which would entail a risk of error). Furthermore, if definitions are not segregated, contracts are open to an interpretive strategy where a use of the term in one part of the contract can more easily be used in interpreting the term in another part of the contract. This type of interpretation involves far more potential interaction – and, hence, more complexity – than in the case of a contract with a section on definitions. Also, in a modular structure, errors in interpreting one part of a contract – here, some part related to a definition of a term – will be less likely to cause ripple errors elsewhere in the contract.

II. Modular Boilerplate

It turns out that boilerplate, although often internally complex, serves a similar role to definitions in promoting modularity and managing complexity in contracts. The word "boilerplate" is used to refer to provisions that typically are found at the back end of a contract and deal with recurring matters such as assignment and delegation, successors and assigns, third-party beneficiaries, governing law and forum selection, waiver of jury trial, arbitration, remedies, indemnities, force majeure, transaction costs, confidentiality, announcements and notices, amendment and waiver, severability, merger, and captions.[11] A quick survey of the use of these provisions reveals a great degree of modularity.

Consider *governing law* or *choice of law* provisions. Most such provisions select the law of a single state or, even more commonly, a single state's law except for that state's conflict of laws rules. In a search of the Contracts and Organizations Research Institute (CORI) contracts library,[12] out of 220 governing law provisions, the largest group specified one jurisdiction (215 out of 220). Of these 215 clauses, there are three types. First, the seemingly simplest choice of law provisions (79 out of the 215 one-state clauses) select the laws of one state without qualification:

> Governing Law. This Agreement shall be construed in accordance with the laws of the State of Nevada.

Second, even more commonly (120), the provision selects one jurisdiction except for that jurisdiction's choice of law, which could otherwise point to the laws of another jurisdiction. This increases modularity and predictability. A typical example of the latter reads:

> Governing Law. This Agreement shall be governed by and construed in accordance with the laws of the State of Ohio, without regard to the choice-of-laws or conflicts-of-laws provisions thereof.

Third, and similarly, some contracts (thirteen) choose the laws applicable to contracts made and to be performed wholly within that state, sometimes along with an agreement that the contract is such a contract:

> Governing Law. The interpretation and construction of this Agreement, and all matters relating hereto, shall be governed by the laws of the State of New York applicable to agreements executed and to be performed solely within such State.

Finally, a few (three) combined the language about applying the laws of one state without regard to conflict of laws with a clause about applying the law of that state that governs contracts made and to be performed entirely within such state.

Very rarely (5 out of 220) did a contract select more than one jurisdiction or tailor the governing law provision by issue. For example, this could be a split by time:

> Governing Law. This Agreement [. . .] shall be governed, construed, and enforced in accordance with the laws of the State of Utah until the finalization of the Fairness Hearing and the entry of order referenced in Paragraph 2 [. . .]; Thereafter, the obligation of the parties shall be governed, construed, and enforced in accordance with the laws of the State of New Mexico and the parties agree that other than as set forth above, any litigation relating directly or indirectly to this agreement must be brought before and determined by a court of competent jurisdiction with the State of New Mexico.

A split of jurisdiction also can be designed by issue. For example, the rights of the primary parties could be subject to the law of one state, whereas rights of the guarantor, or a trustee, are subject to the law of another state.

The overwhelming selection of one state, especially barring choice of law, makes for extreme modularity. By selecting one state, these contracts are displacing off-the-rack law that might involve nonmodular and hard-to-foresee choice of law questions, including the potential of cycling. By blocking a state's conflict of laws rules, the choice of the law of a certain state will not vary with changes in the business or contract context. Here, increased length promotes simplicity through modularity.

Note that it is not writing costs that prevent more tailored governing law provisions. Tailored provisions are not prohibitive to write. Their real problem, I suggest, is nonmodularity, leading to "reading costs" as I interpret that term. The benefits from tailoring do not outweigh the greater complexity stemming from interactions.

Another example for modularity is severability clauses. A typical provision will say:

> SEVERABILITY. If any provision of this Agreement shall be judicially determined to be invalid, illegal or unenforceable, the validity, legality and enforceability of the remaining provisions shall not in any way be affected.

With this term in place, the validity of each provision in the contract can be considered in isolation of other provisions. Here, as in many systems, modularity insulates the system as a whole from the failure of one part. But, interestingly, we do not find provisions that make some proper subset of the contract's provisions severable. In a quick search of a sample of contracts from the CORI database, most (147 of 156) containing a severability clause had the across-the-board type like this one.[13] Again, the problem is not writing costs, especially when one considers that 36 out of the 147 had one of several related extra provisions mostly to the effect that if a provision was severed the parties would bargain in good faith to replace it with a similar but valid one.

Boilerplate contributes to modularity in contracts in specific ways. The functions of modularity can be captured by a variety of "modular operators,"[14] and one can find boilerplate serving these more specific functions as well.

1. Splitting or Decomposition. Modularity involves splitting a system into relatively autonomous components. Decomposability is a matter of degree. The more each module is isolated, the more decomposable the system. The trick is to find the natural fault lines in a problem.[15] In property, these fault lines are around groups of complementary attributes and sometimes track prelegal natural boundaries.[16] To some extent, modularity can be imposed on a system by preventing some communication that would have some positive benefit. Again, taking a property example, surely there would be some benefit in holding people responsible for knowing the particular features of an owner and holding owners responsible for anticipating the torts of others, but this benefit is probably quite small in comparison to the complexity it would add to the problems facing owners and dutyholders.[17] Likewise with the *numerus clausus*, which limits the forms of property to a fixed and finite list: One might be able to find some property arrangement that is made prohibitively costly by the *numerus clausus* principle, but some such frustration costs will be worthwhile to incur in the interests of greater modularization.[18] In the case of property interests, these frustration costs are kept lower than they otherwise would be because the very simple rules for combining basic interests feed each other – and themselves – allowing them, like Lego blocks, to accomplish a surprisingly wide variety of objectives at low cost. In boilerplate, certain parts of the contract are hived off into sections that deal with questions like choice of law or arbitration.

2. Substitution. Because modules only interact in specified ways consistent with an overall general function they are supposed to perform (again, think of a print-control module in a computer program), one module can be substituted for another as long as they perform the specified function. One of the great attractions of boilerplate is that one provision can be substituted for another related provision.

3. Augmentation. If an issue is suitable for modular treatment, a new module can be added to the system without much disruption to the rest. Thus, on some issues like choice of law, boilerplate can be added without having to worry about extensive revisions elsewhere in the contract. Notice that the addition of a module of boilerplate can be regarded as either substitution or augmentation depending on whether the frame of reference is the contract itself or the contract as embedded in the background of the common law or statute. Adding a choice of law provision to a contract that lacks one is augmentation if we are considering the contract as the system. But, if the contract plus off-the-rack law is taken as the system, the addition of the choice of law boilerplate is an example of substitution. Precisely because the law of contractual defaults is supposed to apply trans-substantively to a wide variety of contracts, it is likely to be at least as modular as the boilerplate that might displace it.

4. Exclusion. Likewise, a module can be subtracted without major perturbations. For example, the choice of law boilerplate module can be subtracted and the general off-the-rack choice of law principles will apply. Consider the previous examples of augmentation, which could work in reverse (for example, striking a choice of law boilerplate provision). This is modularity acting through the operator of exclusion.

5. Inversion. The process of inversion takes a previously hidden function, often repeated in many modules, and factors it out, moving it higher up in the hierarchy of the design so that it is visible and can be called on by the various other modules.[19] In software, a typical example would be moving the print function higher up and making it into a module that other modules can use in defined ways. In the realm of contracts, the definition sections can emerge from such a process. Closely related definitions (implicit or explicit) of a given term buried in substantive provisions can be factored out and placed with the definitions in their own module.

6. Porting. Modules can be borrowed from one system and plugged into another. As long as the connections between the module and the exterior world (the rest of the system, especially the contract and the business context) are few and standardized, this process of porting will not cause disruptions. Porting is one of the chief virtues of boilerplate and what allows it to become the subject of a valuable body of judicial interpretations. Form books only make sense with a high degree of portability. Indeed, the complaint of lawyers is that they employ a greater than optimal degree of portability.[20]

III. An Information-Theoretic Model of Contract Boilerplate

In this section, I develop a framework that captures how boilerplate is intermediate between contract and property. Once we apply the tools of information theory, we can show that context-dependence and its converse, formality, are matters of degree. Modularity, like other devices, pushes legal relations away from context-dependence and toward formality, but the real questions are what degree of modularity is optimal in various contexts and who has an incentive to bring modularity in a contract or other instrument toward this optimal point.

The repetition of noun phrases in contracts (for example, the party of the first part commits that the party of the first part will . . .) is an example – some would say an unfortunate example – of formalism.[21] But notice that use of pronouns instead of full noun phrases increases the reliance on context and causes interactions of the type that are inconsistent with stricter forms of modularity. Tracing out all the possible interpretations of a passage with many pronouns can be very complex: There are many phrases requiring the assignment of an interpretation and the interpretations can interact in ways that are sometimes hard to foresee.

Context-dependence and formalism have costs and benefits that are mirror images of each other. It is simply not the case that we always want maximum or minimum context-dependence (minimum or maximum formalism). Context-dependence allows messages to be short given the amount of information conveyed. Where those communicating share a lot of background knowledge, lack of formalism does not lead to misunderstanding because the parties can converge on an interpretation using their background knowledge. This sort of thing happens in everyday conversation in ways that are sophisticated but easy to ignore.

In everyday conversation, a great deal of information can be packed into few words because both parties can rely on what Grice called the Cooperative Principle: "Make your conversational contribution such as is required, at the stage at which it occurs, by the accepted purpose or direction of the talk exchange in which you are engaged."[22] Because of this general principle and the background knowledge shared by the parties to a conversation, much can be communicated via *conversational implicature*.[23] For example, people usually say something such as, "It's cold," in order to get someone standing near an open window to close it, rather than something such as, "I hereby request that you, being closer to the window than I, please close the window." The latter version would be more effective when dealing with someone who has never seen a window before. The second version is more formal because it can work in a wider variety of contexts, but it comes at the greater cost of more length and greater planning (not to mention greater syntactic complexity). The ability to lower the cost of the message itself by using conversational implicature and context but sacrificing portability across those contexts is an example of an informational trade-off: Everyday conversation is informationally dense (what I am calling "intensive") in that it compacts a lot of information per unit of communicative effort. When we want the message to reach a wider audience and more types of contexts, we have to engage in more (not complete) formalism by using messages that are costlier to create and to process.

When stakes are high, parties can invest in developing background knowledge and trust or they can invest in more formalism in the written agreements that govern their relationship. But where parties do not share much background and cannot develop it cost-effectively or have interests antagonistic to each other, it becomes worthwhile to invest in greater formality in order to avoid the high error costs. High stakes thus do not unambiguously point in either direction if we take a very *ex ante* perspective. However, if we take the level of background knowledge as given, then an increase in the stakes as between these parties suggests an increase in formalism. And high-stakes deals are associated with more formal agreements in this relativized sense.

The choice of a degree of formalism is subject to the informational trade-off. Intensive communication involves a lot of information per unit of communicative effort. But, increasing the intensiveness of communication will require either incurring more communication costs or reducing the extensiveness of the audience and the ability to draw on context in general. At a given cost, there is a trade-off between intensiveness and extensiveness of communication. Property is more formal (less context-dependent) and, being in rem, is meant to reach a larger audience. In general, property interests can be mixed and matched and used in a wide variety of contexts. They are very portable in a way that they would not be if they were tailored to individual situations.[24] Certain features of a fee simple of a lease hold true regardless of the nature of the asset and the holder of the interest. This makes property rights very easy to decipher. It also makes furnishing notice to purchasers and potential violators much cheaper.

Modularity is one method of reducing dependence on context. A modular provision in a contract or a modular property right can be added, subtracted, transported, and so on, into new contexts. And the removal or change of a module does not cause problems because the module interacts relatively little with the context. As long as the interface conditions are obeyed, one need not worry further about the context. For example, if a choice of law boilerplate provision is modified or replaced, one need not hunt through a contract to find all the hidden connections that might lead to difficult-to-foresee problems. Some attention needs to be paid to such potential problems because formalism (invariance to context) is not and cannot be complete, but a less modular provision would require a great deal more revising of a holistic sort and would greatly increase reading costs to the other party.

Holding the costs of producing and receiving a message about legal relations constant, one must trade off the intensiveness of the communication with the extensiveness of the set of contexts into which the communication can fit. On the intensive side, a message can have a high information rate and heavy reliance on (specialized) contexts. Think of a highly idiosyncratic contract term. Or, on the extensive side, one can make the message easier to fit into a wider range of contexts but will have to lower the information rate: Spelling things out will cause the rate of information per unit of communication cost to go down. All else equal, increased extensiveness requires decreased intensiveness.

Communication costs should be incurred as long as marginal communication cost is smaller than marginal communication benefit, but the model here emphasizes how costs should be allocated between trying to compact information (intensiveness) or reach a wide set of contexts (extensiveness). For the same cost, one can communicate at a high information rate in specialized contexts or at a low information rate in a large set of contexts.

On the benefits side, different combinations of intensiveness and extensiveness have different values, depending on one's goals. Consider first the contrast of contract and property. In contracts, particularly those involving sophisticated parties, there are large benefits to be gained from error-free communication with one or a few parties – the parties to the contract and perhaps a third-party beneficiary. To some extent, judges have to be communicated to as well. Where someone is claiming a property right, things are very different. Here, one is interested in having the message travel widely, but not much information is needed in order to secure the benefits of property: A message to keep off works to protect investments against all but a few interested parties. Moreover, there are advantages to being able to transfer and compare these rights with similar ones used by other people.

Now consider boilerplate. Like other contractual provisions, it is most useful to the contracting parties. But it deals with matters that could be walled off and dealt with in a modular way. As far as context-dependence within a contract, the benefits of high context-dependence are less than in other matters. Also, it is useful to be able to take a boilerplate term and reuse it, in which case context-dependence is not as beneficial as it might otherwise be. Boilerplate is intermediate between contract and property: It needs to reach an intermediately sized set of contexts (audiences, contracts, business settings). Among contractual provisions, boilerplate is more property-like than others in terms of the informational trade-off.

Conclusion

The modularity of boilerplate is but one aspect of a much larger phenomenon that is pervasive throughout law and the rest of human creation of artifacts. Ultimately, modularity reflects the limits of human cognition. Modularity is a much more promising place to look for the effects of those limits than in many of the behavioral deviations from rationality that have received the most attention in recent years.

One of the most striking implications of the theory and the hypotheses offered about boilerplate, contract, and property in this chapter is that they suggest benefits of formalism that have been overlooked by the realists and formalists (and their successors) alike. Boilerplate is best interpreted in a less holistic, context-dependent manner than are contracts more generally. This differential formalism suggests that images of the law popular with all these types of people are quite misleading. The image of the law as a "seamless web" is appealing and has some truth in it, but it misses an important part of the picture. What is deeply woven into the structure of the law is the modularity that human minds require in order to make legal artifacts useful. Exploiting the benefits of information-hiding and portability can be seen as consequences of bounded rationality. Modularity and other formal devices are more important in some areas, like contracts, than in others, like property, precisely because purposes differ from one area to the next. And boilerplate is interesting and revealing because it is perched somewhere between the poles of contract and property.

THIRTEEN

Contra Proferentem: The Allure of Ambiguous Boilerplate

Michelle E. Boardman

Editor's Note: *In this chapter, Michelle E. Boardman explores the proper interpretation of boilerplate language in insurance contracts. Insurers care a great deal about the certainty of meaning (which they can price). Courts trust that the contra proferentem doctrine will give insurers an incentive to change unclear language, but after a term has been interpreted contra proferentem, insurers may prefer to stick with this more certain pro-consumer meaning.*

Bad boilerplate can shake one's faith in evolution; not only does it not die away, it multiplies. The puzzle is why. Much of boilerplate is ambiguous or incomprehensible. This alienates consumers and is increasingly punished by courts construing the language against the drafter. There must, therefore, be some hidden allure to ambiguous boilerplate. The popular theory is trickery: Drafters lure consumers in with promising language that comes to nothing in court. But this trick would require consumers to do three things they do not do – read the language, understand it, and take comfort in it.

There *is* a hidden allure to ambiguous boilerplate, but the trick lies in the courts, not the consumer. The trick is a private conversation between drafters and courts; excused from the table is the consumer, who could have no fair duty to understand and so has no duty to read. With the consumer out of the room, edits and additions to boilerplate are targeted to courts alone. The new language does not need to make sense to a layman. It does not even need to make sense standing alone; a judge will read the language in the context of precedent, with the aid of briefing.

This chapter evaluates the continued abstruseness of boilerplate language despite incentives, judicial and otherwise, for clarity. Several rules and patterns of judicial interpretation aim for clarity but perversely result in continuity. The linguistic community dwindles to the court and the drafter alone, cutting out the nondrafter, reader, or consumer. This drives drafters deeper and deeper into the arms of existing case law as a primary means of selecting clauses. The danger is that while some consumers may not read the contract, none will read the case law in which any particular turn of phrase is embedded. Precedents speak to the drafter, not to the reader.

I. The Birth of Boilerplate

The infiltration of lawyers in commercial contract drafting, at least in the United States, has led to more than language recycled by a single entity; it has led to communal boilerplate – fixed language that is common to an industry or across industries. The more widely boilerplate spreads, the more it comes to resemble a public statute instead of a private agreement. This, in turn, leads to the common law of common boilerplate.

Corbin drew a distinction between the interpretation and the construction of contracts. An interpretation of contractual language seeks to find the parties' meaning. A construction of the language determines the legally binding meaning, which could bear a number of different relations to the interpretation.

Construing boilerplate rather than interpreting it is sensible. First, given that only one party – the drafter – may have read the language before signing, or even before litigation, a court is unlikely to find an actual joint meaning. Second, boilerplate clauses seem to make up a disproportionate percentage of those clauses courts are unwilling to enforce, even if, or perhaps because their meaning is clear. Third, similar or identical boilerplate language may have already been interpreted by the court at hand or by other courts, so the legal meaning of boilerplate may already be known.

Moreover, the accumulative process by which boilerplate comes to be boilerplate, discussed in detail later, often leads to language a layman will not understand. At this point, many courts will lose all interest in the project of interpretation, if defined as seeking the meaning the parties ascribe to the language. And who can blame them? The nondrafter either will have ascribed no meaning to the inchoate language or will have been misled or confused by it. Given that a court cannot simply refuse to address the case in the absence of meaningful interpretation, it is left with construction.

Once it is accepted that boilerplate is not necessarily the will of the parties, interpretation can be given up in exchange for other values. *Contra proferentem* attempts to value fairness and future clarity and, in the insurance context, the "reasonable expectations" of the policyholder. Farnsworth wrote of *contra proferentem* that although "it can scarcely be said to be designed to ascertain the meanings attached by the parties," at least the "rule may encourage care in the drafting of contracts."[1] This chapter suggests otherwise.

The value of uniform interpretation for the same clause across parties mimics the application of statutory law. Under the Restatement (Second) of Contracts §211(2), "standardized agreements" are "interpreted wherever reasonable as treating alike all those similarly situated, without regard to their knowledge or understanding of the standard terms of the writing." In other words, the language is treated not as a private agreement but as a public statute, with one meaning applied to all.

This approach to the unfortunate aspects of boilerplate can be self-perpetuating. Boilerplate that has repeatedly been construed by courts will take on a set, common meaning, but one that may not be easily understood by reading the language itself. As with judicial interpretation of broad statutes or constitutional provisions, the meaning ascribed to the language by an innocent first reader will differ markedly from the meaning the language is given in court, the meaning upon which drafters rely. With contract clauses, as with such statutes, an outside reader may have an illusion of understanding, but only knowledge of the subsequent case law and regulatory actions can reveal what the language means in the eyes of the law.

For the first nondrafter or consumer before the court, the application of *contra proferentem* is a boon, assuming that the drafter's interpretation was rejected by the court in part to protect the consumer. But, if the court's construction of the language is *acceptable to the drafter*, it will be used in the future, with a corresponding increase in premiums, to the disadvantage of consumers two through two million, who will not understand the language or who will be misled by it into not seeking relief a court would grant. In short, the language takes on a private meaning, not between the two parties to the contract, but rather between the courts and the sophisticated drafter.

II. The Feedback Loop in Policy Drafting

Positive network effects can flow from common or boilerplate clauses in any contract. Widespread, shared contract language is more likely to have taken on a lay meaning and to have been previously interpreted, perhaps definitively, by courts. If courts have fleshed out the application of language, a drafter can be confident about its future application. The value of contract language can therefore increase as the number of others adopting the language increases.

The insurance industry's practices of collective drafting and data pooling creates network effects and path dependence. Network effects in ordinary contracts can stem from language that has become familiar through use, whether or not the language continues to be popular. Just so in insurance, but the learning carries more weight in two ways. First, whether wisdom or paranoia, insurers assume that new language will be systematically construed against their interests. The value of "learning," therefore, is higher relative to the dim alternative for insurers. Second, insurers find greater value in the judicial meaning because, as with statutes but unlike many contracts, a court's interpretation of policy language holds for all those "governed" by the language.

Once the meaning of a clause has been clarified, enlarged, and applied by a court, its value increases, at least for the drafter. The drafter can communicate to courts, if not to policyholders, in one clause what it has taken a court paragraphs – or perhaps an entire opinion – to say. Of course, knowing precisely how courts will interpret a clause can regularly lead to rejecting it. On the other hand, the replacement for a dropped clause might not be a newly minted one but an alteration to the original. The alteration may be crafted in direct response to court opinions, again leaving the nondrafter out of the loop.

The force of path dependence cuts deeper ruts with insurance than ordinary contracts because of the feedback loop of actuarial data. Not only does past language become clearer over time in the insurer's eyes, but the cost of each clause also becomes increasingly clear as actuarial data is collected and pooled. Changing language, even in an effort to decrease coverage, could be more costly. Insurance drafting thus creates more than a set path: It creates a Möbius strip of language reinforcement.

As traditional path dependence teaches, the cost of shifting paths once the journey has begun may be prohibitive unless the value of the alternative path is higher than the collective switching cost. For example, consider the struggle of courts to decide whether destruction of electronic data is covered as property damage. Although large sums of money are at stake in the initial decisions, prospectively the answer doesn't much matter. Either computer files are property, in which case insurers can include the risk in the premium, or files aren't property, in which case insurers will exclude the risk from the premium. Similarly, although with more difficulty, if electronic data is "tangible property" according to case law, insurers can rewrite the definition of "property" or explicitly exclude electronic data from coverage, perhaps selling separate electronic coverage. Once the language has been given meaning by the courts, even if it continues to confuse policyholders, the insurer's path is set.

III. Perverse Incentives

Courts seemingly fail to see how their directives interact with the structure of the insurance-drafting process in particular and the choice of boilerplate in general. As a result, courts either fail to see the weakness of interpretive incentives, or they actively provide incentives to retain murky language. Three of these missteps are identified and explored here.

A. *An Interpreted Clause Is a Good Clause*

As the path-dependency discussion reveals, an interpreted clause is a valuable, predictable clause. With a settled contract term in the hand, even well-drafted new language is in the bush because "the change itself weakens the relevance of the existing stock of dispute-resolving conventions that the traditional language invoked."[2] Ordinary contract drafters thus become attached to clauses that both parties can agree upon and that consistently convey the intended meaning to the court.

Moreover, with insurance, every settled clause has value. Given network effects, path dependence taking the actuarial loop, and the customary preference of insurers for certainty over substance, what's a court to do? Unlike the next two contributions to calcified language, courts may be innocent parties in this debacle. The industry places great value, efficiently and not, on language that has been reliably interpreted by courts. The two obvious "fixes" are for courts to begin interpreting erratically or to refuse to interpret deficient language at all. Neither is tenable. Next best, understanding the self-reinforcing nature of insurance drafting might help relieve courts of the resentment that insurers willfully ignore their directives; in fact, insurers seem to be deaf to all others.

B. *Drafters Will Write Only to Those Who Read*

The reasonable-expectations doctrine belittles the role of the written contract, thereby encouraging drafters to ignore it. In some courts, the focus on reasonable expectations began as a *limitation* on the power of *contra proferentem*. If a term were ambiguous – open to more than one reasonable interpretation – courts would follow the pro-consumer interpretation, but only if the result were within the consumer's reasonable expectation of the clause. In a strong minority of jurisdictions, this has been inverted in the insurance context; the reasonable expectations of the policyholder, as formed by life, can trump what would be a reasonable expectation formed from the policy language.

One given purpose of the reasonable-expectations doctrine is to create "incentives for insurers to clarify language."[3] If only the language could be made clear enough, the contrary expectations of a policyholder would be deemed unreasonable. But in some jurisdictions the doctrine "applies to *all* insurance contracts" because "insurance policies are weighted with such a prolixity of complex verbiage that they would not be understood" and, if read, would present "an inexplicable riddle, a mere flood of darkness and confusion."[4] Here, the incentive fails to promote clarity because of the unrebuttable presumption that insurance language is unreadable; once the application of the doctrine is divorced entirely from the policy language, the insurer has no incentive to make it clear because no level of clarity would help.

For courts that take this position, the "duty to read" either does not arise or is a weak one. This is so for one or several reasons: The policyholder does not receive the actual language until after the policy has been issued; the insurer knows the policyholder does not read the policy when he receives it and therefore cannot rely on his having read it; or the policyholder could not, or does not, understand the language in those rare cases where it is read. In this last case, courts are unwilling to charge policyholders with a "duty to understand" the policy because it is not their fault that the policy is incomprehensible, and if there is no duty to understand the written words, it would be silly to enforce a duty to read.

In its more extreme form, the doctrine allows courts to refuse to enforce policy language that is out of keeping with the policyholder's "reasonable expectations" of what the policy would cover, even if reading the policy would be sufficient to disabuse the policyholder of his expectation. In this scenario, insurers will aim to make policy language clear to the judge who will interpret it, not to the policyholder who is excused from reading it.

C. *Ambiguity by Consensus and the Adverse Possession of Language*

The doctrine of *contra proferentem* has an appealing principal rationale. As the party in control of the drafting process, "it is incumbent upon the dominant party to make terms clear."[5] If the drafter fails in its charge, ambiguous language will be construed against the drafter, in keeping with the reader's reasonable expectations. This provides the drafter an incentive to improve the language and is only fair to the reader, who cannot affect standard-form language. In short, from power comes responsibility: "Convoluted or confusing terms are the problem of the insurer . . . the insured. . . ."[6]

Nicely turned out, but not true. Today, the ambiguity problem may be caused by the drafter, but it belongs to the consumer. The consumer is saddled with the same confusing language time and again, despite the drafter's court-appointed duty. Courts – seemingly unaware of the private nature of their conversation with drafters, insurers in particular – are at wit's end.

The Third Circuit was recently exasperated by a clause that "is widely used in insurance policies and has been the subject of heated litigation throughout the entire country *over the past thirty years*."[7] The relevant clause reads: "'Personal injury' means injury, other than 'bodily injury,' arising out of... [t]he wrongful eviction from, wrongful entry into, or invasion of the right of private occupancy of a room, dwelling or premises that a person occupies by or on behalf of its owner, landlord or lessor."[8] This ambiguous clause was not ambiguous as applied, in an eminent domain case, but that did not stop the court from applying *contra proferentem.*

1. Ambiguous by Consensus. To support its conclusion, the Third Circuit relied on the fact that other courts had found the language ambiguous. A minority of courts found "invasion of private right" ambiguous, a majority found that it unambiguously excludes regulatory decisions, and none found that it unambiguously includes regulatory decisions. The Third Circuit had held in an earlier case that:

> "[t]he mere fact that several... courts have ruled in favor of a construction denying coverage, and several others have reached directly contrary conclusions, viewing almost identical policy provisions, itself creates the *inescapable* conclusion that the provision in issue is susceptible to more than one interpretation," and is therefore ambiguous.[9]

The court's first mistake was to find the clause ambiguous (as applied) by referencing other jurisdictions, none of which had found ambiguity in the regulatory context. Moreover, the perverse incentive of abdicating the ambiguity decision to other courts is apparent. It allows the ordinarily slow process of jurisdiction-by-jurisdiction interpretation to snowball, increasing the predictive power of the language in less time. The follow-the-leader approach also leads to awkward results once a jurisdiction has already ruled that particular language is not ambiguous, only to find a later split among the jurisdictions. Most courts will not reverse course because "conflicting interpretations from other jurisdictions do not create ambiguity where [the] courts have adopted a definitive interpretation under [that state's] law."[10] The somewhat random result is that whether a term is considered ambiguous or not in a given jurisdiction may turn on the order of decisions.

2. The Adverse Possession of Language. The second winning position for the "takings" policyholder was that insurers were on notice that the language was unacceptable. After decades of litigation, while courts have still not settled on a common meaning, insurers know that a decent percentage will find the language ambiguous.

As to why, in the face of this history, insurers had chosen not to clarify the language, or to stop using it, the court admitted that it "cannot conceive of an answer."[11] What the court does not realize is that it has fired its last shot, and the insurer knows it. The threat of construing language against the insurer is mainly in the surprise; the insurer collected premium X but finds it owes coverage X + Y. The next year, the insurer collects premium X + Y, or some calculation thereof, discounting (perhaps) for those policyholders who won't seek Y coverage from X language. One would think that this calculation would become complicated where one-third of the states choose X, one-third choose X + Y, and one-third has yet to rule. Courts are not the only ones stymied that insurers retain the language despite this morass, but consider the insurer's options.

In two-thirds of the jurisdictions, the language has a settled valuable meaning: X in one-third, X + Y in one-third. In the remaining one-third, insurers can guess that more than half will take the jurisdictional split as proof of ambiguity and find X + Y coverage. A settled meaning can therefore be expected in five-sixths of the jurisdictions. In any event, the insurer knows the exact application of the clause (for the disputed facts) in the great majority of jurisdictions; why would it redraft the language now?

We might suspect that insurers would object to the untidy patchwork of interpretations. To get uniform results, the insurer has two options. First, it could introduce new language in every jurisdiction, but this opens it up to a whole new round of the game, without the current interpretation – security found in over two-thirds of cases. Second, it could introduce new language in the X + Y jurisdictions only, aiming to return to the category of X coverage. This choice only makes sense if uniform coverage from varied language is better than varied coverage from uniform language.

Of course, this analysis leaves out a central incentive for insurers – the cost of litigation. Under the current regime, the insurer can handle claims and settlements in at least two-thirds of cases (assuming equal distribution of cases across jurisdictions) without much need for litigation, at least not language-based litigation. The insurer knows how courts will interpret the language without going to court again, and the policyholder, even if confused about the language beforehand, can discover its meaning after the loss. If new language is introduced, however, even relatively clear language, it likely will be litigated in every jurisdiction until a settled meaning is found. This insurers do not want to do.

Finally, some argue that *contra proferentem* should apply equally to unsophisticated and sophisticated parties, in order to maintain a uniform interpretation of the same policy language. Equal application would mean that even if a policyholder could show good reason why it understood the language at hand to have a different meaning, and the specific insurer either shared that meaning at the time (contrary, let us assume, to the drafters and the current precedent) or had reason to know of the policyholder's understanding yet did nothing to fix it, the court should refrain from enforcing the parties' joint intent.

This may be one of the strangest aspects of the statutory nature of boilerplate clauses; as with legislation, but unlike most contracts, a court's interpretation of policy language holds for all those "governed" by the language. But, this additional meaning is semiprivate – the result of an ongoing conversation between insurers and courts – of which policyholders may be unaware. Of course, the meaning is public in that judicial opinions are public, but the public nature of U.S. Supreme Court opinions has not brought constitutional understanding to the streets.

Conclusion: Ending the Private Conversation

Two agents are candidates for evolution in this context, with two potential spheres of efficiency. First, we might expect that over time the courts will develop increasingly efficient rules for the interpretation and application of boilerplate contracts, including insurance contracts. But, this chapter reveals that courts are retaining various inefficient interpretive rules, the goals of which (language alteration) are counter to the incentive created (language perpetuation).

Second, we might hope that as the courts' interpretation of contracts evolves, so would the contracts themselves. If the rules effectively blocked the benefits of misleading language, drafters would draft more direct language. If the rules effectively punished drafters for sloppy language, they would allow less of it to pass once and none of it to pass twice. Poor language avoided is hard to show, and there are examples of helpful redrafts, but contracts do not seem to be swept along in the inexorable march toward clarity, brevity, and efficiency.

There is a difference between missing the basket and making a foul: The lack of efficient evolution in interpretive rules is a missed opportunity, but more, the intentional pursuit of efficiency by courts has resulted in actively perverse incentives in the drafting of policies.

The first outcome no doubt has many causes, but to the extent courts defer to one another's ambiguity rulings, competitive evolutionary pressures are relieved. The second outcome – perverse incentives to retain poor language – stems from the communal structure of boilerplate evolution and the collaborative structure of the insurance market.

Notice that if the incentive given to insurers is to retain language that has increased in certainty value by interpretation, courts seem to assume that all future policyholders will be helped nonetheless. Those who go to court will, and perhaps that is all some courts can see. The remaining policyholders are harmed. Those who do not sue because they do not read the hidden text into the unclear or misleading calcified language are not aided by the fact that, had they sued, coverage would be found. Moreover, these policyholders pay the increased premium for the judicially interpreted clause but only demand coverage for the clause as written. In short, the less sophisticated the policyholder, the greater the risk of harm – again, an outcome opposite courts' intentions.

This chapter uncovers numerous difficulties but points to one fairly obvious solution: Courts should be schooled in the nature of boilerplate creation, including insurance drafting, and be wary of creating perverse incentives to retain the very clauses they seek to change. As the trend in ordinary contract interpretation parallels more closely that already taken with insurance contracts, courts should be aware of the consequences.

Specifically, although the reasonable-expectations doctrine has an established place, its application should not be completely divorced from contract language, or drafters will likewise divorce themselves from improving the language. Moreover, compulsive application of *contra proferentem* to clauses that are not ambiguous but rather simply disputed also can belittle the role of language; to give drafters (and particularly, insurers) an incentive to fix language, language must carry weight with the court.

PART FOUR

COMMENTARY

FOURTEEN

Boilerplate Today: The Rise of Modularity and the Waning of Consent

Margaret Jane Radin

Editor's Note: *In this commentary on the symposium, Margaret Jane Radin discusses how modularity of boilerplate operates in the digital age to diminish the domain of consent and identifies other aspects of the "productization" of contract – the treatment of the text as part of the product. As contracts become less the products of private ordering and more property-like or statute-like, Radin appraises the remaining role of the will theory.*

My commentary relates some of the ideas presented in the symposium to two themes that I think are significant for the groundwork of contract today: The growing modularity of contracts and the waning of consent as the normative basis of legal enforcement. In conjunction with these two themes, I touch on the interplay of standardization and customization; the dialectic of rules and standards; the collapse of the distinction between the contract and the product it relates to; the problem of shoring up (or replacing?) the liberal notion of freedom of the will; and the allied issue of the political status of the regime of private ordering.

I

Henry E. Smith introduced the important topic of legal modularity, although my focus on it is different from his.[1] Modularity refers to the practice of building a whole by fastening together preexisting objects, analogous to construction with building blocks. Modularity became important to physical architecture in the first part of the twentieth century and to the virtual architecture of computer science in the later twentieth century. Now modularity has become important for law.

By legal modularity, I mean the practice of creating a legal document by selecting and cobbling together terms from a source compendium or from different sources. Some model statutes are modular to some extent because they set forth alternate provisions, building blocks from among which enacting jurisdictions may choose. In contractual practice, firms have for a long time maintained form files that facilitate recombination of terms. Organizations such as the American Institute of Architects (AIA) promulgate standardized contractual terms in the form of a compendium where the user may choose among various terms to deploy for a particular transaction.

Boilerplate has long been associated with the idea of standardization. The often-debated question is, "Are standardized adhesion contracts good or bad?" That question – let me call it the standard question – is complicated enough. But once modularity is taken into account, the complex issue of standardization versus customization surfaces. Boilerplate can be used not just for standardization but also, because terms can be used as building blocks, for customization. In fact, as I recount, a number of the articles in this symposium project a somewhat paradoxical quality by focusing more on the possibility of customization than on the standard topic of standardization.

Standardization versus customization is a complex issue. The "versus" can mislead us. The two characterizations are not really opposed to each other. Instead, both apply to the same contracts when viewed with different levels of generality. Standardization serves customization and vice versa. Uniformity at one level facilitates customization at another. Uniform terms serve as building blocks in a customized document. But those uniform terms themselves may be composed of building-block clauses arranged in a customized way. Likewise, the customized document that arranges the uniform terms in a particular way can be used in a uniform manner and can itself become a building block for a still larger particularized transaction. Uniformity at one level, the level of modularity, facilitates customization at the level further up, and the customization at that higher level can facilitate more uniformity at a still higher level. In some instances, recipients of standardized clauses can negotiate over them ("You gave me clause 2.3.1, and I want clause 2.3.3") and thereby achieve a form of customization. A standardized form can be customized in practice, informally and ad hoc, by drawing attention to the beneficial terms for some recipients, forgiving harsh terms for some recipients, or both.

Modularity is greatly facilitated by digitization. The current era has become an era of modularity. Boilerplate, and contract itself, is undergoing a sea change propelled by modularity, a sea change that has yet to be fully recognized and taken into account in legal thought. Recall that the origin of the term "boilerplate" involved a rigid, heavy metal object, the piece of metal produced by a linotype machine.[2] Once this object was produced, recombination of the terms it embodied would be practically impossible. This was the first era of boilerplate.

In the second era of boilerplate, modularity through recombination became possible. Firms maintained form files; by photocopying, then manually cutting and pasting, and then retyping, variant sets of terms were created. Today, in the third era of boilerplate, digitized repurposing – computer reproduction and recombination – is easier and cheaper by many orders of magnitude. Modularity now comes into play much more regularly and with much finer granularity.

What are the implications of the sea change in modularity made possible by digitization? Here, preliminarily, are three: (1) standardized clauses can be routinely cobbled together, even for small transactions; (2) contracts, and the clauses constituting them, can be routinely copied and redeployed by firms other than the one promulgating them; and (3) digital combination facilitates automated contracting.

First, because various clauses can be routinely cobbled together, even for small transactions – because we can standardize modules at a much finer level of granularity – it is now possible to customize transactions that once had to be standardized. When buying a product online, a consumer could check a box to pay an extra seventy-eight cents to extend the warranty from one year to two, or an extra twenty-seven cents to have dispute resolution by litigation rather than arbitration. The determination of what the consumer should pay for each clause and the total of the selected clauses could be outsourced in real time to an actuarial intermediary, and the customized terms could be presented to the consumer in printable form very quickly. So far, this market has not materialized, although in the future it may; there is certainly an analogous market offline for extended warranties and service on big-ticket items, such as cars, and not-so-big ticket items, such as stereo sets and washing machines. If online contracts become customized in this way, there arise possible questions for normative theory that are intertwined with empirical questions: To what extent will firms include the most onerous possible clauses, which will be varied in the consumer's favor only by consumers with more wealth and more knowledge? And to what extent might this practice exacerbate the divide between haves and have-nots?

Second, because digitized clauses can be routinely copied instantly and accurately anywhere in the world, it is possible for the learning effect that leads to widespread standardization to be accentuated. Once a clause has been tested in court, as Michelle E. Boardman argues, its legal effect is understood, and it becomes more valuable to other players in the market.[3] We may see the tendency toward widespread uniform use of successful clauses proceed much more pervasively and rapidly. In this case, modularity could lead, at the level we would be interested in for policy determination, to more standardization rather than more customization.

Third, modularity of digitized contracts facilitates automated contracting. Suppose Firm A routinely buys a certain manufacturing input from several suppliers. Firm A could program its computer with a number of different sets of terms it would find acceptable for purchasing this input. The supply firms would program their computers with sets of terms they each would find acceptable for processing sales. When Firm A's automated assembly line signals that more of the input is needed, Firm A's computer could search among different suppliers for one that offers at least one set of terms in common. With an automated "handshake," the two computers could make the deal, and the supplies would be sent on their way to Firm A. Of course, such a procedure would not be suitable for all transactions, but it would cut the cost of many of the more routine kind. And it would have the beneficial side effect of eliminating the battle of the forms for those transactions.

Modularity, whether in architecture, computer engineering, or law, raises an urgent question of interoperability. We contract theorists have not yet begun to address this kind of question, but we must do so. Standardization at one level permits customization at the next level, but customization does not function if the standardized modules are not interoperable. They just make the project break down: The building will be unusable, the computer program nonfunctional, the legal document inconsistent, confusing, and perhaps useless. The "Frankenstein" contract described by Choi and Gulati is an early example of what happens when interoperability is not a focus of attention.[4]

II

Perhaps a somewhat deeper reflection on modularity involves the dialectic of rules and standards. This dialectic entered the legal literature in the 1970s, initiated by critical legal theorists and later adopted into mainstream discourse.[5] Unfortunately, this terminology is confusing on a practical level and misleading on a philosophical level. It is practically confusing because when engineers and scientists speak of standards, they are referring to rigid parameters that must be implemented precisely; standards are the reason that lightbulbs and plugs fit into their sockets. But that kind of rigid specification is what is meant by "rules" in the rules-and-standards parlance. The rules-and-standards rhetoric is also philosophically misleading because rules and standards form a continuum based upon the degree of vagueness of a word or term, not a conceptual dichotomy.[6] Yet, because the rules-and-standards parlance has become entrenched (standard?) in legal discourse, it seems useful to refer to it in the context of this symposium, as long as its limitations are kept in mind.

It is a commonplace observation that both rules and standards have their efficiency pros and cons. Rules are rigid and uniform, so they may be knowable, predictable, and administrable, but they are under- and overinclusive with regard to their objective. Standards are discretionary and particularized, so they can be more accurate with regard to their objective, but they are less certain and administrable. Which type of directive will function more efficiently seems quite dependent on surrounding circumstances. A number of writers in this symposium seem to be arguing for standards (that is, discretionary implementation), as I discuss shortly. By contrast, Ronald J. Mann offers a nuanced argument that rules will function better than standards in the context of credit card regulation.[7] Other writers such as Ahdieh,[8] Ben-Shahar and White,[9] and Gilo and Porat[10] argue that strict implementation of rules can serve a strategic function that is profit-maximizing for the promulgating firm. One such strategy, sometimes called the positivist kiss-off, is well known in jurisprudence; it is sometimes useful to claim that one's hands are tied by a rule that has previously been laid down.[11] Those who have power in a situation might find their power increased by being able to deny holding it.

Now I come to what I consider a remarkable confluence. A number of the articles in this symposium explore the ramifications of treating boilerplate, considered as a rule-like object, as something that can be informally treated as a standard. Bebchuk and Posner argue that in some contexts, it is efficient for firms to promulgate rule-like boilerplate contracts that are covertly implemented as standards.[12] For example, the hotel that posts the rule-like checkout time of 12:00 noon can implement that directive instead as a standard that would (if expressed explicitly) disallow checking out "unreasonably late." This permits the hotel to be strict with some customers and lenient with others, depending upon what seems advantageous to its profit and reputation. In another example, Jason Scott Johnston argues that under some circumstances, it is efficient for a firm to have strict rules that can be secretly relaxed for those who complain.[13] It is unclear to me that firms would find it useful to incentivize complainers, but perhaps there could be circumstances where that would be true. Other times, it would be useful for firms to enforce rules strictly against quarrelsome or complaining customers and relax them for those who are cooperative or easy to deal with.

If we extend this type of argument, it might be the case that firms can maximize profit by promulgating onerous terms for poor people while routinely relaxing them for wealthier people who might buy more and become repeat customers. This circumstance would raise a normative–empirical question that is similar to the one I noted earlier with respect to the possibility of paying extra for customization of clauses: Will widespread informal implementation of apparent rules as standards exacerbate wealth disparities? Even if so, should we tolerate the practice in the name of efficiency? Selective implementation of rules as standards poses the further issue of leaving enforcement to the discretion of private firms under circumstances in which patterns of discrimination, on the basis of race or other proscribed characteristics, might not be easy to discern. If a firm routinely singles out white people to benefit by nonenforcement of its ostensibly strict rules, that practice might be difficult to remedy. Moreover, disturbing inequalities in practice may arise even if not specifically envisioned, if a firm finds it efficient to reward those who complain or request better treatment and it turns out that white men are more likely to pursue such requests.

Even sticking to efficiency arguments, there is another side to the coin in considering boilerplate as a rule-like object that can be covertly implemented as a standard. In their article, Gilo and Porat argue that one hidden role of boilerplate can be facilitation of rent-seeking by informal customization that is not socially beneficial.[14] Boilerplate may give the appearance of fair contract but may be implemented otherwise. "Beneficial boilerplate" may enable anticompetitive collusion.

In this context, I am reminded of Lon Fuller's concept of congruence, which he elaborated in his description of the Rule of Law.[15] Congruence means that the law on the books must correspond well enough with the law as it is implemented in practice; otherwise, we cannot know and follow the law, as we must be able to do if the Rule of Law is to flourish. When buyers receive confusing or contradictory terms, terms that are too complex to understand, terms that are written as rules but implemented selectively as standards, or terms that mean other than what they say, people cannot follow them and use them to order their affairs, and that is arguably problematic for their autonomy. There seems to be an ironic decision to be made between the amount of choice offered and the practical possibility of actually choosing. Mann, for example, shows that choices involving credit cards are too multifarious and complex – too customized – for people to understand.[16] Would a rigid nonchoice rule be better for autonomy because people would at least be able knowingly to say yes or no to it?

III

Many of the articles in this symposium assume the collapse of any distinction between the product, traditionally thought of as the object of exchange, on the one hand, and the contract, traditionally thought of as the agreement fixing the terms of the exchange, on the other. The collapse of the contract–product distinction is a trope that has become very prominent in contract theory, especially in economic analysis, and I refer to it in shorthand as the contract becoming part of the product, or contract-as-product.[17] It collapses two conceptual categories – an object and a text referring to an object – into one amalgam that obliterates the distinction between text and object.[18] If a cell phone contains a chip that will fail in one year and also comes with boilerplate exonerating the seller of liability for consequential damages, its market value is affected in exactly the same way by these two features; for economic purposes, they are both just features of the product. This idea was clearly stated by Lewis Kornhauser quite awhile ago,[19] by Arthur Leff even longer ago,[20] and by now has become the dominant position of economic analysts. In this symposium, it is resolutely put forward by Douglas G. Baird,[21] explicitly assumed by Bebchuk and Posner,[22] and implicitly assumed by others.

In this dominant economic view, contract terms no longer comprise a separate textual object or artifact that is the repository of independent free wills coming together in exchange. Instead, the terms become part of the product, which is a unified set of disparate features: a battery, a forum-selection clause, a microprocessor, and an anti-reverse-engineering clause. The contract-as-product view denies the traditional liberal normative underpinning of contract as instantiation of freedom of the will or, at least, renders it problematic. Liberal will theory has become vestigial, at least in these quarters, as I mention later.

The collapse of contract into product has conceptually been in the offing for a long time, but it has really come to fruition now that both terms and products are digitized. Now we are presented with a bunch of digitized information, some of which is terms and some of which is functional features. The collapse is now literal and not just conceptual.

The collapse of terms into the product reaches even further fruition, perhaps, with the advent of technological protection measures (TPMs). TPMs are technological self-help. For example, fancy copy protection that disables a program if the user tries to copy it can replace contractual terms that disallow copying. TPMs replace state enforcement with self-enforcement; they substitute an automatic "injunction," implemented by a private firm, for a remedy, implemented by the state, that must be argued for after an alleged breach.[23]

Now, if one accepts the conceptual collapse of contract into product, one could think that TPMs are merely an acknowledgment that all terms are part of the product. When all terms are part of the product, it may seem firms should be allowed to choose whether to implement them as digitized contractual terms or implement them as digitized TPMs. A TPM in this view seems like further "productization" of terms that were formerly contractual. But, there is a significant issue lurking here, because TPMs look like self-help, and uncurtailed self-help undermines social ordering because everyone can engage in self-help in response. When, in the liberal story, we exit the state of nature to implement a polity, we are supposed to renounce self-help, at least to a great extent, to escape the war of all against all. This backdrop of liberal theory may well be the primary reason why self-help has by and large been cautiously treated by legislatures and courts. Unlike machine-implemented self-help, boilerplate that – at least theoretically – can come before a court before it is enforced is – at least theoretically – drafted in the shadow of the law.

But what are the legal limits of self-help? This is a question that will now have to be investigated. Can the ideal of public ordering be salvaged by legislating regulatory limits on TPMs? If contract terms are now fully integrated with products, should their limits be developed by thinking about the law regulating defective products rather than the law regulating unconscionable or otherwise defective contracts? The collapse of the distinction between contract and product, and particularly the advent of TPMs, seems to undermine even further the problematic distinction, central to traditional liberal thought, between public and private ordering.

IV

The traditional picture of contract is the time-honored meeting of the minds. The traditional picture imagines two autonomous wills coming together to express their autonomy by binding themselves reciprocally to a bargain of exchange. The rhetoric of meeting of the minds has not disappeared. But the liberal theory of voluntary exchange transactions between autonomous individuals is now vestigial. The idea of voluntary willingness first decayed into consent, then into assent, then into the mere possibility or opportunity for assent, then to merely fictional assent, then to mere efficient rearrangement of entitlements without any consent or assent.

Because of the historical importance of autonomy and consent, it is evident that many of us are not yet ready to give up the rhetoric. Consent seems obviously fictional in a great many transactions, however, and that is one reason I say that consent is vestigial. Consent is fictional when the terms are filed somewhere we cannot access, as in airline tariffs. Consent is fictional when almost all of us click onscreen boxes affirming that we have read and understood things we have not read and would not understand if we did. Consent is fictional on Web sites whose terms of service state that just by browsing the site, whether or not one ever clicks on the terms, one has agreed to whatever the terms say, now or as they may be changed in the future. Consent is fictional when the contract ends, as one I saw recently did, with "By reading the above you have agreed to it."

Not everyone is willing to give up on consent. Robert A. Hillman wants to rescue it. He proposes some legal and practical strategies for making it possible for recipients to read and understand the significance of boilerplate terms before they become bound by them.[24] For example, the idea of placing terms on a Web site for anyone who wishes to view them in advance seems easy to implement. Firms may have incentives to do this. Firms might write contracts that look reasonable and be happy to post them, hoping to enhance their reputation and also hoping the contract will proliferate and become a widespread standard, thereby enhancing its effectiveness.

It is less clear, as Hillman ruefully realizes, that making terms more easily available will result in more people reading them. Hillman wants to shore up vestigial will theory when possible, although his caveats and worries show that it is an angst-ridden endeavor. In a similar vein, Michelle E. Boardman worries about notice and the ability of insurance policy recipients to understand what their policy covers; she, too, clings to will theory.[25] Others in this symposium seem willing to bite the bullet and abandon will theory in favor of pervasive liability rules: If the market price is correct for the product-cum-terms, it doesn't matter whether any given individual understands the features that we used to call contract terms.

If we accept the collapse of the terms into the product, is there any remaining role for liberal will theory? It is attractive to try to retain liberal will theory somehow, and I am thus sympathetic to Hillman's project, because it is still our leading candidate for what justifies rearranging entitlements among private parties.

If we want to rely on efficiency to justify rearranging entitlements without consent yet avoid abandoning a commitment to autonomy, we could try saying that there is autonomous bargaining over the total product – consisting of the concatenation of terms and functional features – or at least consent to the attributes of the total product. We can imagine that the user is bargaining over or, at least, consenting to the battery plus forum-selection clause plus microprocessor plus anti-reverse-engineering clause, and so on. But this picture does not seem normatively promising. What determines the willingness to pay for the total product and, hence, the price of the product is not the consent of each individual, as in will theory. Instead, it is some other kind of thing, having to do with how a market functions in the aggregate. We do not "knowingly" accept a total product in the sense of "knowing" how the battery will function or how the forum-selection clause will function. The buyer does not knowingly accept the whole product in the way that liberal-will theory postulates in order to justify the transfer of entitlement by the buyer's free will. Even if we think that something about an aggregation of individuals and their knowledge does determine willingness to buy the product at what turns out to be the market price – that is, a demand curve – that something does not map onto traditional will theory. Traditional will theory is individualistic in a way that economic analysis is not. The aggregate analysis does not support a notion that in the process by which the market price of a product is determined, individuals are each expressing their free will by means of voluntary interaction or even by means of a relatively robust and not merely rhetorical understanding of consent.

V

The liberal public–private distinction has been central to the notion of public enforcement of private ordering. Hence, it is central to the traditional notion of contract. Private ordering has been thought of as the expression of free will privately but in the context of a juridical infrastructure. The juridical infrastructure is necessary to set out the limits of contract – delineate what is off the bargaining table, such as baby-selling, contracts in restraint of trade, murder for hire – and also to police transactions for coercion and fraud. These limits, I would say, are necessary to the idea of private ordering.

The legal realists deconstructed the public–private distinction by showing that contract, which is supposed to be private, cannot exist without its public infrastructure, its infrastructure of legality. The public–private distinction may have been deconstructed enough that it is no longer a workable conceptual distinction. But I still think a pragmatic version of it has remained necessary in order to understand and justify the legal institution of contract and the notion of private ordering in the context of the democratic state and the Rule of Law. Certain functions belong primarily to the state, and certain functions belong primarily to individuals to accomplish without immediacy of state involvement, even though the state supports the background infrastructure. There are borderline cases in which we can't tell whether to call an interaction public or private, but the borderline cases must not overwhelm the system. If the notion of private ordering is to remain viable, then the pragmatic version of the public–private distinction must remain viable.

Here, I think certain conceptual moves made by some participants in this symposium tend to undermine the pragmatic public–private distinction and, hence, to weaken the normative justification of private ordering within the Rule of Law. Contract is moving toward property; contract is moving toward legislation by trade groups; contract is moving toward productization featuring machine-implemented self-enforcement. All of these conceptual changes signify moves that previously belonged to the sovereign infrastructure but are now going over to the firm. For example, in IP law, contract is moving toward property because mass-market end-user licenses are superseding whatever user rights are granted by the federal IP regimes; and those background regimes become in practice irrelevant to the extent that the user's property rights are determined by the mass-market contract and not by the legislated background law.[26] The law of the legislature is being superseded by the law of the firm. Legislative rules are tied up with democracy in a way that rules promulgated by firms are not, even though democracy in practice, as the positive political theorists show us, is nonideal. I think we do not yet have a satisfactory way of theorizing this metamorphosis. The only thing I want to say here is that this tendency to migrate sovereign functions to firms puts pressure on the last vestiges of liberal-will theory. Boilerplate in the contemporary context is clearly raising the question; we have not yet talked about the kinds of principles we ought to use to think further about it.

FIFTEEN

The Law and Sociology of Boilerplate

Todd D. Rakoff

Editor's Note: *In this commentary on the symposium, Todd D. Rakoff concludes that a major theme confirmed by many of the articles is that boilerplate ought to be understood in the particular context in which it operates, rather than in general abstract terms. To generate proper legal results, dynamic models of the various contexts have to be developed; although, we do not think of that as an ordinary judicial task, courts should, in fact, be trusted to conduct such context-specific inquiries.*

In my view, the scholarship presented at this symposium demonstrates that in order to analyze form contracts and boilerplate successfully, one must carry out a set of operations that embodies an approach I call law and sociology. But I presume I was invited to be a commentator at this conference on boilerplate not because the article I wrote on one branch of the subject a while back exemplified this methodological approach but rather because it took a rather strong substantive position.[1] And so I think I ought first to say a brief word about that.

The article in question concerned contracts of adhesion in, roughly speaking, the consumer context,[2] and the position I took was that what I called the "invisible" terms of those contracts – the large number of terms not disciplined by the actual bargaining or shopping behavior of consumers even in price-competitive markets – ought to be treated by the law as presumptively unenforceable. The burden should be put on drafting firms to show their form terms were worth judicial enforcement rather than on adherents to the forms to show the terms were unconscionable; and, if this burden were not met, the courts should apply the general, legally implied default terms instead of the drafters' terms. This was not then and is not now the law, but I would not be candid if I did not say that I still think that, in regard to the domain I was addressing, I was right.

In particular, I am not persuaded by the article presented at this symposium that seems to me most directly to challenge my thesis (although by no means aimed at me personally): Lucian Bebchuk and Richard Posner's *One-Sided Contracts in Competitive Consumer Markets.*[3] As I understand it, Bebchuk and Posner assert that what appear to be "one-sided" consumer contracts in fact function to allow firms, concerned about their reputations, to satisfy those consumers who have worthy complaints while resisting other customers who present complaints that are overblown or unjustified. In such circumstances, Bebchuk and Posner say, the "courts would do well to take a hard line in enforcing the terms of one-sided consumer contracts in the absence of evidence of fraud."[4] For if this is done, then in the shadow of the law where most cases will be decided, the one-sided terms of the form contracts will be counterbalanced by the other-sided nature of the market in reputation, in which sellers worry about their good name much more than consumers do theirs. Apparently, this approach is to apply without regard to how harsh the content of the form terms is because the primary function of the form terms is to give firms the room they want in which to maneuver.

Without belaboring the issue, Bebchuk and Posner seem to me to do nothing to show that this combination of judicial enforcement and the reputational concerns of firms will produce systematically desirable results. There is no reason to think it will in any way lead firms to recognize voluntarily the supposed legitimate claims of decent consumers at a volume or a value that is congruent with or even regularly near to any known measure of a proper number – resembling, that is, either any known legal measure of harm or any known economic measure of an incentive for efficient behavior. They offer no model of how the market in reputation works, or of why the values it generates are responsive to anything other than firms' fears of how much reputational damage particular claimants are, for a myriad of possible reasons, in a position to cause. Nor do they consider whether the existing transaction costs of the legal system might allow firms to differentiate between merited and unmerited claims even if consumers are able to claim reasonable legal rights. Finally, on a somewhat different dimension, Bebchuk and Posner do not consider the impact on the individual liberty of consumers of a practice of giving firms (with the help of the proposed standard for legal enforcement) a blank check so blank that, when after-contracting disputes do arise, consumers are forced to be nothing more than supplicants.

I now turn to address the broader range of issues raised by the rest of this collection of articles. Although it is too much to hope to find a unified conclusion that all the articles would support, I do think there is a single thread that appears in the fabric of many of them that is worth teasing out. It is, as I have already suggested, a methodological thread, and the essence of it can be stated simply: To understand boilerplate and to determine the law's proper response to it, one must approach it by building a structural model of how it is produced and used that goes beyond the model assumed both in ordinary contract law and in much of the economic analysis of law as well. Or, more simply, what the articles reveal is the need for a sophisticated and differentiated law and sociology of boilerplate.

Indeed, the traditional justifications for enforcing contracts already rest on implicit institutional dynamics. Viewed as a dyadic interaction, contracts are assumed to be the product of bargaining and mutual assent. Enforcing their terms presumptively enhances welfare because parties generally know what is good for them. When they trade quid pro quo, each party choosing what he is to get over what he is to give, each party comes out better off, and the same set of resources produces greater satisfaction overall. And, enforcing the terms of contracts also presumptively enlarges freedom because each party chose to enter the arrangement. Taking someone's voluntary commitments seriously both dignifies his freedom and enhances his opportunities for expressing that freedom.

Viewed now as part of a working social system, contracts are assumed to be the products of competition in the marketplace. Speaking systemically, enforcing the terms of contracts presumptively enhances welfare because competition establishes conditions under which the individual deals people make lead, as if guided by an invisible hand, to an efficient use of society's resources to satisfy wants. Enforcing contractual terms under these conditions also presumptively enhances freedom because competition among the participants on one side of the market (for instance, among employers or producers) creates, as much as possible, choice and an absence of duress for those on the other side (for instance, workers or consumers).

Many rules of the general law of contracts reflect these assumptions in doctrinal form. The modern theory of consideration, which makes a promise presumptively worthy of enforcement merely because it was bargained for a return promise or performance, is one. The refusal to treat general social circumstances as constituting duress, so long as a competitive market is in place, is another. If we assume that these doctrines are intended to further freedom and welfare, they do so only because of the postulated underlying dynamics.

Any such model, of course, never matches all the features of the circumstances to which it is applied; to require that would be to demand an infinity of models to match the innumerable quirks of life. Fit is always to some extent a matter of judgment. But the question of the fit of this standard contractual sociology in regard to boilerplate has been an explicit topic of concern for contracts scholars – especially with regard to consumer contracts but also, for example, with regard to franchise arrangements – at least since Friedrich Kessler's famous article on contracts of adhesion.[5]

Unless we say that the value of simplicity is so great that we will apply the traditional model even when it fits very poorly, we have two main choices. Either we can take the elements of the standard model – individual actors, bargains, and markets – and try to have a more subtle understanding of them; or we can introduce additional structural features. To some degree, of course, the two paths merge; the dividing line between additional subtlety and additional features is a blurry one. But it seems to me that the older articles that discussed boilerplate in terms of markets dominated by monopolies or oligopolies,[6] and the recent articles that expanded the "rational actor" with ideas of "bounded rationality," "satisficing" instead of maximizing, and the numerous heuristic mistakes ordinary people make,[7] fall within the "standard model, more subtlety" group. So do some of the articles at this symposium. But many of the articles herein collected do something different. Looking at the facts regarding how, in particular contexts, boilerplate is produced and used, their authors have found that the gap between the assumed general model underlying contract law and the phenomena to be addressed is so great as to be unbridgeable simply by positing deviations from perfect contractors or perfect markets. Instead, they have had to take note of and build models based on additional institutional and cultural structures. In doing so, although I do not say that they will adopt the term, they seem to me to have crossed into terrain best labeled "law and sociology."

Let us look at the range of issues that these essays suggest ought to be addressed. As I count them, there are four sorts of considerations that go into the making of the more complex types of model. First, if we are to cover the range of situations in which boilerplate appears, we need a particularized identification of the parties involved. The characters that stalk the Restatements of Contracts are the well-known acontextual "A" and "B"; prior thinking about boilerplate has extended this to "firm" and "consumer" and sometimes "insurance company." But, on the evidence of these papers, prior thinking has not gone nearly far enough. The model that Omri Ben-Shahar and James J. White present in *Boilerplate and Economic Power in Auto-Manufacturing Contracts*,[8] for example, is not just a model of "sophisticated businesses" making deals with "sophisticated businesses"; it is specifically a model of "Original Equipment Manufacturers" doing business with their "tier-1" suppliers. At least some of their explanations for what they find in the parties' contract forms turn on the particularity of this relationship.[9]

Moreover, the portraits of parties drawn in these more complex designations often have reference not to how the parties are situated vis-à-vis a contractual or market relation but rather to other features of their social or institutional positions. Much of the mystery that Stephen J. Choi and G. Mitu Gulati investigate relates specifically to sovereign issuers of debt using language that has in view nonsovereign issuers.[10] The alternatives that Kevin E. Davis discusses relate specifically to nonprofit drafters of form contracts.[11] Or, to use other words, implicit in the analysis of many of the articles is the claim that, in order to determine the law rightly, we need to consider the particular institutional location of the parties involved.

Second, to understand many of the dynamics of the use of boilerplate, it seems we need to consider the broad network of relationships that these institutionally located entities have. The law of contracts usually focuses, and focuses rather narrowly, on the direct relationship of the entities that are making a deal (who are typically, in the litigation context, the juridically defined parties). When we build models of what is actually going on regarding boilerplate, however, we find that what those who make deals do is greatly influenced by what others are doing – others with whom they are not making deals but with whom they are linked in systematic relationships.

Of course, a dynamic of this sort was to some degree implicit in the traditional view that parties were greatly affected by the market. This approach remains important for considering the uses of boilerplate too. We find, for example, that boilerplate used to define the obligations undertaken in some instruments is standardized because standardization facilitates creation of a market for these contractual instruments, which are meant to be publicly traded.[12] But many of the essays in this collection consider other, rather particular, institutional contexts that structurally link drafters or users of boilerplate. Thus, we find that the boilerplate used by any one insurance company will tend to be the same as that used by another in good part because that standardization enables actuarial data to be collected and shared across a much larger set of language-defined "events."[13] Meanwhile, in yet other industries, such as construction or real estate – in which contractual instruments are neither put on the market nor subject to an actuarial risk analysis – contractual terms are often standardized for the yet different reason that they are drafted by one or a few trade associations.[14] Yet, elsewhere, perhaps because none of these dynamics is in play, the terms used by any one firm may be standardized for its customers but quite different from the terms insisted on by its competitors.[15]

Third, the implication of several of these essays is that the category "boilerplate" has itself taken on a cultural meaning, and that that fact is of practical significance. A set of contractual words represented to be and accepted as boilerplate – accompanied by the meaning (articulated or implied) that "this is boilerplate" or "these are standard terms" or "we always use terms like these" or "everyone uses terms like these" – is different in important ways from the same set of words absent those assertions.

Indeed, there are at least three sorts of differences. First, lawyers in a position unilaterally to draft contracts treat boilerplate differently. Indeed, we have the suggestion that even when premier law firms draft instruments running to billions of dollars, it may be true that "no one will have an incentive to figure out the true meaning of such terms. Instead, attorneys will uncritically include the terms in all their contracts."[16] Second, as some of the essays point out, the fact that language is boilerplate can be used strategically in negotiating deals and contracts. The assertion "this is boilerplate" can be used to signal that certain terms are not negotiable[17] or to create favorable focal points in negotiations that are inherently cooperative and distributive at the same time.[18] Third, partly as a result of the preceding dynamics, boilerplate may not relate to the resulting document in the same way that the same words, if not boilerplate, would. If the purpose of a paragraph was to be the "x" boilerplate term, perhaps subtle differences in expression between it and other contracts' ways of saying "x" are not significant.[19] Or if, as Henry E. Smith suggests, various structural forces will lead a contract made of boilerplate to be more modular than a bespoke one is, more an agglomeration of different clauses not strongly connected to each other, then perhaps we should simply expect more disjointedness in the document viewed as a whole.[20]

Fourth, as is perhaps already clear, boilerplate, seen in light of the institutional and cultural points already made, sometimes intersects with legal rules differently from the way ordinary contract language does. If Henry E. Smith's point, just mentioned, is right, then we should perhaps depart from the usual rule of contract construction that expects the same word in different parts of a document to mean the same thing. To follow our usual practice may misinterpret the actual meaning of the language in light of the dynamics involved in its creation.

Perhaps of greater importance, several of the chapters make a special point of the need to pay close attention to the incentives created by ordinary legal rules when applied to the particular institutional context at hand. They want us to consider the real possibility that the dynamics created by a rule may in context produce a result that is quite different from, possibly opposite to, what was intended. For example, Robert A. Hillman worries that a rule requiring ongoing Web site disclosure of a firm's standard terms for its e-sales might not only fail to achieve its intended goal of generating market forces adequate to discipline the terms but also might give firms an argument that will insulate their terms from being disciplined by the doctrine of unconscionability.[21]

Of course, the possibility that the rules of contract law might be counterproductive is not new; there have long been claims that, for instance, the Statute of Frauds enables more frauds than it prevents.[22] But the point the present articles seem to bring home is that it is not possible to trace the actual incentive effects of various rules of the game without a considerable amount of institutional specificity. Thus, for example, Michelle E. Boardman points out that when courts interpret ambiguous language in insurance policies distinctly against the drafting companies, intending to teach them a lesson and to spark clearer redrafting, the courts in fact add value, as the insurance companies themselves see value, to the very language that they have now made clear. Construing it against the drafting party, but construing it clearly, thus makes redrafting less, not more, likely.[23]

To summarize, if we are to build an adequate descriptive model of how boilerplate is produced and used and of the effect of legal rules on the process, we need to consider the types of parties involved in the transaction, described with some degree of institutional specificity; the structured ways in which they interact with other parties, including parties not involved in the deals at issue; the cultural meaning of boilerplate in the particular context; and the various incentives (intended or unintended) any proposed rules will create in light of the actual use being made of boilerplate. Seen in this light, the traditional model of transactions incorporated in contract law represents just one of the possible models of the relevant social dynamics; indeed, as applied to boilerplate, it might even be thought of as the corner solution that abstracts most completely from the phenomena to be observed. As I have already said, the articles presented here do not come together to suggest a single alternative. Instead, the overall conclusion to be drawn from the work of this symposium is that we need to construct many – or at least several – structural models if we are rightly to understand and respond to the phenomena at issue.

Turning now to the prescriptive part of the matter, contract law, as already discussed, traditionally has been justified by connecting its rules, through its relatively simple view of personal dealings and market interactions, with individual freedom and the general welfare. These two broad ideals remain relevant to the world of boilerplate. Although many of the symposium articles take a general welfare norm as their criterion of good law, or at least good contract law, enough is said or noticed to remind us that the legal system has other goals as well – and especially, in regard to boilerplate, that we might care about its effects on freedom in one or another of its guises. As Douglas G. Baird suggests, this point is of great relevance to perhaps the most heated current debate regarding form contracts – the use of boilerplate to remove large swathes of contracts from the courts to the arbitrators.[24]

To complete our job, then, we need to consider how the law can connect boilerplate as it works in several different dynamic situations with the overall goals of furthering freedom and welfare. As some of the chapters suggest, a first approach to this problem in any particular instance is to look at the existing rules and the existing institutional arrangements to see if the on-the-ground situation as it presently exists does enough to police the private use of boilerplate.[25] If so, fine; if not, we need to consider the alternatives.

Some of the essays in this collection describe the alternatives in terms of the substantive rules that should apply to specific situations – for example, Douglas G. Baird's interesting reanalysis of the illegitimacy of the contract clause at stake in *Williams v. Walker-Thomas Furniture Co.*[26] But, by and large, the alternatives are what might be thought of as legal-process alternatives: recommendations regarding the different law-making or law-applying institutions that might best be given the job of drafting, interpreting, applying, or rejecting boilerplate. In addition to the obvious possibilities of legislation and judicial decision, the authors suggest in one setting or another turning matters over to expert administrative agencies,[27] nonprofit trade associations,[28] law firms that are leaders in a field,[29] and even (although somewhat uncertainly) publicity-minded watchdog groups.[30] (This profusion also, I think, reflects the sensibility of law and sociology.)

How should we decide whether judges should decide a matter themselves or instead defer to a trade association by choosing to give it the power to offer authoritative interpretations of common language? And how should we decide whether legislators should take an issue away from judges through legislation – and then either decide the matter themselves or in their turn delegate it to an administrative agency?

In one sense, this is not at all a new problem in the law of contracts. "Who should authoritatively decide?" was necessarily an issue in, for example, the replacement in large part of the common law of sales by the Uniform Sales Act and then the Uniform Commercial Code; in the supercession in large part of the common law of securities transactions by acts of Congress and rules of the S.E.C.; and in other like actions. If it be thought that the driving force behind these movements was that different and specialized dynamics were present in the sale of goods, in transactions for securities, and so forth, then perhaps we are simply facing a new instance of an old trend.

If so, probably the most traditional analysis of the conclusions we have reached about boilerplate in terms of appropriate legal process would be that, as it seems that we need different models to fit various phenomena throughout the economy, primary emphasis should be put on action by legislatures and administrative agencies. It is not that judges cannot build models – they do it, sometimes very self-consciously, when deciding which rules to apply to specific types of transactions, and they sometimes consider specifically the role of boilerplate within those models.[31] But looked at comparatively, specialized administrative agencies – and to some extent the staffs of legislative committees – can become expert about matters in their particular domains in a way that general-jurisdiction judges cannot. The processes used in agencies and legislatures allow for the development of a scope of information and variety of methodology beyond what litigants typically develop in a traditional lawsuit.

On this view, the judges would continue to apply to boilerplate the general common law model of contract, with its standard tests for enforceability and its standard modes of interpretation, and would continue to police only the outer margins of commercial practices through the doctrines of unconscionability or undue surprise. It would be left to legislatures to address particular sectors of the economy in which the "general rules" of contract fit so poorly that there was real distress, and they might do so either by enacting different rules on their own or by authorizing administrative agencies to do so. The agencies could, in turn, decide when deference to the views of private trade groups and the like was appropriate.

Perhaps that is the right analysis, but there are also real costs to viewing judicial action so narrowly. Legislation directly, and administrative action derivatively, depend on political action; and, rightly or wrongly, in the United States, we have a set of political institutions intentionally structured to make it difficult to develop the necessary political will. If we think application of the single legal framework of tradition to the manifold varieties of boilerplate is often greatly overbroad, there are many "wrong" outcomes lurking within that institutional conservatism. Moreover, the percentage of contractual disputes that implicate boilerplate is so large, and the present law, based on its simple model, fits them so poorly, that even if the judges do only somewhat better than they are now doing, the improvement in the law can be great. Even modestly sophisticated models ought to generate better results in many cases.

In short, I fear that the traditional analysis of what is "best" may cause us to lose sight of what is only "better." It is a mistake to assume that because the judges cannot do everything, therefore they can do, or ought to do, nothing. In much of the writing on boilerplate – not necessarily in this collection – one senses just below the surface (and sometimes right on the surface) a looming fear that if the judges are unleashed, they will simply muck up a situation in which the private parties are producing, if not a great solution, at least a tolerable one. This attitude seems to me to hold the judges to a higher standard than it holds those responsible for the boilerplate. The question is whether the judges can improve on the product produced by those who write and use the boilerplate. If the dynamics of the on-the-ground situation do not do much to police the private use of boilerplate, then it seems to me wrong to fear the judges' efforts.

Perhaps this phobia is fueled by a mistaken belief that, if the judges err, there will be no further correction. But this is, of course, not true. Judges in other jurisdictions may disagree; later judges in the same jurisdiction may overrule. More generally, although what the judges say in interpreting, displacing, or revising boilerplate may constitute mandatory rules (or mandatory allocations of powers to interpret) in regard to the private parties, judicial decisions, except in constitutional cases, represent only default rules in regard to the legal system as a whole. They are always subject to revision by legislation or by properly authorized administrative action. Of course, there will be some stickiness in getting these other institutions to act, and that may mean that only if the judges produce a really bad result will they be corrected. But, as has already been said, the same stickiness means, if the judges are not supposed to act, that only if the drafters of boilerplate produce a really bad result will they be corrected. It is a question of who in the system is allowed to take the initiative. If we think on balance that judges will improve outcomes by trying to build models like those suggested by the authors in this symposium rather than by simply applying doctrines based on the truncated model of ordinary contract law, then we should not only let them but indeed ask them to try.

Moreover, if we are to sort out the welter of possible models regarding boilerplate – if we are to develop an informed view of how many and what sort of models are needed – participation by the judges offers us some important intellectual advantages. Because they have a general jurisdiction and because they have to explain and not merely declare the rules they apply, judges in their ordinary work have to take a broad view of the whole terrain and consider what the crucial features are that differentiate situations. By contrast, law that depends on legislation or administrative regulation tends to become (if I may borrow a term I have used elsewhere) "sectorized."[32] A different set of rules governs each sector of the economy and, for their legitimacy, these rules trace back to specific enactments rather than to general principles. Because each rule ultimately derives from a legislative enactment representing a particular political moment, there is no reason why the rules in different sectors should represent similar analyses or methodologies or cohere in any way with each other. The structure of the legal materials defeats rather than encourages development of a general understanding of the phenomena.

It seems to me, therefore, that there is still a considerable role, practical and intellectual, for judicial action. The alternative, it seems, is for the courts to go on treating boilerplate and standard forms as if they were ordinary clauses in ordinary contracts. In many cases, in light of all that has been said at this symposium, that will produce the wrong result; and even in the cases in which it produces the right result, that right result will be rationalized on traditional grounds and, therefore, intellectually speaking, accidental. The legal system as a whole certainly can do better and, in my view, the judges can too.

The recognition that boilerplate has an institutional context – that how it is written and used, why it is written and used, and by whom it is written and used make a difference – is both true and important. That it makes life more complicated for those who study, teach, and write about contract law only proves its worth. That it also makes life more complicated for the existing institutions of the law cannot be denied, but it does not make sense to respond by pretending that what is true is not so. Rather, we have to think about the best way to pursue enough complexity to capture what is true while at the same time generating law that is clear enough for practical social purposes.

NOTES

PREFACE

1. Compare the California Supreme Court's holding in Armendariz v. Foundation Health Psychcare Services, Inc., 99 Cal. Rptr. 2d 785 (2000) with the Seventh Circuit's view in Oblix v. Winiecki, 374 F.3d 488 (7th Cir. 2004).
2. Robert A. Hillman, *Online Boilerplate: Would Mandatory Web site Disclosure of E-Standard Terms Backfire?* (in this volume).
3. Michelle E. Boardman, *Contra Proferentem*: The Allure of Ambiguous Boilerplate (in this volume).
4. Omri Ben-Shahar, *Forward – Freedom from Contract, in Symposium on Freedom from Contract*, 2004 Wisc. L. Rev. 261.
5. Lucian A. Bebchuk & Richard A. Posner, *One-Sided Contracts in Competitive Consumer Markets* (in this volume).
6. Jason Scott Johnston, Cooperative Negotiations in the Shadow of Boilerplate (in this volume).
7. Ronald J. Mann, *"Contracting" for Credit* (in this volume).
8. Florencia Marotta-Wurgler, *"Unfair" Dispute Resolution Clauses: Much Ado About Nothing?* (in this volume).
9. Omri Ben-Shahar & James J. White, *Boilerplate and Economic Power in Auto-Manufacturing Contracts* (in this volume).
10. Douglas G. Baird, *The Boilerplate Puzzle* (in this volume).
11. David Gilo & Ariel Porat, *The Unconventional Uses of Transaction Costs* (in this volume).
12. Omri Ben-Shahar & James J. White, *Boilerplate and Economic Power in Auto-Manufacturing Contracts* (in this volume).
13. Kevin E. Davis, *The Role of Nonprofits in the Production of Boilerplate* (in this volume).
14. Stephen J. Choi & G. Mitu Gulati, *Contract as Statute* (in this volume).
15. Gilo & Porat, *supra* note 11, show various ways in which boilerplate reduces competition and thus reduces total welfare; Ben-Shahar & White, *supra* note 12, suggest that standard-form purchase orders in the automotive business exhibit various inefficient terms.
16. Choi & Gulati, *supra* note 14.
17. Henry E. Smith, *Modularity in Contracts: Boilerplate and Information Flow* (in this volume).
18. Gilo & Porat, *supra* note 11.

19. Margaret Jane Radin, *Online Standardization and the Integration of Text and Machine*, 70 Fordham L. Rev. 1125 (2002); Margaret Jane Radin, *Humans, Computers, and Binding Commitment*, 75 Ind. L. J. 1125 (2000); Margaret Jane Radin, *Regime Change in Intellectual Property Law: Superseding the Law of the State with the "Law" of the Firm*, 1 U. Ottawa L. & Tech. J. 173 (2003–2004).
20. Todd D. Rakoff, *Contracts of Adhesion: An Essay in Reconstruction*, 96 Harv. L. Rev. 1174 (1983).
21. Margaret Jane Radin, *Boilerplate Today: The Rise of Modularity and the Waning of Consent* (in this volume); Todd D. Rakoff, *The Law and Sociology of Boilerplate* (in this volume).

ONE. ONE-SIDED CONTRACTS IN COMPETITIVE CONSUMER MARKETS

1. See, e.g., Stewart Macaulay, *Non-Contractual Relations in Business: A Preliminary Study*, 28 Am. Soc. Rev. 55 (1963); Charles J. Goetz & Robert E. Scott, *Principles of Relational Contracts*, 67 Va. L. Rev. 1089 (1981); Lisa Bernstein, *Merchant Law in Merchant Court: Rethinking the Code's Search for Immanent Business Norms*, 144 U. Pa. L. Rev. 1765 (1996). The paper closest to our analysis in its emphasis on problems of observability by courts is Benjamin Klein's analysis of franchise agreement. See Benjamin Klein, *Transaction Cost Determinants of "Unfair" Contractual Arrangements*, 70 Am. Econ. Rev. 356 (1980).

   In his contribution to this symposium, Jason Johnston seeks, like us, to analyze the distinction between the language and the actual implementation of contracts in the context of contracts between businesses and consumers. See Jason Scott Johnston, *The Return of Bargain: An Economic Theory of How Standard-Form Contracts Enable Cooperative Negotiation between Businesses and Consumers*, 104 Mich. L. Rev. 857 (2006). The only prior paper of which we know to have explored this issue is Clay Gillette's study of rolling contracts that consumers enter into online. See Clayton P. Gillette, *Rolling Contracts as an Agency Problem*, 2004 Wis. L. Rev. 679 (2004).
2. See, e.g., Richard A. Posner, Economic Analysis of Law 115 (6th ed. 2003).
3. See Florencia Marotta-Wurgler, *Competition and the Quality of Standard Form Contracts: An Empirical Analysis of Software License Agreements* (NYU Law and Econ. Research Paper No. 0511, 2005), available at http://ssrn.com/abstracts=799274 (citing relevant sources).
4. See, e.g., Michael I. Meyerson, *The Efficient Consumer Form Contract: Law and Economics Meets the Real World*, 24 Ga. L. Rev. 583, 594–603 (1990).
5. See, e.g., Oren Bar-Gill, *Seduction by Plastic*, 98 Nw. U. L. Rev. 1373 (2004); see also Paul Bennett Marrow, *The Unconscionability of a Liquidated Damages Clause: A Practical Application of Behavioral Decision Theory*, 22 Pace L. Rev. 27 (2001).
6. See, e.g., Phillipe Aghion & Benjamin Hermalin, *Legal Restrictions on Private Contracts Can Enhance Efficiency*, 6 J. L. Econ. & Org. 381 (1990); Eric A. Posner, *Contract Law in the Welfare State: A Defense of the Unconscionability Doctrine, Usury Laws, and Related Limitations on the Freedom to Contract*, 24 J. Legal Stud. 283 (1995).
7. See, e.g., Meyerson, *supra* note 4, at 608–22.
8. See, e.g., Williams v. Walker-Thomas Furniture Co., 350 F.2d 445 (D.C. Cir. 1965); Galligan v. Arovitch, 219 A.2d 463 (Pa. 1966); Sosa v. Paulos, 924 P.2d 357 (Utah 1996); State ex rel. Dunlap v. Berger, 567 S.E.2d 265 (W. Va. 2002); Pittsfield Weaving Co. v. Grove Textiles, Inc., 430 A.2d 638 (N.H. 1981) (per curiam).
9. E. Allen Farnsworth, Farnsworth on Contracts §4.28, at 560–61 (2d ed. 1998); see, e.g., Monsanto Co. v. McFarling, 302 F.3d 1291 (Fed. Cir. 2002); Seekings v. Jimmy GMC of Tuscon, Inc., 638 P.2d 210 (Ariz. 1981).

10. See *Agreement between Harvard University Press and Lucian Bebchuk and Jesse Fried* (Mar. 23, 2004) (on file with authors).
11. Richard A. Posner, The *Law and Economics of Contract Interpretation*, 83 Tex. L. Rev. 1581, 1585–86 (2005).
12. Margaret N. Kniffin, Corbin on Contracts §§24.7, 24.9 (Joseph M. Perillo ed., rev. ed. 1998).
13. There is a sense in which our explanation is information-based, too; but the information deficit in our analysis is not a deficit of either party to the contract but rather of the court that may be called on to enforce the contract.

TWO. COOPERATIVE NEGOTIATIONS IN THE SHADOW OF BOILERPLATE

1. See, e.g., Galligan v. Arovitch, 219 A.2d 463 (Pa. 1966).
2. Alan Schwartz & Louis L. Wilde, *Imperfect Information in Markets for Contract Terms: The Examples of Warranties and Security Interests*, 69 Va. L. Rev. 1387 (1983).
3. George L. Priest, *A Theory of the Consumer Product Warranty*, 90 Yale L. J. 1297, 1298 (1981).
4. Carnival Cruise Lines, Inc. v. Shute, 499 U.S. 585, 593–94 (1991) (citations omitted) (relying on and citing the reasoning in Nw. Nat'l Ins. Co. v. Donovan, 916 F.2d 372, 378 (7th Cir. 1990)). For an argument that the market assent reasoning in Shute and similar cases is consistent with classical contract notions of assent, see Randy E. Barnett, *Consenting to Form Contracts*, 71 Fordham L. Rev. 627 (2002).
5. See, e.g., Robert A. Hillman & Jeffrey J. Rachlinski, *Standard-Form Contracting in the Electronic Age*, 77 N. Y. U. L. Rev. 429 (2002); Russell Korobkin, *Bounded Rationality, Standard-Form Contracts, and Unconscionability*, 70 U. Chi. L. Rev. 1203 (2003).
6. Julie Appleby, *Hospital Bills Spin Out of Control*, USA Today, Apr. 13, 2004, at A1.
7. *Reducing Hospital Bills, Dollar Stretcher*, http://www.stretcher.com/stories/980923c.cfm (last visited Nov. 20, 2005).
8. Harris Interactive, *"Haggling" with Health Care Providers About Their Prices Likely to Increase Sharply as Out-of-Pocket Costs Rise*, www.harrisinteractive.com/news/allnewsbydate.asp?NewsID=443 (Mar. 6, 2002).
9. Ronald Mann, *Contracting for Credit* (in this volume).
10. See, e.g., Beth Kobliner, Get a Financial Life: Personal Finance in Your Twenties and Thirties 62 (2000) (encouraging negotiation with credit-card issuers for lower rates); Suze Orman, The Money Book for the Young, Fabulous & Broke 88–89 (2005) (encourages using the threat of transfer to get a lower credit-card rate); Steven Strauss & Azriela Jaffe, The Complete Idiot's Guide to Beating Debt 81–90 (2000) (an entire chapter on negotiating with creditors); Eric Tyson, Personal Finance for Dummies 76 (4th ed. 2003) (encouraging negotiation with creditors).
11. Letter from Paul A. Smith, Senior Counsel, Am. Bankers Ass'n., to David D. Gibbons, Deputy Comptroller for Credit Risk, Office of the Comptroller of Currency, et al. 2 (Sept. 23, 2002), available at http://www.aba.com/NR/rdonlyres/DC65CE12-B1C7-11D4-AB4A-00508B95258D/26583/CreditCardLendingGuidancefinalcmt9230993.pdf; see also Letter on Behalf of the Financial Services Roundtable (Sept. 23, 2002) (on file with author).
12. See Evan Schuman, *The War Against Retail Return Abuses*, eWeek, Dec. 17, 2004, http://www.eweek.com/article2/0,1759,1743671,00.asp.
13. This important general result is due to Joseph Stiglitz & Andrew Weiss, *Credit Rationing in Markets with Imperfect Information*, 71 Am. Econ. Rev.393 (1981).

14. Calling the situation on this particular issue a "split" may be going too far because even the strongest judicial statement in favor of holding that a merger clause bars evidence of fraud, UAW-GM Human Res. Ctr. v. KSL Recreation Corp., 579 N.W. 2d 411 (Mich. Ct. App. 1998), has already been subject to the limiting interpretation that it is inapplicable to frauds that allegedly nullify assent to an entire contract, as opposed to assent to a particular term. See Star Ins. Co. v. United Commercial Ins. Agency, 392 F. Supp. 2d 927, 928–29 (E.D. Mich. 2005).
15. Compare Van Der Stok v. Van Voorhees, 866 A.2d 972, 975–76 (N.H. 2005), and Snyder v. Lovercheck, 992 P.2d 1079, 1084–85 (Wyo. 1999), with Danann Realty Corp. v. Harris, 157 N.E.2d 597, 599 (N.Y. 1959).
16. See Towers Charter & Marine Corp. v. Cadillac Ins. Co., 894 F.2d 516, 522 (2d Cir. 1990) (citing Rose v. Spa Realty Assocs., 366 N.E.2d 1279, 1283 (N.Y. 1977)).
17. Conclusions reached in a survey of empirical findings of arbitration versus civil litigation are presented in Lewis L. Maltby, *Employment Arbitration and Workplace Justice*, 38 U. S. F. L. Rev. 105, 108–17 (2003).

THREE. BOILERPLATE AND ECONOMIC POWER IN AUTO-MANUFACTURING CONTRACTS

1. Benjamin Klein, Robert G. Crawford & Armen A. Alchian, *Vertical Integration, Appropriable Rents, and the Competitive Contracting Process*, 21 J. L. & Econ. 297 (1978).
2. Oliver Hart, Firms, Contracts, and Financial Structure 7 (1995); Oliver Williamson, The Economic Institutions of Capitalism 114–15 (1985).
3. Courts that have adjudicated such termination provisions in lower-tier cases and one recent OEM–tier-1 case have held the contracts to be unenforceable. See, e.g., Dedoes Indus. v. Target Steel, No. 254413, 2005 WL 1224700 (Mich. Ct. App. May 24, 2005); Gen. Motors Corp. v. Steel Dynamics, No. CR-04-056983-CK (Cir. Ct. Oakland County, Mich. Aug. 4, 2004).
4. Jane Spencer, *The Best Car Deal Around: Never Paying for Repairs – New Longer Warranties Open Door to Car Hypochondriacs*, Wall St. J., Nov. 12, 2002, at D1.
5. Craig Fitzgerald, *Getting Serious About Quality*, Auto. Indus., July 2004, at 45. A different source suggests that American OEMs spend on warranty claims between $537 and $628 per vehicle, whereas Japanese vehicles average only $226 per vehicle sold in the United States. See *Auto Warranties*, Warranty Week, January 27, 2004, http://www.warrantyweek.com/archive/ww20040127.html.
6. Fitzgerald, *ibid.*
7. There are many theoretical accounts of this "stickiness" of boilerplate. See, e.g., Omri Ben-Shahar & John Pottow, *On the Stickiness of Contractual Default Rules*, 33 Florida St. L. Rev. 651 (2006); Stephen J. Choi & G. Mitu Gulati, *Contract as Statute* (in this volume); Marcel Kahan & Michael Klausner, *Standardization and Innovation in Corporate Contracting*, 83 Va. L. Rev. 713 (1997) at 761–64.
8. See Klein et al., *supra* note 1. The Klein account of the Fisher Body–GM merger and its illustrative role for the theory of the firm has been widely embraced. See, e.g., Dennis W. Carlton and Jeffrey M. Perloff, Modern Industrial Organization 13 (2d ed. 1994).
9. In recent studies, Ronald Coase and others have argued that GM's takeover of Fisher Body did not intend to solve contractual hold-up by Fisher Body – in fact, no such hold-up ever occurred – but, rather, to secure GM's stronghold over a critical supplier vis-à-vis other OEMs. See R. H. Coase, *The Acquisition of Fisher Body by General Motors*,

43 J. L. & ECON. 15 (2000); Douglas G. Baird, *In Coase's Footsteps*, 70 U. CHI. L. REV. 23 (2003); Ramon Casadesus-Masanell & Daniel F. Spulber, *The Fable of Fisher Body*, 43 J. L. & ECON. 67 (2000); Robert Freeland, *Creating Holdup Through Vertical Integration: Fisher Body Revisited*, 43 J. L. & ECON. 33 (2000).

10. OLIVER HART, FIRMS, CONTRACTS, AND FINANCIAL STRUCTURE 7 (1995).
11. Johnson Controls v. A.P.T. Critical Sys., 323 F. Supp. 2d 525 (S.D.N.Y. 2004).
12. See Coase, *supra* note 9.
13. See Baird, *supra* note 9, at 26 (noting that the GM–Fisher hold-up account is not plausible because GM could have retained ownership of dies, which it would be able to retrieve in case Fisher engaged in hold-up).
14. See Coase, *supra* note 9.
15. During the time that we conducted this study, five major automobile suppliers filed in Chapter 11: Delphi (the world's largest tier-1 supplier), Tower Automotive, Intermet, Meridian, and Collins and Aikman.
16. One prominent example is Collins and Aikman ("C&A"), a tier-1 supplier that entered bankruptcy in May 2005. When C&A filed for bankruptcy under Chapter 11, it threatened to stop performance unless its contracts were renegotiated and the prices increased – that is, it engaged in classic hold-up. The payoff was quick: The three OEMs agreed to give C&A $82.5 million by raising the prices on their existing supply contracts with C&A by 15 percent, to purchase $140 million of tooling, and to make a loan of $82.5 million. See Jeffrey McCracken, *Plan OK'd for Aid to Keep C&A Supplying*, DETROIT FREE PRESS, July 8, 2005, available at 2005 WLNR 10705184.

FOUR. "UNFAIR" DISPUTE RESOLUTION CLAUSES: MUCH ADO ABOUT NOTHING?

1. This view was adopted by the Supreme Court in Carnival Cruise Lines v. Shute, 499 U.S. 585 (1991). Justifying its decision to enforce a forum selection clause printed on a cruise ticket, the Court stated that "[I]t stands to reason that passengers who purchase tickets containing a forum clause like that at issue in this case benefit in the form of reduced fares reflecting the savings that the cruise line enjoys by limiting the fora in which it may be sued." See also Clayton P. Gillette, *Rolling Contracts as an Agency Problem*, 2004 WIS. L. REV. 679.
2. See Larry E. Ribstein & Bruce H. Kobayashi, *State Regulation of Electronic Commerce*, 51 EMORY L. J. 1 (2002).
3. William J. Woodward, Jr., *Contractual Choice of Law: Legislative Choice in an Era of Party Autonomy*, 54 S.M.U.L. REV. 697 (2001); William J. Woodward, Jr., *"Sale" of Law and Forum and the Widening Gulf Between "Consumer" and "Nonconsumer" Contracts in the UCC*, 75 WASH. U. L. Q. 243 (1997).
4. America Online v. Booker, 781 So. 2d 423 (Fla. App. Ct. Feb. 7, 2001). It has been argued that sellers' aggressive use of mandatory and choice of forum clauses has led to a significant reduction in judicial opinions, a consequent slowing down in the development of common law, and a disruption in consumers' ability to obtain compensation for damages. See Rex R. Perschbacher & Debra Lynn Bassett, *The End of Law*, 84 B. U. L. REV. 1, 30 (2004).
5. Samuel Issacharoff & Erin F. Delaney, *Credit Card Accountability*, 73 U. CHI. L. REV. 157 (2006).
6. William J. Jr., Woodward, *Finding the Contract in Contracts for Law, Forum, and Arbitration*, 2 HAST. BUS. L. J. 1 (2006).

7. For a detailed account of these issues in the credit-card market, see Oren Bar-Gill, *Seduction by Plastic*, 98 Nw. U. L. Rev. 1373 (2004). See also Robert Hillman & Jeff Rachlinski, *Standard Form Contracts in the Electronic Age*, 77 N. Y. U. L. Rev.429 (2002) (providing an overview of the behavioral biases that might lead buyers to underestimate the implications of contractual limitations).
8. UCC §1–105; RESTATEMENT (SECOND) OF CONFLICT OF LAWS §188(2) (1971).
9. A narrow restriction is that the law chosen should not violate a fundamental of the jurisdiction whose law would otherwise apply. UCC §1–103.
10. V.I. CODE ANN. tit. 11A, § 1–301 (2003).
11. VA. CODE ANN. §§ 59.1–501.1 to 59.1–509.2 (2001 & Supp. 2005); MD. CODE ANN., COM. LAW §§ 22–101 to 22–816 (LexisNexis Supp. 2003). This proposed law provides rules governing fair use, reverse-engineering consumer protection, and the enforceability of shrinkwrap licenses.
12. UCITA 109 (2000).
13. An exemption is a recent study by Geoffrey Miller and Theodore Eisenberg of the use of choice of law and forum clauses by large corporate parties in merger agreements. Theodore Eisenberg & Geoffrey P. Miller, *Ex Ante Choices of Law and Forum: An Empirical Analysis of Corporate Merger Agreements*, NYU Law and Economics Research Paper No. 06-31 (August 2006).
14. Florencia Marotta-Wurgler, *Competition and Quality of Standard Form Contracts: An Empirical Analysis of Software License Agreements*, NYU Law and Economics Paper No. 05–11 (2005); Florencia Marotta-Wurgler, *Are "Pay Now, Terms Later" Contracts Worse for Buyers? Evidence from Software License Agreements*, NYU Law and Economics Paper No. 05–10 (2005). Because the sample in this chapter overlaps heavily with that used in previous papers, I refer the reader to those papers for further details on the data-collection procedure.
15. Although the inclusion of class-action waivers in credit-card form contracts has attracted a lot of attention from legal academics, I find no evidence of their use in software license contracts. For this reason, I don't record whether the EULA has a class-action waiver. The same is true for clauses requiring that the parties meet with a mediator before going to court. I found only one EULA that required mediation.
16. Some companies have offices in several states but, for practical purposes, I only record the location of their headquarters.
17. For example, a scrapbooking software product would be categorized as a "consumer" product and a client management product would be categorized as a "business" product.
18. See Eisenberg & Miller, *supra* note 13.
19. In most states, forum selection clauses are per se enforceable absent unconscionability. The same is true for forum selection clauses in software license agreements and online contracts. See, e.g., Cairo, Inc. v. Crossmedia Serv., Inc., 2005 WL 756610 (N.D. Cal. Apr. 1, 2005) (upholding forum selection clause in license agreement). However, the states of Idaho, North Carolina, and Montana have enacted statutes prohibiting the enforcement of forum selection clauses in consumer transactions. In addition, Georgia courts have refused to enforce forum selection clauses in consumer contracts. See, e.g., Fidelity & Deposit Co. v. Gainesville Iron Works, Inc., 125 Ga. App. 829 (Ga. Ct. App. 1972).
20. *Supra* note 14.
21. As an alternative to simple "linear probability" models, I have also estimated logit models, with virtually identical results in terms of statistical significance and implied

economic significance. I report the linear probability models because they are simpler to interpret.

22. See Section IV, *infra.*
23. A choice of law clause, if priced, would probably have an effect of price of a few cents of the dollar for most products. See James J. White, *Contracting Under Amended 2–207*, 2004 WIS. L. REV. 723, 742 (stating that "[f]or a nickel or a dime, almost all of us would [. . .] agree to arbitrate").
24. This finding is consistent with my earlier finding that the EULAs of larger companies tend to have more restrictive contracts than those of smaller companies. See Marotta-Wurgler, *supra* note 14.
25. I am grateful to Jean Braucher and Bill Woodward for providing this taxonomy.
26. When incorporation alone is the sole relationship to the selected law, there has been disagreement among courts on whether that state is "reasonably related" to the transaction. Thus, enforcement will depend on the forum that hears the dispute. For cases in which incorporation alone suffices to establish a relationship, see, e.g., CIENA Corp. v. Jarrard, 203 F.3d 312, 324 (4th Cir. 2000) and Valley Juice Ltd. v. Evian Waters of France, Inc., 87 F.3d 604, 608 (2d Cir. 1996). See also Restatement (Second) of Conflicts of Laws §187.
27. Eisenberg & Miller, *supra* note 13, also find that companies are more likely to select Delaware for incorporation than they are likely to select Delaware law in their choices of law and forum. The remaining off-diagonal 14 percent includes a number of U.S. subsidiaries of foreign-owned firms whose EULA specifies the law of the firms' home country and firms that have been acquired in the recent past but whose EULAs still stipulate the law of the state of the original firm.
28. Lucian Bebchuk and Alma Cohen, *Firms Decisions Where to Incorporate*, 46 J. OF L. & ECON 383 (2003).
29. For example, the California Arbitration Act mandates a waiver of arbitration fees for low-income consumers and requires arbitration organizations to publish its consumer arbitration decisions. See California Code of Civil Procedure Sections 1284.3, 1281.96.
30. The consumer section of the AAA Web site reads: "The AAA will only administer your dispute if the arbitration clause meets certain fairness standards that are contained in the AAA's Consumer Due Process Protocol. . . . [U]under the AAA's procedures, you may claim any amount of special damages such as attorney's fees or punitive damages, without an increase in fees." At http://www.adr.org/Consumer.

FIVE. THE UNCONVENTIONAL USES OF TRANSACTION COSTS

1. See David Gilo & Ariel Porat, *The Hidden Roles of Boilerplate and Standard Form Contracts: Strategic Imposition of Transaction Costs, Segmentation of Consumers, and Anticompetitive Effects*, 104 MICH.L.REV. 983, 990-1 (2006).
2. See, e.g., Educational Housing Services, http://www.studenthousing.org/ (last visited Dec. 2, 2005). See also job search sites on the Internet, Monster, http://www.monster.com (last visited Jan. 8, 2006), and Career Builder, http://www.careerbuilder.com (last visited Jan. 8, 2006).
3. See, for example, the boilerplate terms of sale of Speakeasy, offering broadband Internet services: "Speakeasy offers a 25-day Trial Period on all ADSL services. . . . If you feel that you must cancel within 25 calendar days of your Activation Date you may do so without being subject to a Disconnection Fee." Speakeasy, Terms of Service (Sept. 28, 2005), http://www.speakeasy.net/tos/ (last visited Dec. 1, 2005).

4. The "Help" devices of Microsoft Office programs are too complicated for some users, who would prefer to pay for support or to learn about operation of the programs in special courses.
5. See, e.g., See David Gilo, *The Anticompetitive Effect of Passive Investment*, 99 MICH. L. REV. 1, 17–18 (2000); David Gilo, Yossi Moshe & Yossi Spiegel, *Partial Cross Ownership and Tacit Collusion*, 37 RAND J. ECON.81 (2006); Jonathan B. Baker, *Vertical Restraints with Horizontal Consequences: Competitive Effects of "Most-Favored-Customer" Clauses*, 64 ANTITRUST L.J. 517 (1996).
6. Note that not all firms need to offer complex contracts in order for the anticompetitive effects of complexity to exist. As long as complexity is abundant enough, it would be useless for a rival offering a simple contract to try to steal customers from suppliers who offer complex contracts.
7. See Simon P. Anderson & Régis Renault, *Pricing, Product Diversity, and Search Costs: A Bertrand-Chamberlin-Diamond Model*, 30 RAND J. ECON. 719 (1999) (showing that prices in oligopoly rise when search costs rise); Christopher R. Knittel, *Interstate Long Distance Rates: Search Costs, Switching Costs, and Market Power*, 12 REV. INDUS. ORG. 519 (1997) (showing that search costs and switching costs have enabled long-distance carriers in the United States to raise prices after the dissolution of AT&T).
8. In this sense, hiding benefits in boilerplate language is a stronger facilitator of collusion than price-matching policies, in which the supplier promises to match a rival's price cut. With price matching, a price matcher's rival can still make considerable profits from deviating from collusion, due to the consumers' hassle in going to the rival and then back to the price matcher in order to invoke the price match. See Morten Hviid & Greg Shaffer, *Hassle Costs: The Achilles' Heel of Price-Matching Guarantees*, 8 J. ECON. & MGMT. STRATEGY 489 (1999); Aaron S. Edlin, *Do Guaranteed-Low-Price Policies Guarantee High Prices, and Can Antitrust Rise to the Challenge?*, 111 HARV. L. REV. 528 (1997), at note 24. In contrast, with hidden benefits in boilerplate language, the rival cannot steal readers because they are already enjoying the competitive benefits.
9. See Gilo & Porat, *supra* note 1, at 1013.
10. As we show elsewhere, not only is deviation from collusion less profitable when benefits are hidden in boilerplate, but collusion itself also is more profitable. See Gilo & Porat, *id.* at 1012.
11. See HUGH COLLINS, REGULATING CONTRACTS 260–66 (1999) (explaining that unfairness cannot be detected by analyzing specific terms as seemingly unfair because these terms are usually concessions granted in exchange for other advantages).
12. See Douglas Baird, *Commercial Norms and the Fine Art of the Small Con*, 98 MICH. L. REV. 2716, 2724 ("Unsophisticated consumers are often better off in a market in which no one can bargain for special terms than in a market where everyone can.").
13. See, e.g., Plain Language Contract Act, Minn. Stat. Ann. §§325G.29–.36 (West 2004 & Supp. 2006). Section 325G.35, entitled "Review by the attorney general," states: "Any seller, creditor or lessor may submit a consumer contract to the attorney general for review as to whether the contract complies with the requirements of section 325G.31.... Any consumer contract certified pursuant to subdivision 1 is deemed to comply with section 325G.31 ... "
14. See Robert A. Hillman & Jeffrey J. Rachlinski, *Standard-Form Contracting in the Electronic Age*, 77 N.Y.U.L. Rev. 429, 468 (2002) ("[E]-consumers cannot negotiate because web pages and installation software do not allow for interaction with a live agent.").

15. See David Gilo, *Retail Competition Percolating Through to Suppliers and the Use of Vertical Integration, Tying, and Vertical Restraints to Stop It*, 20 YALE J. ON REG. 23, 25–75 (2003), and the literature cited there, *ibid.* at note 9.
16. Indeed, McAfee & Schwartz claim that franchisors use uniform and rigid contracts with franchisees in order to better commit not to negotiate them. However, they discuss uniformity alone, rather than mechanisms that raise the costs of negotiation. R. Preston McAfee & Marius Schwartz, *Opportunism in Multilateral Vertical Contracting: Nondiscrimination, Exclusivity, and Uniformity*, 84 AM. ECON. REV. 210, 213 (1994).
17. This term is taken from the standard-form contract of Novell, a software vendor. See http://www.novell.com/licensing/eula/securelogin_35.pdf. It shows how the supplier may also want to credibly commit toward noncommercial consumers that it will not discriminate among them.
18. Most-favored-nation clauses, which contractually bind the supplier to grant similar concessions to all of his buyers, could also facilitate tacit collusion, but they are difficult to implement and could draw antitrust scrutiny. The strategy of term-rigidity and difficulty of negotiation, on the other hand, could more easily and credibly be implemented and does not currently draw antitrust attention.
19. For instance, the Truth in Lending Act is aimed at increasing disclosure of credit costs to borrowers. Truth in Lending Act, 15 U.S.C. §§1601–07(c) (2000). Similarly, the Equal Credit Opportunity Act mandates that an applicant for credit is entitled to disclosures explaining the reasons why credit has been denied or revoked. Equal Credit Opportunity Act, 15 U.S.C. §1691(a)–(f) (2000).
20. See, e.g., Plain Language Contract Act, Minn. Stat. Ann. §§325G.29–36 (2005) (enacted in 1981).
21. See, generally, United States ex rel. Bussen Quarries, Inc. v. Thomas, 938 F.2d 831, 834 (8th Cir. 1991); Merrill Lynch, Pierce, Fenner & Smith, Inc. v. First Nat'l Bank of Little Rock, Ark., 774 F.2d 909, 913 (8th Cir. 1985); Restatement (Second) of Contracts §161 (1981); Restatement (Second) of Torts §551 (1977).
22. See Restatement (Second) of Contracts §303(b) (1981); Restatement of Restitution §8 cmt. e, §28 (1937); E. ALLAN FARNSWORTH, FARNSWORTH ON CONTRACTS §§4.11, 4.15 (1999) (discussing the effects of nondisclosure and the remedies for misrepresentation).
23. Cf. Restatement (Second) of Torts §551 (1977), Farnsworth, *ibid.*, at §§ 4.15, 4.29.
24. See Gilo & Porat, *supra* note 1, at 1025–29.

SIX. ONLINE BOILERPLATE: WOULD MANDATORY WEB SITE DISCLOSURE OF e-STANDARD TERMS BACKFIRE?

1. See Robert A. Hillman & Jeffrey J. Rachlinski, *Standard-Form Contracting in the Electronic Age*, 77 N.Y.U.L. REV. 429, 464 (2002). In contrast, in a "browsewrap" transaction, a consumer who is downloading software or purchasing goods electronically views a screen that refers to terms that can be found elsewhere. Browsewrap, therefore, permits consumers to bypass the standard form and to "agree" to the terms without ever seeing them.
2. See Jean Braucher, *Amended Article 2 and the Decision to Trust the Courts: The Case Against Enforcing Delayed Mass-Market Terms, Especially for Software*, 2004 WIS. L. REV. 753, 768 ("Advance disclosure in the age of computers and the Internet is simple and cheaper than printing copies and getting them into boxes.").

3. Robert A. Hillman, *On-Line Consumer Standard-Form Contracting Practices: A Survey and Discussion of Legal Implications*, *in* Is Consumer Protection an Anachronism in the Information Economy? (forthcoming 2006).
4. My survey results show that only 4 percent of purchasers generally read their e-purchase contracts beyond price and product description. See Hillman, *supra* note 3; *see also* Clayton P. Gillette, *Rolling Contracts as an Agency Problem*, 2004 Wis. L. Rev. 679, 687–88 (2004) ("It is unlikely that the Internet buyer will devote more time to reading text on the website than more traditional buyers devote to reviewing the terms of tangible [standard forms].").
5. Even consumers who read their terms do not necessarily account for them in their decisionmaking. See generally Russell Korobkin, *Bounded Rationality, Standard Form Contracts, and Unconscionability*, 70 U. Chi. L. Rev. 1203 (2003).
6. Hillman & Rachlinski, *supra* note 1, at 478 (footnotes omitted).
7. Lee Goldman, *My Way and the Highway: The Law and Economics of Choice of Forum Clauses in Consumer Form Contracts*, 86 Nw. U. L. Rev. 700, 720 (1992).
8. Hillman, *supra* note 3, at 12 tbl.5C.
9. *Id.* at 481; see also Anonymous Posting to ContractsProf Blog, http://lawprofessors.typepad.com/contractsprof_blog/2005/04/paper_not_plast.html (Apr. 27, 2005) ("The 'cautionary' functions of a contract are easier to achieve through the formalities of a written document . . . " (relying on a report in BNA's Electronic Commerce and Law journal)).
10. *Ibid.* at 485. Few empirical studies examine consumer reading of standard forms in the paper world. Most commentators merely cite or quote Todd Rakoff's piece on contracts of adhesion for the proposition that consumers do not read standard forms. See Todd D. Rakoff, *Contracts of Adhesion: An Essay in Reconstruction*, 96 Harv. L. Rev. 1173, 1179 (1983); see also Korobkin, *supra* note 5, at 1217 n.45.
11. Hillman, *supra* note 3. The survey inquired, among other things, about the frequency of electronic contracting, the subject matter (purchases or subscriptions), the place and time of making such contracts, the extent to which participants read forms, the particular terms read, the reasons for not reading, and conditions and mechanisms that would promote reading. The survey also compared the practices of men and women and of frequent and occasional users. Respondents could select more than one response to many of the questions discussed in the survey.
12. Sixty-five percent of the respondents failed to read for this reason. *Ibid.* at 10.
13. *Ibid.* at 13. PC Pitstop's licensing agreement promised a "consideration" to anyone who read their terms and sent an email to an address listed in the agreement. It took four months and more than three thousand downloads before anyone wrote the e-mail. Larry Magid, *It Pays to Read License Agreements*, PC Pitstop, http://www.pcpitstop.com/spycheck/eula.asp (last visited Oct. 14, 2005). My colleague Doug Kysar points out that PC Pitstop is a free site and people are therefore unlikely to read the terms of use.
14. See, e.g., Alan Schwartz & Louis L. Wilde, *Imperfect Information in Markets for Contract Terms: The Examples of Warranties and Security Interests*, 69 Va. L. Rev. 1387, 1409 (1983).
15. Hillman & Rachlinski, *supra* note 1, at 470; Avery Wiener Katz, *Standard Form Contracts*, 3 The New Palgrave Dictionary of Economics and the Law 502, 505.
16. There is ample evidence that some businesses seek to take advantage of consumers. See, e.g., Jeff Sovern, *Towards a New Model of Consumer Protection: The Problem of Inflated Transaction Costs*, 47 Wm. & Mary L. Rev. (forthcoming 2006) (marshaling evidence

of businesses' strategies to increase consumer transaction costs, such as by utilizing rebates). Businesses that seek to defraud customers are beyond the scope of this chapter.

17. Gillette, *supra* note 4, at 695.
18. Hillman & Rachlinski, *supra* note 1, at 471–72; see also Donnavieve N. Smith & K. Sivakumar, *Flow and Internet Shopping Behavior: A Conceptual Model and Research Propositions*, 57 J. Bus. Res. 1199, 1207 (2004) ("To ensure the desired shopping behavior, e-tailers should attempt to manage the shoppers' flow states on an individual basis. They should invest in tools that enable them to develop personal profiles of their customers, while garnering information regarding the consumers' skills and their perceptions of the challenges presented by shopping the site.").
19. Hillman & Rachlinski, *supra* note 1, at 479.
20. Hillman, *supra* note 3.
21. See Korobkin, *supra* note 5, at 1234 ("'Notice' is a prerequisite of salience, but notice is not a sufficient condition of salience."). See also David Frisch & John D. Wladis, *General Provisions, Sales, Bulk Transfers, and Documents of Title*, 46 Bus. Law. 1455, 1495–96 (1991) (discussing courts' varying requirements regarding "conspicuousness" in disclaimers of implied warranties under the UCC).
22. See generally Christian J. Meier-Schatz, *A Fresh Look at Business Disclosure*, 51 Am. J. Comp. L. 691 (2003) (book review).
23. See Annalee Newitz, *Dangerous Terms: A User's Guide to EULAs*, Elec. Frontier Found., http://www.eff.org/wp/eula.php (last visited Oct. 28, 2005).
24. Karl Llewellyn, The Common Law Tradition: Deciding Appeals 370–71 (1960).
25. Lon L. Fuller, Legal Fictions 84 (1967).
26. According to one study, e-shoppers may be confident or apprehensive, and highly involved or apathetic. Letecia N. McKinney, *Internet Shopping Orientation Segments: An Exploration of Differences in Consumer Behavior*, 32 Fam. & Consumer Sci. Res. J. 408, 418–421 (2004). Such attitudes may have a significant effect on reading habits, as well as purchasing frequency.
27. Braucher, *supra* note 2, at 768. Few software vendors currently display their terms on their Web site. See Jean Braucher, *Delayed Disclosure in Consumer E-Commerce as an Unfair and Deceptive Practice*, 46 Wayne L. Rev. 1805, 1806–07 (2000) [hereinafter Braucher, *Delayed Disclosure*] (reporting the author's finding that 87.5 percent of software companies did not make precontract disclosures of their terms).
28. "There are design prescriptions gleaned from empirical studies of web-searching behavior that claim that if in three clicks users do not find information that at least suggests they are on the right track, they will leave the site." Gary M. Olson & Judith S. Olson, *Human-Computer Interaction: Psychological Aspects of the Human Use of Computing*, 54 Ann. Rev. Psychol. 491, 500 (2003). The Federal Trade Commission has promulgated rules of Web site disclosure. Federal Trade Commission, Dot Com Disclosures, http://www.ftc.gov/bcp/conline/pubs/buspubs/dotcom/index.html (last visited Dec. 21, 2005). For a discussion, see Christina L. Kunz et al., *Browse-Wrap Agreements: Validity of Implied Assent in Electronic Form Agreements*, 59 Bus. Law. 279, 302 (2003).
29. Junghyun Kim & Robert LaRose, *Interactive E-Commerce: Promoting Consumer Efficiency or Impulsivity?* 10 J. Computer-Mediated Comm., Nov. 2004, http://jcmc.indiana.edu/vol10/issue1/kim_larose.html.
30. *Ibid.* (citing Dennis W. Rook & Robert J. Fisher, *Normative Influences in Impulsive Buying Behavior*, 22 J. Consumer Res., Dec. 1995, at 305–13).
31. *Ibid.*

32. *Ibid.* Reluctance to purchase because of fear of disclosing information diminishes when firms have good reputations, when the consumer is familiar with a site, and even when sites have "visually pleasing" layouts, including easy navigation and "professionalism." See Miriam J. Metzger, *Privacy, Trust, and Disclosure: Exploring Barriers to Electronic Commerce*, 9 J. COMPUTER-MEDIATED COMM., July 2004, http://jcmc.indiana.edu/vol9/issue4/metzger.html ("Web sites of respected organizations that were visually pleasing were rated high in trustworthiness and expertise.").
33. Kim & LaRose, *supra* note 29; see also Robert LaRose & Matthew S. Eastin, *Is Online Buying Out of Control? Electronic Commerce and Consumer Self-Regulation*, 46 J. BROADCASTING & ELECTRONIC MEDIA 549, 559 (2002) ("[D]eficient self-regulation . . . may be a more important determinant of online buying activity than either rational or economic expectations about the cost and convenience of Internet shopping or the personal and economic characteristics of e-commerce consumers.").
34. LaRose & Eastin, *supra* note 33, at 552; see also Robert LaRose, *On the Negative Effects of E-Commerce: A Sociocognitive Exploration of Unregulated On-Line Buying*, 6 J. COMPUTER-MEDIATED COMM., Apr. 2001, http://www.ascusc.org/jcmc/vol6/issue3/larose.html.
35. Paul Markillie, *Crowned at Last*, Economist, Apr. 2, 2005, at 3, 4; see also Alan Mitchell, *Marketers Must Face Up to the Buyer's Side of the Coin*, MKTG. WEEK, Apr. 14, 2005, at 32 (discussing how the Internet "turns the tables" on businesses). But see Victoria Murphy, *The Revolution That Wasn't*, FORBES, Oct. 27, 2003, at 210 (asserting that the anticipated benefits of online shopping have failed to materialize).
36. Kim & LaRose, *supra* note 29 (citing Sharon E. Beatty & M. Elizabeth Ferrell, *Impulse Buying: Modeling Its Precursors*, 74 J. RETAILING 169–91 (1998)).
37. Metzger, *supra* note 32.
38. For example, at the moment that I am typing this, I am experiencing pain in my shoulder and neck from looking at this manuscript on the screen. This is likely bad for my tennis.
39. See Kunz et al., *supra* note 28, at 280–81 ("[T]he terms most commonly providing the impetus to challenge the validity of electronic standard-form agreements are dispute resolution clauses, forum selection clauses, disclaimers of warranty, limitations of liability, and prohibitions on the commercial use of the data or software available on the site." (footnotes omitted)).
40. Magid, *supra* note 13 (discussing the licensing agreement that accompanies Gain Publishing's eWallet software, which authorizes the collection of data about a consumer's reading behavior, TV interests, and communication partners, effectively allowing the company to "follow [the transferee] around").
41. See, e.g., Comb v. PayPal, Inc., 218 F. Supp. 2d 1165, 1172–76 (N.D. Cal. 2002); *In re* RealNetworks, Inc., Privacy Litigation, No. 00 C 1366, 2000 WL 631341 (N.D. Ill. May 8, 2000); Strand v. U.S. Bank Nat'l Ass'n ND, 693 N.W.2d 918, 924 (N.D. 2005).
42. See Robert A. Hillman, *Debunking Some Myths About Unconscionability: A New Framework for U.C.C. Section 2–302*, 67 CORNELL L. REV. 1, 42 (1981).
43. Armendariz v. Found. Health Psychcare Servs., Inc., 6 P.3d 669, 690 (Cal. 2000).
44. Magid, *supra* note 13 (quoting the licensing agreement that accompanies Gain Publishing's eWallet software).
45. See Florencia Marotta-Wurgler, "Are 'Pay Now, Terms Later' Contracts Worse for Buyers?" Evidence from Software License Agreements (Aug. 22, 2005) (unpublished manuscript, on file with author) (noting that evidence suggests that "sellers whose boilerplate is more one-sided tend to make their contract harder to challenge by requiring buyers to unequivocally accept it").

46. Cain et al., *supra* note 73, at 3 n.2 (*quoting* Action on Smoking and Health, Warning: History of Tobacco Manipulation of Congress (Sept. 11, 1997), http://www.no-smoking.org/sept97/9–11-97–1.html).

SEVEN. PREAPPROVED BOILERPLATE

1. See, e.g., Robert A. Hillman & Jeffrey J. Rachlinski, *Standard-Form Contracting in the Electronic Age*, 77 N.Y.U.L. Rev. 429, 432–33 (2002) (noting businesses' ability to take advantage of consumers in standard-form contracts).
2. See, e.g., Oren Bar-Gill, *Seduction by Plastic*, 98 Nw. U. L. Rev. 1373, 1407 (2004); Russell Korobkin, *Bounded Rationality, Standard Form Contracts, and Unconscionability*, 70 U. Chi. L. Rev. 1203, 1205–06 (2003); Ronald J. Mann, *"Contracting" for Credit* (in this volume).
3. See generally Clayton P. Gillette, *Rolling Contracts as an Agency Problem*, 2004 Wis. L. Rev. 679; Alan Schwartz & Louis L. Wilde, *Intervening in Markets on the Basis of Imperfect Information: A Legal and Economic Analysis*, 127 U. Pa. L. Rev.630 (1979).
4. Robert Hillman, *Online Boilerplate: Would Mandatory Web Site Disclosure of e-Standard Terms Backfire?* (in this volume).
5. See Mann, *"Contracting" for Credit* (in this volume).
6. Standard Contracts Law, 5743–1982, 37 LSI 6 (1982) (Isr.); see Sinai Deutch, *Controlling Standard Contracts – The Israeli Version*, 30 McGill L. J. 458, 473, 475 (1985); Shmuel I. Becher, Going Beyond the Traditional Approaches to Standard Form Contracts: The "Good Housekeeping Law" 11–12 (Mar. 2005); Kenneth Frederick Berg, *The Israeli Standard Contracts Law 1964: Judicial Controls of Standard Form Contracts*, 28 Int'l & Comp. L.Q. 560, 561 (1979).
7. See Council Directive 93/13, 1993 O.J. (L 95) 29 (EC), *available at* http://europa.eu.int/eur-lex/lex/LexUriServ/LexUriServ.do?uri=CELEX:31993L0013:EN:HTML.
8. *Id.* art. 3, § 1, at 31; see *id.* annex at 33 (listing seventeen unfair terms).
9. The role of trade associations in drafting standard-form contracts is studied in another contribution to this volume. See Kevin Davis, *The Role of Nonprofits in the Production of Boilerplate* (in this volume).
10. In the credit card context, Ronald Mann suggests that the credit card networks could draft standardized terms for their members and implies that some "non-price terms" could be subject to variation by individual issuers. See Mann, *supra* note 5.
11. Dix v. ICT Group, 106 P. 3d 841, 844 (Wash. Ct. App. 2005).
12. See *Discover Bank v. Superior Court*, 30 Cal. Rptr. 3d 76, 87 (2005).
13. See Michelle E. Boardman, *Contra Proferentem: The Allure of Ambiguous Boilerplate* (in this volume).
14. Williams v. Walker-Thomas Furniture Co., 350 F.2d 445 (D.C. Cir. 1965).
15. The clause at issue, of dubious readability to the average consumer, recited that: "The amount of each periodical installment payment to be made by [purchaser] to the Company under this present lease shall be inclusive of and not in addition to the amount of each installment payment to be made by [purchaser] under such prior leases, bills or accounts; and all payments now and hereafter made by [purchaser] shall be credited pro rata on all outstanding leases, bills and accounts due the Company by [purchaser] at the time each such payment is made." Id. at 447 (alterations in original) (internal quotation marks omitted).
16. 16 C.F.R. § 433.2 (2005).

17. *Id.* § 429.1.
18. Council Directive 93/13 1993 O.J. (L 95) 29 (EC).
19. Thomas L. Gais et al., *Interest Groups, Iron Triangles and Representative Institutions in American National Government*, 14 Brit. J. Pol. Sci. 161, 177 (1984) (showing the modern rise of "representatives of the public interest" and their increasing effectiveness in dealing with government regulation).
20. See, e.g., AARP v. EEOC, 383 F. Supp. 2d 705, 706, 712 (E.D. Pa. 2005); *Public Citizen: 30 Years*, Pub. Citizen News, Anniversary Issue 2001, at 16, 19.
21. See Gillette, *supra* note 3, at 703–12; see also Jason Scott Johnston, *Cooperative Negotiations in the Shadow of Boilerplate* (in this volume); Lucian A. Bebchuk and Richard Posner, *One-Sided Contracts in Competitive Consumer Markets* (in this volume).

EIGHT. "CONTRACTING" FOR CREDIT

1. See The Nilson Report No. 828, at 9 (Feb. 2005).
2. See Oren Bar-Gill, *Seduction by Plastic*, 98 Nw. U. L. Rev. 1373 (2004); Susan Block-Lieb & Edward Janger, *The Myth of the Rational Borrower: Rationality, Behaviorism, and the Misguided "Reform" of Bankruptcy Law*, 84 Tex. L. Rev. (forthcoming 2006); Ron Harris & Adu Einat Albin, *Bankruptcy Policy in Light of Persuasion in Credit Advertisement*, 7 J. Theoretical Inquiries in L. (forthcoming 2006); Cass R. Sunstein, *Boundedly Rational Borrowing: A Consumer's Guide*, 73 U. Chi. L. Rev. (forthcoming 2006).
3. Jeffrey Davis, *Protecting Consumers from Overdisclosure and Gobbledygook: An Empirical Look at the Simplification of Consumer-Credit Contracts*, 63 Va. L. Rev. 841 (1977).
4. See Thomas H. Jackson, *The Fresh-Start Policy in Bankruptcy Law*, 98 Harv. L. Rev. 1393, 1410–14 (1985).
5. See Xavier Gabaix & David Laibson, *Shrouded Attributes, Consumer Myopia, and Information Suppression in Competitive Markets* (Mass. Inst. of Tech. Dep't. of Econ. Working Paper Series, Paper No. 05–18, 2005), available at http://papers.ssrn.com/abstract_id=728545 (summarizing literature).
6. Stewart Macaulay, *Private Legislation and the Duty to Read – Business Run by IBM Machine, the Law of Contracts and Credit Cards*, 19 Vand. L. Rev. 1051, 1069–74 (1966).
7. See Bar-Gill, *supra* note 2.
8. Truth in Lending Act (TILA) §132, 15 U.S.C. §1642 (2004); Regulation Z, 12 C.F.R. §§225, 226 (2005). The Uniform Commercial Code does not cover payment cards. See U.C.C. §4–104(a)(9) (2002) ("'Item'... does not include... a credit or debit card slip."). But see Broadway Nat'l. Bank v. Barton-Russell Corp., 585 N.Y.S.2d 933, 938 (Sup. Ct. 1992) (reaching a contrary conclusion under pre-revision Article 4). Although some states have enacted statutes that govern certain aspects of the issuer/cardholder relationship, it seems fair to say that none of those statutes has any significant impact, largely because the National Bank Act would preempt any substantial regulation. See Mark Furletti, *The Debate over the National Bank Act and the Preemption of State Efforts to Regulate Credit Cards*, 77 Temp. L. Rev. 425 (2004). To the extent that there is any substantive regulation by the states, it tends to be very specific statutes authorizing specific business practices.
9. Council Directive 93/13/EEC, Unfair Terms in Consumer Contracts, 1993 O.J. (L 95) 29.
10. See Philip Schuchman, *Consumer Credit by Adhesion Contracts*, 35 Temple L.Q. 125, 130 (1962).

NINE. THE ROLE OF NONPROFITS IN THE PRODUCTION OF BOILERPLATE

1. Charles J. Goetz & Robert E. Scott, *The Limits of Expanded Choice: An Analysis of the Interactions Between Express and Implied Contract Terms*, 73 Cal. L. Rev. 261 (1985); Henry T. Greely, *Contracts As Commodities: The Influence of Secondary Purchasers on the Form of Contracts*, 42 Vand. L. Rev. 133, 160–61 (1989); Marcel Kahan & Michael Klausner, *Standardization and Innovation in Corporate Contracting (Or "The Economics of Boilerplate")*, 83 Va. L. Rev. 713 (1997); Michael Klausner, *Corporations, Corporate Law, and Networks of Contracts*, 81 Va. L. Rev. 757 (1995); Mark C. Suchman, *The Contract as Social Artifact*, 37 L. & Soc'y Rev. 9, 102 (2003).
2. The role of nonprofits in the production of boilerplate has been described by authors such as Karl Llewellyn and Lisa Bernstein. See, generally, K. N. Llewellyn, *The Effect of Legal Institutions Upon Economics*, 15 Am. Econ. Rev. 665, 672–74 (1925); Lisa Bernstein, *Private Commercial Law, in* 3 The New Palgrave Dictionary of Economics and the Law 108 (Peter Newman, ed., 1998). A few of the reasons why it may matter whether boilerplate is produced by nonprofits or for-profits are discussed in Goetz & Scott, *supra* note 1, at 293, 303; Kahan & Klausner, *supra* note 1, at 762; Lisa Bernstein, *id.* at 110–11; Lisa Bernstein, *Private Commercial Law in the Cotton Industry: Creating Cooperation Through Rules, Norms, and Institutions*, 99 Mich. L. Rev. 1724, 1742–43 (2001); and Robert B. Ahdieh, *The Role of Groups in Norm Transformation: A Dramatic Sketch, in Three Parts*, 6 Chi. J. Int'l L.231, 249–252 (2005). The analysis in this chapter extends this literature in ways that find close analogues in the literature on production of goods besides boilerplate. See, for example, Henry Hansmann, The Ownership of Enterprise 227–45 (1996); Josh Lerner & Jean Tirole, *Some Simple Economics of Open Source*, 50 J. Indus. Econ. 197 (2002); Josh Lerner & Jean Tirole, *A Model of Forum-Shopping with Special Reference to Standard Setting Organizations*, National Bureau of Economic Research Working Paper No. 10664; Emmanuel Farhi, Josh Lerner & Jean Tirole, *Certifying New Technologies*, 3 J. Eur. Econ. Ass. 734 (2005).
3. The American Law Institute and the National Conference of Commissioners on Uniform State Law have somewhat arbitrarily been excluded from the following discussion. These organizations draft the Uniform Commercial Code, which, to the extent that it contains default rules that parties are free to exclude, is functionally equivalent to boilerplate drafted by trade associations. However, the fact that some of the rules drafted by these and similar organizations are mandatory rules (or at least "sticky" defaults) that are ultimately enacted as statutes seems to make their activities qualitatively different from those of the other entities discussed in this chapter (although the distinction becomes blurred in cases in which boilerplate comes to be treated as binding custom). Moreover, the drafting activities of these entities have been analyzed in some depth by other commentators. See, generally, George G. Triantis, *Private Lawmaking and the Uniform Commercial Code in* 3 New Palgrave Dictionary of Economics and the Law 117 (Peter Newman, ed., 1998).
4. Trade associations also may find it relatively easy to translate benefits and costs that accrue to their members into financial returns because they may be able to recover the net benefits that accrue to their members by imposing some sort of levy. This technique is unlikely to be available to a for-profit firm.
5. Eric Bennett Rasmusen, *Explaining Incomplete Contracts as the Result of Contract-Reading Costs*, 1 Advances in Economic Analysis & Policy Issue 1, Article 2 (2001) at 9–10, 28.

6. Yochai Benkler, *Coase's Penguin, or, Linux and The Nature of the Firm*, 112 Yale L. J. 369 (2002).
7. Some for-profit firms clearly have access to volunteers. Examples include software developers, publishers of academic journals, and any firm that has ever relied upon the results of a customer satisfaction survey. Benkler, *supra* note 6, at 440–41; Dietmar Harhoff, Joachim Henkel & Eric von Hippel, *Profiting from Voluntary Information Spillovers: How Users Benefit by Freely Revealing Their Innovations*, 32 Res. Pol'y 1753 (2003).
8. Frances R. Hill & Barbara L. Kirschten, Federal And State Taxation Of Exempt Organizations 14.04 (1994).
9. I.R.C. §501(c) (2000).
10. I.R.C. §511(a) (2000).
11. I.R.C. §512(a), (b)(2) (2000).
12. Hugh Collins, *The Freedom to Circulate Documents: Regulating Contracts in Europe*, 10 Eur. L. J. 787 (2004).

TEN. THE BOILERPLATE PUZZLE

1. This idea that contract terms are embedded in products, rather than the result of a discrete transaction between autonomous individuals, looms larger in the digital age. For a discussion of this point, see Margaret Jane Radin, *Humans, Computers, and Binding Commitment*, 75 Ind. L. J. 1125 (2000).
2. See, e.g., Alan Schwartz & Louis L. Wilde, *Intervening in Markets on the Basis of Imperfect Information: A Legal and Economic Analysis*, 127 U. Pa. L. Rev. 630 (1979). For a lucid overview of the terrain, see Robert A. Hillman, *Rolling Contracts*, 71 Fordham L. Rev. 743 (2002).
3. 161 A.2d 69 (N.J. 1960).
4. 350 F.2d 445 (D.C. Cir. 1965).
5. (1893) 1 Q.B. 256 (U.K.).
6. See, e.g., N.Y. Gen. Bus. Law §350-a (McKinney 2004).
7. I developed this idea in Douglas G. Baird, *Commercial Norms and the Fine Art of the Small Con*, 98 Mich. L. Rev. 2716 (2000).
8. For example, disclaimers of liability for consequential damages in consumer transactions might seem a form of advantage-taking, but such disclaimers are commonplace between sophisticated parties and likely show that buyers are better positioned to guard against them than sellers. More generally, there are many risks that buyers are simply better positioned to bear than sellers. See George L. Priest, *A Theory of the Consumer Product Warranty*, 90 Yale L. J. 1297 (1981).
9. Payday lending is a potential place for useful regulation precisely because of the danger that the borrowers in such a market (those who live from one paycheck to the next) are not likely to include any sophisticated parties. See Creola Johnson, *Payday Loans: Shrewd Business or Predatory Lending*, 87 Minn. L. Rev. 1 (2002). One cannot justify regulation on this account alone, but it becomes a factor to consider once one pays attention to the market as a whole.
10. See, e.g., FTC Rule Concerning Cooling-Off Period for Sales Made at Homes or Certain Other Locations, 16 C.F.R. §429 (2005).
11. 161 A.2d 69 (N.J. 1960).
12. *Id.* at 86.

13. See Robert E. Scott, *A Relational Theory of Secured Financing*, 86 Colum. L. Rev. 901, 930 (1986).
14. See Lon L. Fuller, *Consideration and Form*, 41 Colum. L. Rev. 799, 800 (1941).
15. 350 F.2d 445 (D.C. Cir. 1965).
16. Sunstein and others have unpacked the idea of paternalism into strong and weak forms. See Cass R. Sunstein, *Boundedly Rational Borrowing*, 73 U. Chi. L. Rev. 249 (2006).
17. (1893) 1 Q.B. 256 (U.K.).
18. See, e.g., *Carlill*, 1 Q.B. at 264 (discussing, in the course of establishing the requisite consideration, the seller's need for the public to have confidence in the efficacy of the product).
19. See A. W. B. Simpson, *Quackery and Contract Law: The Case of the Carbolic Smoke Ball*, 14 J. Legal Stud. 345, 372 (1985).
20. 15 U.S.C. §§2301–12 (2000).
21. §2304.
22. U.C.C. §2–316 (2000).
23. U.C.C. §2–317(a) (2000).
24. See Writers' Guild of America, West, Screen Credits Manual II.A.d.1 (2002), available at http://www.wga.org/subpage_writersresources.aspx?id=170.
25. *Ibid.* For a case upholding these rules, see Ferguson v. Writers Guild of Am., W., Inc., 277 Cal. Rptr. 450, 453 (Ct. App. 1991).
26. See Fed. Trade Comm'n, Report on Automobile Warranties 11 (1970).
27. See, e.g., Les Jackson, *Warranties Get Better with Cars*, Wash. Times, Jan. 16, 2004, at G10.
28. See FTC Credit Practices Rules, 16 C.F.R. §§444.1(i), 444.2(a)(4) (2005).
29. See Susan Lorde Martin & Nancy White Huckins, *Consumer Advocates vs. the Rent-to-Own Industry: Reaching a Reasonable Accommodation*, 34 Am. Bus. L. J. 385 (1997). The abuse in this industry first came to light in an exposé in the *Wall Street Journal*. See Alix M. Freedman, *Peddling Dreams: A Marketing Giant Uses Its Sales Prowess to Profit on Poverty*, Wall St. J., Sept. 22, 1993, at A1.

ELEVEN. CONTRACT AS STATUTE

1. See Broad v. Rockwell Int'l. Corp., 642 F.2d 929, 947 (5th Cir. 1981) (en banc) for textual interpretation; Morgan Stanley & Co. v. Archer Daniels Midland Co., 570 F. Supp. 1529, 1541–42 (S.D.N.Y. 1983) for deference to prior interpretations; CIBC Bank & Trust Co. (Cayman) v. Banco Cent. do Brasil, 886 F. Supp. 1105, 1115 n.8 (S.D.N.Y. 1995) for reluctance to apply good-faith duties; and Sharon Steel Corp. v. Chase Manhattan Bank, N.A., 691 F.2d 1039, 1048–51 (2d Cir. 1982) for analysis of economic interests.
2. The discussion in this section is based on Stephen J. Choi & G. Mitu Gulati, When Sophisticated Parties Fail to Cure Ambiguities Caused by a Litigation Shock: The Puzzle of the Pari Passu Case (Dec. 22, 2005).
3. 194 F.3d 363 (2d Cir. 1999).
4. This is not to say that there won't be rent-acquisition opportunities for these same elite lawyers to take control of the standard-setting process. See Alan Schwartz & Robert E. Scott, *Contract Theory and the Limits of Contract Law*, 113 Yale L. J. 541, 598 (2003) (concluding that rent-seeking by interest groups can occur in expert advisory processes such as those set up by the ALI).

5. For a discussion of the Eternity cases and the interpretation issue therein, see James Warnot & Justin Williamson, *ISDA Definitions Unclear, Says U.S. Court, Int'l Fin. L. Rev.* Sept. 2004, at 27; Felix Salmon, *Sovereign Market Awaits Court Verdicts*, EUROMONEY, May 2002, at 32.
6. See Lisa Bernstein, *The Questionable Empricial Basis of Article 2's Incorporation Strategy: A Preliminary Study*, 66 U. OF CHI. L. REV. 710 (1999) (questioning whether industry-wide customs exist). But see Richard Epstein, *Confusion about Custom: Disentangling Informal Customs from Standard Contractual Provisions*, 66 U. OF CHI. L. REV. 821 (1999), who makes the distinction between the pre-standard-form period, where understandings of custom are in flux, and the post-standard-form period that Bernstein's article does not address. Epstein, though, seems to assume that once custom morphs into a standard form, the understandings of what the standard-form term means will remain.
7. See Sharon Steel Corp. v. Chase Manhattan Bank, N.A., 691 F.2d 1039, 1048 (2d Cir. 1982).
8. For discussions of this negative signaling effect as a cause of contract stickiness, see Omri Ben-Shahar & John Pottow, *On the Stickiness of Default Rules*, 33 FLA. ST. U. L. REV. 651 (2006).
9. We do not mean to suggest that contract law should incorporate the entire debate over statutory interpretation. Indeed, we recognize that there is a strain of statutory interpretation that prescribes strict textualism and abhors historical inquiry into legislative intent. Our point instead is to suggest that, at least in the boilerplate context, it is worth having the kinds of debates over textualism versus historical understandings versus contemporary understandings that take place in the statutory context.
10. See Bernstein, *supra* note 6, at 754–56.

TWELVE. MODULARITY IN CONTRACTS: BOILERPLATE AND INFORMATION FLOW

1. For development of this theory in which context is defined by audience type, see Henry E. Smith, *The Language of Property: Form, Context, and Audience*, 55 STAN. L. REV. 1105, 1125–28 (2003).
2. See, e.g., 1 CARLISS Y. BALDWIN & KIM B. CLARK, DESIGN RULES 6–11, 169–94 (2000); *Managing in the Modular Age: Architectures, Networks and Organizations* (Raghu Garud, Arun Kumaraswamy & Richard N. Langlois eds., 2003); Richard N. Langlois, *Modularity in Technology and Organization*, 49 J. ECON. BEHAV. & ORG. 19 (2002). See also HERBERT A. SIMON, THE SCIENCES OF THE ARTIFICIAL (2d ed. 1981).
3. See, e.g., Carol M. Rose, *The Several Futures of Property: Of Cyberspace and Folk Tales, Emission Trades and Ecosystems*, 83 MINN. L. REV. 129, 169–70 (1998); Henry E. Smith, *Exclusion Versus Governance: Two Strategies for Delineating Property Rights*, 31 J. LEGAL STUD. S453, S470–71 (2002).
4. J. E. PENNER, THE IDEA OF PROPERTY IN LAW 29–30, 71 (1997); Thomas W. Merrill & Henry E. Smith, *The Property/Contract Interface*, 101 COLUM. L. REV. 773, 794–95 (2001); Thomas W. Merrill & Henry E. Smith, *What Happened to Property in Law and Economics?*, 111 YALE L.J. 357, 359 (2001); Smith, *supra* note 3, at S475; Smith, *supra* note 1, at 1151.
5. Henry Hansmann & Reinier Kraakman, *The Essential Role of Organizational Law*, 110 YALE L.J. 387 (2000); see also Claire A. Hill, *Securitization: A Low-Cost Sweetener for Lemons*, 74 WASH. U. L.Q. 1061 (1996).

6. Hansmann & Kraakman, *supra* note 5, at 399–405, 424–25.
7. Baldwin & Clark, *supra* note 2, at 5.
8. This is also a rule for drafters of statutes. For a very interesting article on statutory drafting that recognizes the benefits of modularity through an analogy to object-oriented programming, see Thomas F. Blackwell, *Finally Adding Method to Madness: Applying Principles of Object-Oriented Analysis and Design to Legislative Drafting*, 3 N.Y.U.J. Legis. & Pub. Pol'y 227 (2000).
9. See Eric Kades, *The Laws of Complexity and the Complexity of Laws: The Computational Complexity Theory for the Law*, 49 Rutgers L. Rev. 403, 445–66 (1997).
10. Smith, *supra* note 1 at 1177–83. One aspect of differential formalism is the type of evidence admitted on contract-interpretation questions. See Alan Schwartz & Robert E. Scott, *Contract Theory and the Limits of Contract Law*, 113 Yale L.J. 541, 568–94 (2003).
11. See, e.g., Tina L. Stark, Negotiating and Drafting Contract Boilerplate, at vii–xxii, 5 (2003). In the broader sense, "boilerplate" refers to any standardized term in a contract.
12. The Digital Contracts Library of the Contracting and Organizations Research Institute (CORI) (http://cori.missouri.edu).
13. CORI, Contract Search, http://ronald.cori.missouri.edu/cori_search_client_search.php (last visited Jan. 11, 2006). The initial search, performed on December 2, 2005, was for "severability" in contracts filed between January 1, 2003, and December 31, 2004 (15502 contracts), taking the first of every group of 100 along with the first contract of the last group, listed by CORI ID number, for a total of 156 contracts.
14. Baldwin & Clark, *supra* note 2, at 12–13, 123–46.
15. See, e.g., Langlois, *supra* note 2, at 24–26; Simon, *supra* note 2, at 195–98. This is sometimes called "factoring."
16. See *supra* note 3.
17. See *supra* note 4.
18. Thomas W. Merrill & Henry E. Smith, *Optimal Standardization in the Law of Property: The Numerus Clausus Principle*, 110 Yale L.J. 1, 35–38 (2000).
19. Baldwin & Clark, *supra* note 2, at 138–40.
20. For advice on how to pay attention to the ramifications of boilerplate, see Stark, *supra* note 11, at 5.
21. See Peter M. Tiersma, Legal Language 71–73 (1999). The use of noun phrases instead of pronouns is a familiar aspect of context-dependence (called indexicality) and features in Dewaele's constructed variable of formalism. See Jean-Marc Dewaele, *How to Measure Formality of Speech? A Model of Synchronic Variation*, in Approaches to Second Language Acquisition 119 (Kari Sajavaara & Courtney Fairweather eds., 1996); see also Francis Heylighen, *Advantages and Limitations of Formal Expression*, 4 Found. Sci. 25, 49–53 (1999).
22. H. P. Grice, *Logic and Conversation*, in 3 Syntax and Semantics 41, 45 (Peter Cole & Jerry L. Morgan eds., 1975), reprinted in Paul Grice, Studies in the Ways of Words 22, 26 (1989).
23. Grice, *supra* note 22, at 30; see also Stephen C. Levinson, Presumptive Meanings: The Theory of Generalized Conversational Implicature (2000) (recent development of Gricean theory).
24. The types of property rights are limited to a fixed and finite number under the numerus clausus, and the ones allowed first should be the most widely useful. Merrill & Smith, *supra* note 18, at 39.

THIRTEEN. CONTRA PROFERENTEM: THE ALLURE OF AMBIGUOUS BOILERPLATE

1. E. Allan Farnsworth, Contracts §7.11, at 474 (3d ed. 1999).
2. Charles J. Goetz & Robert E. Scott, *The Limits of Expanded Choice: An Analysis of the Interactions Between Express and Implied Contract Terms*, 73 Cal. L. Rev. 261, 301 (1985).
3. John L. Romaker & Virgil B. Prieto, *Expectations Lost: Bank of the West v. Superior Court Places the Fox in Charge of the Henhouse*, 29 Cal. W. L. Rev. 83, 103 (1992) (citing Keeton, *supra* note 56, at 968).
4. Storms v. U.S. Fid. & Guar. Co., 388 A.2d 578, 579–80 (N.H. 1978) (quoting De Lancey v. Ins. Co., 52 N.H. 581, 588 (1873)) (emphasis added) (citations omitted).
5. Penn Mut. Life Ins. Co. v. Oglesby, 695 A.2d 1146, 1150 (Del. 1997).
6. Penn Mut. Life, 695 A.2d at 1150.
7. New Castle County, Del. v. Nat'l. Union Fire Ins. Co. of Pittsburgh, Pa., 243 F.3d 744, 747 (3d Cir. 2001)) (emphasis added).
8. *Id.* at 756–57 n.1 (Scirica, J., dissenting) (quoting insurance policy).
9. Little v. MGIC Indem. Corp., 836 F.2d 789, 796 (3d Cir. 1987) (quoting Cohen v. Erie Indem. Co., 432 A.2d 596, 599 (Pa. Super. Ct. 1981)) (emphasis added).
10. E.g., Beretta, U.S.A., Corp. v. Fed. Ins. Co., 117 F. Supp. 2d 489, 495 (D. Md. 2000).
11. New Castle County, Del. v. Nat'l. Union Fire Ins. Co. of Pittsburgh, 243 F.3d 744, 755 (3d Cir. 2001).

FOURTEEN. BOILERPLATE TODAY: THE RISE OF MODULARITY AND THE WANING OF CONSENT

1. See Henry E. Smith, *Modularity in Contracts: Boilerplate and Information Flow* (in this volume).
2. James P. Nehf, *Writing Contracts in the Client's Interest*, 51 S. C. L. Rev. 153, 158 n.9 (1999).
3. Michelle E. Boardman, *Contra Proferentem: The Allure of Ambiguous Boilerplate* (in this volume).
4. Stephen J. Choi & G. Mitu Gulati, *Contract as Statute* (in this volume).
5. Duncan Kennedy, *Form and Substance in Private Law Adjudication*, 89 Harv. L. Rev. 1685 (1976); Kathleen M. Sullivan, *Foreword: The Justices of Rules and Standards*, 106 Harv. L. Rev. 24, 57 (1992).
6. Margaret Jane Radin, *Reconsidering the Rule of Law*, 69 B. U. L. Rev. 781 (1989).
7. Ronald J. Mann, *"Contracting" for Credit* (in this volume).
8. Robert B. Ahdieh, *The Strategy of Boilerplate*, 104 Mich. L. Rev. 1033 (2006).
9. Omri Ben-Shahar & James J. White, *Boilerplate and Economic Power in Auto-Manufacturing Contracts* (in this volume).
10. David Gilo & Ariel Porat, *The unconventional uses of Transaction Costs* (in this volume).
11. Frederick Schauer, Playing by the Rules: A Philosophical Examination of Rule-Based Decision-Making in Law and in Life (1991); William Simon, *The Ideology of Advocacy: Procedural Justice and Professional Ethics*, 1978 Wis. L. Rev. 29, 39–91.
12. Lucian A. Bebchuk & Richard A. Posner, *One-Sided Contracts in Competitive Consumer Markets* (in this volume). In an earlier article, Clayton Gillette advanced a similar idea.

See Clayton P. Gillette, *Rolling Contracts as an Agency Problem*, 2004 Wis. L. Rev. 679, 706.
13. Jason Scott Johnston, *Cooperative Negotiations in the Shadow of Boilerplate* (in this volume).
14. Gilo & Porat, *supra* note 10, at 1010.
15. Lon L. Fuller, The Morality of Law 81–90 (rev. ed. 1969).
16. Mann, *supra* note 7.
17. See Margaret Jane Radin, *Humans, Computers, and Binding Commitment*, 75 Ind. L.J. 1125 (2000).
18. See Margaret Jane Radin, *Online Standardization and the Integration of Text and Machine*, 70 Fordham L. Rev. 1125 (2002).
19. Lewis A. Kornhauser, *Unconscionability in Standard Forms*, 64 Cal. L. Rev. 1151 (1976).
20. Arthur Allen Leff, *Contract as Thing*, 19 Am. U. L. Rev. 131, 144–51, 155 (1970).
21. Douglas G. Baird, *The Boilerplate Puzzle* (in this volume).
22. Bebchuk & Posner, *supra* note 12, at 829.
23. See Margaret Jane Radin, *Regulation by Contract, Regulation by Machine*, 160 J. Inst. & Theoretical Econ. 1 (2004).
24. Robert A. Hillman, *Online Boilerplate: Would Mandatory Web Site Disclosure of e-Standard Terms Backfire?* (in this volume).
25. Boardman, *supra* note 3, at 1115, 1117–18.
26. See Radin, *supra* note 18. The acronym I coined for this situation, "EPSER," for "Efficacious Promulgated Superseding Entitlement Regime," will probably not become a household word.

FIFTEEN. THE LAW AND SOCIOLOGY OF BOILERPLATE

1. Todd D. Rakoff, *Contracts of Adhesion: An Essay in Reconstruction*, 96 Harv. L. Rev. 1173 (1983).
2. More precisely, the situation discussed was defined by seven attributes involved in mass contracting, of which the last was: "The principal obligation of the adhering party in the transaction considered as a whole is the payment of money." *Ibid.* at 1177.
3. Lucian A. Bebchuk & Richard A. Posner, *One-Sided Contracts in Competitive Consumer Markets* (in this volume). See also Jason Scott Johnston, *Cooperative Negotiation in the Shadow of Boilerplate* (in this volume).
4. Bebchuk & Posner, *supra* note iii, at 834.
5. Friedrich Kessler, *Contracts of Adhesion – Some Thoughts about Freedom of Contracts*, 43 Colum. L. Rev. 629, 636 (1943).
6. E.g., Kessler's article, *ibid.* at 632.
7. E.g., Robert A. Hillman & Jeffrey J. Rachlinski, *Standard-Form Contracting in the Electronic Age*, 77 N.Y.U.L. Rev. 429 (2002).
8. Omri Ben-Shahar & James J. White, *Boilerplate and Economic Power in Auto-Manufacturing Contracts* (in this volume).
9. See, e.g., their discussion of the degree to which tier-1 companies can successfully hold up the Original Equipment Manufacturers for additional benefits after the contracts have been signed. *Ibid.* at 974–76.
10. Stephen J. Choi & G. Mitu Gulati, *Contract as Statute* (in this volume).
11. Kevin E. Davis, *The Role of Nonprofits in the Production of Boilerplate* (in this volume).

12. Choi & Gulati, *supra* note 10 (swaps and derivatives); Douglas G. Baird, *The Boilerplate Puzzle* (in this volume) (commodities contracts).
13. Michelle E. Boardman, *Contra Proferentem: The Allure of Ambiguous Boilerplate* (in this volume).
14. Davis, *supra* note xi, at 1078.
15. Ben-Shahar & White, *supra* note 8 (automobile manufacturers); Ronald J. Mann, *"Contracting" for Credit* (in this volume) (credit card issuers).
16. Choi & Gulati, *supra* note 10.
17. David Gilo & Ariel Porat, *The Hidden Roles of Boilerplate and Standard-Form Contracts: Strategic Imposition of Transaction Costs, Segmentation of Consumers, and Anticompetitive Effects*, 104 MICH. L. REV.983, 987 (2006).
18. Robert B. Ahdieh, *The Strategy of Boilerplate*, 104 MICH. L. REV. 1033, 1053–66 (2006).
19. Choi & Gulati, *supra* note 10.
20. Henry E. Smith, *Modularity in Contracts: Boilerplate and Information Flow* (in this volume).
21. Robert A. Hillman, *Online Boilerplate: Would Mandatory Web Site Disclosure of e-Standard Terms Backfire?* (in this volume).
22. See 2 E. ALLAN FARNSWORTH, FARNSWORTH ON CONTRACTS §6.1, at 105–06 (3d ed. 2004).
23. Boardman, *supra* note 8.
24. See Baird, *supra* note xii. On the "mandatory arbitration" issue in general, see Charles L. Knapp, *Taking Contracts Private: The Quiet Revolution in Contract Law*, 71 FORDHAM L. REV. 761 (2002), and the several articles in *Symposium, Mandatory Arbitration*, 67 LAW & CONTEMP. PROBS. 1 (2004).
25. See Mann, *supra* note 15; see also Hillman, *supra* note xxi.
26. 350 F.2d 445 (D.C. Cir. 1965); Baird, *supra* note xii.
27. Mann, *supra* note 15.
28. Davis, *supra* note 11; Choi & Gulati, *supra* note 10.
29. See Choi & Gulati, *supra* note 10.
30. See Hillman, *supra* note xxi.
31. See, e.g., Ellsworth Dobbs, Inc. v. Johnson, 236 A.2d 843 (N.J. 1967).
32. Todd D. Rakoff, *The Shape of the Law in the American Administrative State*, 11 TEL AVIV U. STUD. L. 9, 18 (1992).

INDEX